UNDER A BLACK STAR

UNDER A BLACK STAR

THE MAROON IMPULSE IN NEW ORLEANS

Amari Johnson

UNIVERSITY OF MINNESOTA PRESS
MINNEAPOLIS • LONDON

Excerpt from "Loma y Machete" by Anónimo Consejo from *Hablando de Algo*, copyright 2007; reprinted with permission from Yosmel Sarrias. Excerpt from "We Know This Place" by Sunni Patterson in *We Know This Place*, copyright 2022 University of New Orleans Press; reprinted with permission from Sunni Patterson. Excerpts from "Hole in the Wall" by Melvin Waiters copyright 1999 by Peermusic III Ltd / Deltaboy Music Company; reprinted by permission, all rights reserved.

Copyright 2025 by the Regents of the University of Minnesota

All rights reserved. No part of this publication may be reproduced, stored in a retrieval system, utilized for purposes of training artificial intelligence technologies, or transmitted, in any form or by any means, electronic, mechanical, photocopying, recording, or otherwise, without the prior written permission of the publisher.

Published by the University of Minnesota Press
111 Third Avenue South, Suite 290
Minneapolis, MN 55401-2520
http://www.upress.umn.edu

ISBN 978-1-5179-1653-4 (hc)
ISBN 978-1-5179-1654-1 (pb)

A Cataloging-in-Publication record for this book is available from the Library of Congress.

Printed in the United States of America on acid-free paper

The University of Minnesota is an equal-opportunity educator and employer.

To my parents
My first community builders

Contents

	Introduction: Beyond the Gong	1
1.	No Place in Babylon: The Maroon Impulse	21
2.	West Bank Is the Best Bank: Algiers and the Unseen Presence as Landscape	39
3.	Black Star, Keep Shining: Invisibility as Cloak	59
4.	"They Ain't Talkin' 'bout Nothin', Y'heardme?": Fugitivity and the Educational Landscape	77
5.	The Seed of Our Ancestors: Kamali Academy and Navigating the Impulse	93
6.	Black in the Whirlwind: Hole in the Wall as Portal	117
	Coda: BlackStar Forever	133
	Acknowledgments	141
	Appendix	147
	Notes	151
	Bibliography	165
	Index	185

Introduction

Beyond the Gong

> The music is different here. . . . We set up a colony for Black people here. See what they could do on a planet all their own without any white people there.
>
> —Sun Ra, *Space Is the Place*

My grandfather only went to New Orleans once. During World War II, he and his military buddies passed through the Crescent City for a night before moving on. With the time off, they decided to enjoy themselves and catch a movie. Like nearly everywhere in the 1940s South, the segregated theater condemned the Black soldiers to balcony seats and rear entrances. He was accustomed to this, having been born to a sharecropping family and raised on a farm in North Carolina. He wasn't as familiar, however, with the gong placed conspicuously down in the front of the theater. The movie was a comedy. During any humorous scene, my grandfather would learn, the Black viewers were required to hold their laughter until after the whites had finished theirs. The gong would sound, and the Black people, my grandfather included, would be free to express themselves. He vowed to never return to New Orleans. Wartime in America.[1]

He shared this story with me in early September 2005 as he and I sat glued to a television in his living room in a small town outside Greensboro. It had been several days. They're still on the roof. Why are they talking about them like this? How can the media get reporters on the ground, but evacuation crews are absent? All these Black faces. Why are they showing floating bodies on national television in the middle of the afternoon? How many days has it been?

Until then, Katrina was a nice name. Its abbreviated version, Trina, was a familiar sound on the New Jersey playgrounds where I grew up. Now it would forever be marred by water stains, death, and state-sanctioned neglect. A bad rap, really, because the hurricane was not itself directly responsible for the destruction that grew synonymous with its name. By the time it reached New Orleans, it was varyingly classified as a category one or two storm, of which the city had seen plenty (Knabb, Rhome, and Brown 2023). The deluge that flooded the Big Easy was the result of cut corners, risky engineering, and losing bets—an outdated and insufficient levee system that engineers had been calling attention to for many years leading up to the storm. After all was said and done, the devastation was absolute—brick, mortar, spirit, memory.

Before the water receded and the breadth of the destruction could be rendered incomprehensible, I returned to New York—enraged—for my senior year in college. The federal government's lethargic response to the needs of the people of the Black city of New Orleans, coupled with the media's malicious depiction of survivors as looters and thugs, confirmed to me what I had long believed: we, Black people, are on our own. Kanye West's impromptu statement that "George Bush doesn't care about Black people," when considered in conjunction with Bush's foreign and domestic policies and practices, was a matter of fact that should have garnered attention only for its veracity.[2] So, once back in New York, I joined an organization working for the self-determination of the Black nation and began organizing directly with hurricane survivors evacuated to the Big Apple as the Federal Emergency Management Agency (FEMA) threatened to terminate their funding in yet another demonstration of the government's absent desire to protect its Black subjects. I also doubled down on my studies of marronage in an attempt to develop viable solutions to the issues we were facing.

I had spent the year before Katrina studying in Cuba, Ghana, and Brazil, where I researched legacies of marronage, or the process and practices by which African people escaped from the dominant social and political order to build autonomous and independent communities. What initially served as a historical boost of self-esteem—groups of Black people undermining the plantation order by reclaiming their autonomy and wreaking havoc on plantation owners—had grown into an unshakable series of questions: Why did African people from varying parts of the continent express their resistance to enslavement in remarkably similar ways? Why do historians and anthropologists only speak of marronage as a past phenomenon? If the power relations that structure society have remained consistent—that is, Black people's collective relationship to a white power establishment has not changed—could marronage prove useful for shaping our contemporary reality? What would that require? I carried these questions into graduate school at the University of Texas at Austin. On my drive to Austin, two Augusts after Katrina, I spent my first night in New Orleans.

Growing up, I didn't know much about the city. My father used to tell me it was shaped like a bowl with most of it below sea level; the ninth season of *The Real World* was filmed there, featuring a character named David who created the underground classic "Come On Be My Baby Tonight"; my brother and I, in our northeastern arrogance, *refused* to give Master P and No Limit a chance; and Mardi Gras had something to do with beads. By the time I made it to Canal Street, however, the city had come to occupy my mind as an embattled terrain containing clues to understanding our relationship to both the African Diaspora and freedom.

A few days after arriving in Austin, I met Samori Camara, a New Orleans native in the history department with a commitment to the liberation of African people that matched my own. We became fast friends and began making regular trips to his hometown. When I completed my coursework, I moved to the city's Algiers section. For the following three years I immersed myself in what is easily one of the most remarkable places I had ever been.

The BlackStar Community

Under a Black Star: The Maroon Impulse in New Orleans tells the story of a group of people whom I call the BlackStar community. They formed around and were associated with the sibling institutions of BlackStar Books and Caffé and Kamali Academy. They came from varying educational, geographical, philosophical, and socioeconomic backgrounds but shared both an evolving identity and a common interest: a broadly defined—and often debated—idea of freedom. While BlackStar sold books and coffee, its primary function was that of a gathering place. Kamali Academy was a systematic homeschool collective for K–12 students and offered an "education for liberation." They were seeking liberation at most and autonomy at least. They engaged with various traditions of Black struggle in a dynamic blend of revolutionary and cultural nationalisms in a way that challenged false binaries and invigorated stale tropes (S. Brown 2003; Konadu 2004; Joseph 2007). They debated ideas of Malcolm X, Ella Baker, Marcus Garvey, Elijah Muhammad, Queen Mother Moore, Amos Wilson, Toni Cade Bambara, the Black Panther Party for Self-Defense, Kwame Nkrumah, Thomas Sankara, and the various educational formations associated with the Council of Independent Black Institutions. They experimented with the effectiveness of revolutionary art. While their rhetoric was largely informed by the Black Power movement, their vision was set on a "Black heaven" lying somewhere in the future. Kamali was intent on breaking the corporate model of education so prominent in the city in order to prepare its students for the world they would seek to build. This included regular participation from neighbors and community members in a collective reimagining of the possibilities of a liberatory model of education.

I was an active participant in the physical and ideological development of both Kamali Academy and BlackStar Books and Caffé. Kamali operated out of my living room and was run by my roommate and friend, Samori. I taught language arts and physical education and worked with Samori to develop the school's philosophical foundation. In addition, I, along with Samori and a small group of others, helped Baakir Tyehimba with renovations to the space that would become BlackStar. Baakir was Samori's former substitute teacher, and the two had been making plans for a school and bookstore in the year leading up to Samori's return to the city. Now that things were in motion, BlackStar had become our default hangout. Located less than a half-mile from my house and Kamali Academy, we spent most of our nonschool hours there. Students would head to the café after school to eat snacks, play chess, use the computers, or wait for their parents—many of whom were regular participants in the book store's events. People would have business meetings there or stop by out of curiosity. When it first opened its doors, I committed several days a week to working behind the counter, eventually spending most of my formal time with the shop as the guitar player in the house band for its Liberation Lounge open-mic nights. BlackStar and Kamali worked to secure autonomous community for Black people in a New Orleans attempting to drive them out through denied employment, insufficient education, and an ensuing housing crisis. Rather than appeal to the city, BlackStar and Kamali chose to build for themselves the community they desired.

Human beings have always gathered in pursuit of shared objectives. Today the term "intentional communities" has become quite chic, identifying groups forming around specific interests. In another sense, so-called marginalized groups have long sought protection and preservation through proximity to one another. In this way, the BlackStar community was not unique. We were like any other group of Black people coming together to meet common needs. This community was noteworthy, however, at least significant enough to study, for three central reasons. First, Hurricane Katrina's aftermath set the ground for an experiment in neoliberal reform that would have international ramifications.[3] The state takeover of the public schools and its subsequent granting of charters to private organizations would culminate with the country's first all-charter-school city in 2019. Those who attended Kamali Academy would recognize the draconian and deleterious impact of the charter schools' ominous presence as early as 2009. Furthermore, the storm would open the floodgates for northern and western investors whose real estate speculation would rapidly diminish the Crescent City's historically Black population through an increased cost of living and decreased inventory of affordable housing. This also included the obliteration of Black cultural institutions and continued challenges to "Black place" (Purifoy 2021). The BlackStar community came together in the midst of this tempestuous period to secure *something* for ourselves and exercise a form of control over our lives.

Second, this community did not form through formal, political mobilization or grassroots organizing techniques. There was no "community outreach" or, as some activist circles might state it, efforts toward "consciousness raising." This was not a "social movement," which in many ways has become the lingua franca when discussing groups of people working toward collective—often politically defined—goals. Rather, this community grew organically through a shared need for quality education and affirming social spaces. While there were common values—an emphasis on an African cultural identity, shared intent for self-determination, centralization of study, absent desire of government/NGO assistance, skepticism of white "allyship"—these values were certainly not above debate, nor necessary for participation. BlackStar Books and Caffé and Kamali Academy met a series of needs, and as such the community was able to cultivate an autonomy built around ideas and actions, offering an alternative model of community organizing that extends beyond the narrow confines of protest politics and focuses, instead, on community construction.

Third, through our particular practices of building and maintaining autonomous institutions, the BlackStar community was experimenting with a cultural tradition of marronage—which, I argue, consists of varying degrees of disengagement, flight, and reengagement.[4] While we did practice elements of what Yarimar Bonilla (2015) calls "strategic entanglement"—having parents register as homeschoolers with the State of Louisiana, paying taxes, maintaining various forms of employment, and so forth—we exhibited acts of refusal and appealed to practices that do not fit easily into the mouth of political discourse. The BlackStar community offered a respite, a space from which to plot and plan. As such, the practices of this community help us theorize a contemporary marronage that is not limited to myopic concepts of democracy, justice, activism, social movements, or civic engagement.

Sketches of Marronage

Under a Black Star explores the ways in which the institutional lives of BlackStar and Kamali demonstrate an engagement with marronage in the twenty-first century. Marronage often refers to the practices of those Africans (and their descendants) who escaped the plantation in order to establish free societies elsewhere—whether it be the hills, mountains, swamps, jungles, or cities in some cases. For Carolyn Cooper, it is "that tradition of resistance science that establishes an alternative psychic space both within and beyond the boundaries of the enslaving plantation" (1995, 5). This is a useful definition in that it accounts for tradition while locating power within its very fluidity. Marronage involves escape, rejection, refusal, and embrace. I argue that this *escape,* however, has never been as central as *pursuit:* the pursuit of autonomy, community, and freedom. Put differently, marronage is not about moving from, but rather advancing toward. This reveals an epistemological nuance that extends beyond semantics and has much to suggest about the viability of marronage as an ongoing liberatory praxis. It does not simply represent a separation from the plantation complex, although this is not of negligible importance; it demonstrates an engagement with a safe and sacred space, free from external determination and domination in which participants can effectively exercise autonomy through a process of both escape and arrival. In form, marronage has been amorphous, taking on the different shapes and structures of its particular climate, both politically and geologically. More vitally, marronage unveils a collective understanding that the complete and uninhibited well-being of its participants cannot be met within the dominant social order. It is an African Diasporic cultural tradition that informs and is informed by contemporary efforts toward Black self-determination.

Scholars, particularly in the fields of anthropology, history, and literature, have engaged with this concept for decades.[5] There are, however, at least four significant shortcomings within these engagements. First, the term *marronage* describes the *practice* that results in a *product* of a maroon formation (society, community, camp). In much of the literature, however, the process becomes subsumed by the product, and the two are often used interchangeably. Here, I argue that marronage is more appropriately understood as a process that *may* result in the formation of a maroon community but does not necessarily have to. In other words, this process of disengagement, flight, and reengagement may yield more outcomes than a rigid commitment to a narrowly defined "maroon community" allows for. Shifting the focus to the *process* instead of the *product* opens new avenues of exploration and expression.

Second, for many scholars, marronage is inextricably linked to chattel enslavement. This implies that once chattel enslavement was abolished, the impetus for marronage disappeared, forever remaining the sole patrimony of those maroons and their descendants. Anthropological treatments of those descendants in places like Suriname, Jamaica, and Brazil evince this belief. This understanding falsely interprets the ultimate motivation for marronage as that of escaping enslavement. My objective is to remove marronage from the conceptual bondage of the matrix of chattel enslavement. Instead, I agree with Willie Jamaal Wright that marronage exists "beyond the embodied realities of racial slavery in the Western Hemisphere" (2019, 1136).

Third, due to this association with chattel enslavement, marronage is largely regarded as a historical phenomenon relegated to the past. The first documented evidence of marronage in a New World context of chattel enslavement occurred in the early 1500s in Hispaniola. For nearly the next four centuries, marronage abounded throughout the Americas and on the African continent (Hueman 1986). It took different forms and shapes, but one thing remained consistent: the quest for autonomous community. To suggest that this impulse ceased with the abolishment of slavery is to ignore overwhelming evidence of the opposite—the refusal of recognized maroon communities to vacate their lands, the establishment of Black townships, mutual aid societies, spiritual temples, churches, and other social, political, and cultural institutions (Du Bois 1907; Purifoy and Seamster 2020; Gordon Nembhard 2014). In keeping with what Saidiya Hartman (2007) describes as the afterlife of slavery, I argue that the power relations that characterized the world of slavery persist in the present moment. Marronage contributes to a legacy of collective autonomy and is one characteristic found among Black communities throughout the African Diaspora. Rather than a coincidental response to enslavement and oppression, marronage is in fact a transtemporal, African diasporic cultural tradition with considerable implications for the present. While referencing historical examples is useful for contextualization, these examples are not the only means of assessment, as marronage is a living praxis that is constantly evolving.

Fourth, in identifying marronage, scholars have worked with general typologies that describe the size, longevity, scope, and nature of these formations. From *grand* to *petit,* borderland to hinterland, sociogenic and sovereign, these typologies offer a broad-stroke usefulness but fall apart under closer scrutiny (Diouf 2014; Price 1996; Roberts 2015). Marronage is amorphous and in dynamic interplay with its environment. As such, it does not lend itself to neat categorization. Furthermore, when understanding marronage as a process, size and longevity become ineffective means of measuring significance, success, or effectiveness. Rather, this is but a step on a larger journey, demonstrating the *vem e vai* of life. There is no arrival, but rather a constant arriving.[6]

Work in the field of Black geographies has provided key interventions in our thinking around marronage over the past several years. These scholars are expanding our conceptualizations beyond the historical and into the spatial (D. Allen 2022; Bledsoe 2017; Bledsoe and Wright 2018; Hosbey and Roane 2021; Malm 2018; Winston 2021; Wright 2019). My study makes use of these interventions, which challenge many of the outdated yet pervasive groundings mentioned previously. They offer vibrant insights by engaging what Adam Bledsoe calls the "spatial figure of the maroon community" (2017, 30). This includes a transtemporality that allows for a more nuanced and expansive view of marronage that escapes from the tethers of colonial archives. I am cautious of what still seems to be a heavier emphasis on escape and fugitivity than on pursuit, and I find great use in Celeste Winston's designation of marronage as "not just a fleeting practice but also as a significant method of producing place" (2021, 2186).

My intention in this study is neither to glorify marronage nor to uncritically celebrate the study's subjects. Marronage is a tool, a method, and a cultural practice. As with anything involving human participation, it is susceptible to misdirection, misgivings, and failure. My objective here is to identify the promise that an expanded understanding of marronage offers as a diasporic practice of autonomous community construction. While this book focuses specifically on the United States, I recognize and draw upon similar manifestations throughout the Black world. Exploring the potential of this process offers new directions for research while also providing a lens through which to interpret Black diasporic cultural expression.

Against the Canvas of Night

Across the twentieth century, numerous social and political movements in Africa and throughout the Diaspora have made use of the black star as a symbol of liberation. While these were certainly in my orbit as a child, I didn't become fully aware of them until I was in high school when my brother shared with me the album *Mos Def and Talib Kweli Are Black Star* (1998). In this, their debut album, Mos Def (now known as Yasiin Bey) and Talib Kweli address themes of cultural pride, self-determination, the challenges and triumphs of urban life, knowledge of self, and more. The group's name is an explicit reference to Marcus Garvey and the Universal Negro Improvement Association's Black Star Line—the shipping vessels intended to bring Blacks of the Diaspora back to Africa in a massive venture of commerce and leisure. The album's second track, "Astronomy (8th Light)," opens with Bey: "Against the canvas of the night appears a curious celestial phenomenon called the black star. But what is it?" The duo then trade bars that speculate about its wide-ranging possibilities. The concept of a black star is, indeed, peculiar: How can a black something on the black background of night still *shine* "from very far to where you are"? It is an oxymoron that almost makes for bad poetry. Its literal and figurative meanings—as well as its cultural significance—however, suggest a world that exists beyond the earthly and the logical. This curious celestial phenomenon of a black star reveals two themes that are central to this study: a maroon impulse and the unseen presence.

The BlackStar community set out to build for itself the world it desired. In *Under a Black Star,* I am less concerned with the community's successes and failures than with the anatomy of this desire (Kelley 2002). I argue that this desire is more than a whimsical yearning and that it reflects a *maroon impulse,* or a shared and active/acted-upon drive to create and maintain beneficial forms of autonomous community, usually by extracting oneself from vexed social, political, and/or cultural arrangements. To do this, I explore the ways this group of people pursued autonomy through an engagement with the praxis of marronage. This maroon impulse drives individuals to seek such communities and offers alternative avenues for exploring African diasporic quests for liberation. In places like the United States, where dominating narratives characterize this journey as one whose objectives include assimilation into a hostile mainstream society, this maroon impulse provides us with a framework and language for interpreting alternative forms of community construction, such as BlackStar and Kamali, and places them within larger traditions that traverse both space and time (Joseph 2010; Hahn 2009; Wright 2019).

To be effective in the midst of a hostile society, a maroon impulse must necessarily make use of what I refer to as an *unseen presence,* or clandestine community creation and maintenance. It is the maroon camp, the underground, the hole in the wall, the Black commons (Roane 2018) hiding in plain sight. It is a world in the darkness, yet it is visible to those eyes equipped to see it. In the case of BlackStar Books and Caffé, this meant limiting interactions with the city government and avoiding invasive licensing procedures. For Kamali Academy, it meant utilizing a loophole in Louisiana homeschooling processes to reduce scrutiny. This study explores the creative potential of strategic invisibility as a means of securing autonomy, rather than seeking amelioration and running toward the mirage of mainstream acceptance. The curious celestial phenomenon contains a world within itself. It is a Black world where a maroon impulse flourishes under the cover of an unseen presence.

A Live(d) Black World

In *Black Aliveness, or A Poetics of Being* (2021), Kevin Quashie begins with a prompt: imagine a Black world. For Quashie, it is a world in which "what we expect and get from Black people is beingness" (10). His text is a refreshing alternative to the growing literature that centers Black death, nonbeing, and anti-Blackness. These works offer useful insights into assessing the metastructures of a governing libidinal economy.[7] I can't help but read at least part of their underlying arguments, however, as laments of exclusion. In this literature, Black is necessarily nonbeing. The issue, it seems, is not so much with the fraught nature of Being—often beautifully articulated with labyrinthine prose and nuance that only great intimacy affords. Rather, the problem is that "the Black" does not have access to this beingness. We, Black people, are ontologically marked outside of the family of humanity, resulting in a dialectical quandary that leaves us in a perpetual state of social death and nonbeingness. While I am sympathetic toward much of these theoretical lines in inquiry, my disagreement rests with their commitment to their conclusion: the impossibility of Blackness. I take issue with this *commitment* insofar as it either accepts the parameters of the constructed order as primordial and, as such, fixed, or is resigned to the will and whim of those whom they identify as possessing constitutive power. It would seem there is a phrase missing: impossibility of Blackness so long as we are wed to—and can therefore only understand ourselves in relation to—whiteness. This expanded phrase unearths epistemological assumptions about position, power, and possibility that have far-reaching implications and speak to the heart of this work.

So readily available are the words to describe Black death and suffering. We are left searching, however, when engaging life beyond the gong. This is underscored by my having resisted throughout this writing a persistent, knee-jerk tendency to describe the time and place of my study as "post–Hurricane Katrina New Orleans." Certainly, the hurricane and its aftermath were life-altering events of unspeakable and unknowable calamity, the consequences of which have surely shaped the lives of all affected—both directly and not. During my time in the Crescent City, Hurricane Katrina was indeed mentioned regularly. It was most commonly referred to as "the storm" and discussed with the assumed familiarity of a collective family member. Its utterance was met with an unspoken understanding by those who lived through it. Ironically, it was those who hadn't—those who, like me, watched it play out on television screens in air-conditioned comfort—who imposed what they thought was an appropriate level of indignation and sorrow. Katrina was, for me, first and foremost a political assault in the ongoing war against Black people, made all the more infuriating by the changing landscape of the city we saw playing out before our very eyes. I would get nods of agreement from New Orleanians as I broke into my diatribes. Then they would shift the conversation. They agreed there was a political element, but it wasn't first and foremost for them. It was, above all else, something that happened. It was part of an immutable past that, whether right, wrong, or indifferent, contributed to the tapestry of collective experience and settled into their daily lives as something they either had to or had not to deal with. What an anthropological sin it would be to force my fury onto their experience, with such a neat yet indistinct categorization as "post-" anything. The ease with which this shorthand obfuscates is cause for concern. "Post-Katrina" does not only signal an event, but suggests a rupture in time. Its imposition subsumes and defines. This facility of reduction limits the vocabulary available to me to tell this story. It leaves only synonyms of death and destruction, mourning, trauma, and devastation—concepts rendered legible by a "commonsense" understanding of Black-life-as-Black-death. These concepts—death, destruction, mourning, trauma, devastation—do not, however, overdetermine the world into which I entered in New Orleans. They offer only a grayscale pallet to depict the blooming kaleidoscope that was the BlackStar community.

This returns us to Quashie's prompt to imagine a Black world. I am encouraged by his "attempt to displace anti-blackness from the center of [his] thinking" (2021, 9). What is peculiar is what appears to be a presumption on Quashie's part that a Black world must be imagined. The prompt suggests that such a world—and there must necessarily be multiple—is only accessible through imagination. My world—and that of the BlackStar community—is and was Black. And while we certainly engaged in collective imaginings, we did so from the comfort and safety of our Black world. The "Black" of this world does not function as a racial marker. In fact, the conversations and ideas circulating in the community began moving beyond a racial paradigm for understanding ourselves in relation to our world. Black speaks not to the opposite of white—a sociological artifact of a failed social order—but to an incalculable totality as both aspiration and manifestation, that which I call the *unseen presence*.

In the film *Space Is the Place* (1974), philosopher and jazz musician Sun Ra sets out to transport Black people to a "planet of our own." He uses his music to do so. Ra is clear, however, that this is not a multicultural utopia where all are welcomed and may leave their troubles behind: "My kingdom is the kingdom of darkness and blackness. And none can enter except those who are of the Black spirit." For Sun Ra, race alone does not cover the cost of admission. It is not enough to be Black racially. One must be of Black *spirit*.[8] In the film's final scene, as people are boarding the spacecraft, they pass through what resembles a TSA body scan machine. Using a scepter and crystal ball, Ra measures potential passengers by the "discipline of their Black ancestors." If they are in possession of a Black spirit, it is separated from their body and allowed to board the ship. Not everyone will make it, though. Here I am reminded of Marcus Garvey's statement that he had no desire to take all Black people back to Africa. Some, for him, were "no good here, and will naturally be no good there" (Garvey 1986). In contemporary parlance, this is to say that "skinship don't equal kinship."

Some may lambast both Sun Ra and Garvey as gatekeepers guilty of policing the borders of "Blackness" as they attempt to determine for themselves who is of Black spirit or usefulness. I would like to offer that such a critique suffers from its own limitations—namely, an implied idea of a "universal Blackness" whose borders can indeed be patrolled. Sun Ra, Garvey, and even the BlackStar community identified the world they sought, and they pursued it on their own terms. This did not include *all* Black people. That would be a racial definition too limited for their aspirations. It would be a reactionary identity based on what one is not (non-being) rather than what one is. Instead, they engaged in self-definition that advanced beyond legal classifications imposed for purposes of taxation. Sun Ra's kingdom of darkness and Blackness exists outside of a racial paradigm wherein "Black" is reduced to the confines of social definition. It embraces an "alter-destiny" in which power and potential are limited only by desire and effort. I argue that this desire for a Black world inhabited by Black spirits is and has been commonplace, though often underacknowledged in an era of "diversity and inclusion" and beyond. While Sun Ra's artistic rendering presents an ideal type, *Under a Black*

Star accompanies the BlackStar community's practical efforts to create and maintain such a world as an expression of a maroon impulse.[9]

Coming to New Orleans

I moved to New Orleans in the summer of 2009 to begin dissertation research on the city's housing crisis. It had been four years since the storm, and the city was still attempting to recover. I was interested in the connections between the historical legacy of marronage and the ways that Black grassroots organizations were mobilizing resources to construct autonomous communities in the city. Due to the municipal government's denial of displaced residents' right to return to their property, in tandem with the destruction of available public housing and the aggressive corporate takeover of housing reconstruction, the city's homeless population—an overwhelming majority of whom were Black—doubled shortly after the storm and remained consistent through my arrival (Rameau 2013; People's Hurricane Relief Fund 2008). The organization with which I was working was attempting to mobilize housing and workers' cooperatives to provide a temporary solution that would insert the issue into public debate while making provisions to advance a larger struggle of urban land reform.

I had visited the city several times over the previous two years, was relatively familiar with its layout, and had already established some working relationships. Samori and I became roommates upon my arrival. He was working with a friend, Baakir Tyehimba, to draft plans for BlackStar Educational Cooperative, a homeschool collective for high school students that would operate out of our house. These plans also included a bookstore and café to provide financial support for the school. Although I did not participate formally in the cooperative, Samori and I spent many hours discussing its mission, vision, structure, content, format, and recruitment strategies. I spent that academic year (2009–10) working as a literacy specialist at an all-Black, all-boys charter school, Henson Academy. This was my formal introduction to both New Orleans's youth culture and the charter school system that flourished in the city after Hurricane Katrina (D. Cooper 2008; Cedric Johnson 2015; Sanders 2015; Tompkins 2015; Rosario-Moore 2015; Lipsitz 2015).

Henson Academy was a middle and high school. The majority of my students were sixth and tenth graders, but their reading levels fell far below. As I began to teach with the goal of improving these students' reading levels, I quickly noticed the administration's preference for disciplinary excellence over academic achievement. It was rare that I had all of my students in class at the same time, as one or another would almost always be suspended or absent. Beyond that, there were several occasions when I would walk into classrooms looking for students and find teachers talking on the phone or listening to music. I had long heard about charter schools being the "privatization of public education," and my experiences at Henson only confirmed this idea. The lengths to which administrators went to maintain funding—suspending students who were in danger of failing the state exams so as not to reflect poor performance, providing students with answers to standardized tests, and so forth—had proven the school to be an unhealthy environment for students and teachers. After months of mounting frustrations, I left the position at the completion of the academic year—just a few months before the school was wrought with cheating and nepotism scandals.

BlackStar also had a challenging year. After working through incongruent schedules, Samori and Baakir decided that Samori would run the school while Baakir focused on the café. The number of students at the school was inconsistent. At its height, there were three of them, with only one paying the monthly $150 cash or in-kind tuition. At the end of the year, none of them would be returning. When BlackStar Books and Caffé opened six months after the start of the school year, we quickly realized that the revenue was not enough to sustain the café, so supporting the school was out of the question. Samori spent that summer honing his vision of a new school with a more sustainable model. It would be called Kamali Academy. No longer working at Henson, I was ready to commit full-time and joined as a language arts teacher. Meanwhile, Baakir—a perpetual optimist—worked through the financial and personnel struggles at the café, and by midsummer the first Liberation Lounge took place. This bimonthly-turned-weekly open-mic jam would become the anchor of the café and serve as a platform for displaying the artistic possibilities of the world BlackStar sought to build. As BlackStar and Kamali headed into the new school year, both institutions did so sure-footedly.

At the same time, my work with the housing organization was inconsistent. New Orleans is a seasonal city. From Thanksgiving through Mardi Gras (February through early March), people and businesses are occupied with the holidays, making organizing work difficult. A number of major festivals take place from Mardi Gras through May, also complicating organizing efforts through the massive influx of tourists and greater availability of temporary work. From June through September the summer heat is excruciating. There are more festivals from August through October, leading right back into Thanksgiving. The organization could never seem to maintain momentum and, marred by miscommunication, internal power struggles, and disorder, took an extended hiatus in the winter of 2010, forcing my research to a halt. I saw in this an opportunity, however, to shift my study to where my energies were already being directed: Kamali Academy.[10] The core elements of my research remained consistent: independent Black spaces, autonomous communities, and marronage. While my research site may have been adjusted, I was already studying the school and larger community around it for the purposes of becoming a more effective participant in the work we were doing. I was immersed in the world of the BlackStar community, splitting my time between the school and the café. We spent late nights planning, plotting, and debating. New ideas were constantly being tossed out to see what stuck. While there was a rotating cast of people taking part in these discussions, Samori, Baakir, his friend Baba El, and I were the most regular.

As I explore throughout the text, silence and clandestinity are pillars of an unseen presence. This poses a challenge when producing a public-facing project such as an academic book, where a level of invasiveness into the inner worlds of interlocutors is expected as fodder for theorization. Their lives become abstractions for consumption and judgment. My first loyalty, however, is to the BlackStar community. To honor them and their trust, I have shifted the lens to the only story that is mine to tell, employing elements of ethnographic memoir not as representative of the BlackStar experience but as an entry point into a discussion on the practical and theoretical import of a maroon impulse. Naturally, members of the community—students, parents, artists, and architects—feature prominently throughout, but I have implied little beyond what they offered through formal interviews, conversations, or written correspondence. I have used pseudonyms to protect the privacy of all youth and adult participants, with the exceptions of Samori Camara, Baakir Tyehimba, and a few others whose roles in Kamali Academy and BlackStar Books and Caffé are publicly known. Henson Academy and Roberts High School are also fictitious names of real places. As part of reckoning with the public-facing nature of this project, there is a hint of Édouard Glissant's *right to opacity* (Glissant 1997) at play to the extent that I am questioning the false assumption that one should be knowable simply because of another's curiosity. For Glissant, transparency—through definition and quantification—is reductive and rests on the faulty premise that "the Other" can, if fact, be known or represented. Transparency works against my purposes. Marronage flourishes in obfuscation. Glissant's opacity functions here, however, only insofar as I am addressing the public nature of this book. I am less concerned with explaining why we need to remain obscure than with how that obscurity may be put to use in the service of autonomous community construction. To whatever extent explanation or representation appears, this story is intended for those who find shelter under the cloak of invisibility.

I am committed to the aspirations of the BlackStar community. That is, I am dedicated to the world that this community sought to build, a world where Black people could live collective and individual lives of autonomy and self-determination. In *Under a Black Star*, I explore the BlackStar community's journey toward its realization. What can we learn from their efforts?

Figure 1. Baakir Tyehimba leading a procession around the perimeter of Little Afraka during the Second Annual Little Afraka Street Festival. Photograph by Jafar M. Pierre.

Book Outline

This study addresses questions about a maroon impulse and contemporary institutional formation. What forms might this impulse take in the twenty-first century? How—if at all—did the BlackStar community in New Orleans respond to this impulse and mobilize the tradition of marronage to create autonomous spaces within the context of an aggressively gentrifying city? What can BlackStar teach us about strategies available to similar communities across the country and throughout the world? Ultimately, this book seeks to highlight the potential for self-determination through the African Diasporic cultural tradition of marronage. In chapter 1, I sketch a definition of marronage. Furthering my argument that it is a transtemporal cultural expression, I discuss the ways my travels throughout the Black world have shaped and been shaped by a maroon impulse that has, in turn, informed and expanded my understanding of marronage as process and practice. Using music, film, literature, and family history, this chapter establishes a maroon impulse as a driving force for community autonomy and self-determination that we see in the BlackStar community.

Chapter 2 explores the spatial significance of the BlackStar community's location as a site ripe for the unseen presence. Algiers is New Orleans's only neighborhood on the west bank of the Mississippi River. It was settled as an outpost to support the thriving economy across the river. Its primary function, however, was to import and warehouse enslaved Africans who would provide forced labor for the colony of Louisiana and beyond. While the two sides of the river were mutually dependent, each developed on its own, with Algiers largely viewed as existing in the East Bank's shadow. The river became a stand-in for a cultural divide that a bridge—built nearly two and a half centuries after their settlement—could not wholly mend. For African people, the West Bank was both hell and haven. Vicious living conditions and violence bred widespread and chronic marronage where families and networks thrived in inhospitable swamps. White terrorism persisted through Hurricane Katrina when groups of vigilantes actively hunted Black survivors of the storm. This was the raw material with which the BlackStar community built its world of invisibility and brilliance.

Chapter 3 highlights the role of invisibility and the unseen presence in Black world-making. I examine the concept of a black star—as theory and icon—in order to discuss the creative potential of invisibility. BlackStar was proactive in its efforts to build a community on its own terms and with its own resources at a time when Black people in New Orleans were being neglected and overlooked by local and federal governments. Rather than engaging in protest politics or lobbying efforts, BlackStar opened itself up to its local community outside of the direct knowledge or purview of the municipality. By inserting and asserting itself in such a manner, the café embraced the invisibility present in its name and offers insight into the effectiveness of an unseen presence.

In chapter 4, I present an overview of the educational landscape in New Orleans in the years immediately following Hurricane Katrina. To do this, I jump between my experiences teaching Black boys at Henson Academy and the sight of students hopping the fence to escape Roberts High School, which was located across the street from my home. Henson provides specific examples of some of the many concerns that students, community members, and activists have voiced about the charter school movement. Roberts demonstrates the lengths to which students would go to get out. Both of these acts can be viewed as expressions of a fugitive practice. This chapter explores both the potential and the shortcomings of fugitivity as a liberatory praxis. Fugitivity accounts for disengagement and flight, but it does not allow for a reengagement into mutually affirming community.

Through an ethnographic treatment of Kamali Academy, chapter 5 explores the process and attendant challenges of establishing such a community. We inherited a tradition of independent education that extends to pre-Emancipation and created a space with families needing a quality and caring learning environment for their students. These needs weren't being met in the mainstream education system, so faculty and families sought to break away. While our visions for breaking away often overlapped, they were not identical, and this sometimes caused friction and frustration. I discuss some of the practical issues and concerns that accompany a response to a maroon impulse and establishing a life beyond fugitivity, while exposing the processual nature of marronage.

In chapter 6, I use the concept of the "hole in the wall"—a descendant of the juke joint—as a means of contextualizing time travel and contemporary efforts at community formation and world-making through the creation and maintenance of underground cultural institutions. I do this through BlackStar's flagship event, Liberation Lounge, a weekly open mic, as well as my experiences as a touring musician playing throughout the South. Ultimately, the hole in the wall offers an example of communal actualization through a maroon process of disengagement, flight, and reengagement.

My grandfather passed away a few months after I moved to New Orleans in 2009. I never got to tell him about the city. He never found out about the people I came to know and love. He couldn't know about the summer night's air blowing through your hair as you drive down Elysian Fields Avenue. The way the sky turns purple at sunset over the Mississippi River. Wearing all white as a brass band plays Frankie Beverly and Maze. He didn't know about the Mardi Gras Indians, social aid and pleasure clubs, the Black Panther Party's standoff with the NOPD in the Desire Housing Project, Mark Essex, or Ahidiana. He would not know about Kamali Academy or BlackStar Books and Caffé, about Community Book Center, Ashé Cultural Arts, or the Burrito Juke Joint. It was still wartime in America. Louisiana had one of the largest incarceration rates in the world. The homicide rates remained among the highest in the country. Carpetbaggers were flooding the city with capital to drive the locals away. The education system was being auctioned to the highest bidder through state- and private-managed charter systems. The city, as my grandfather certainly believed, was no paradise. But I never got to tell him, in the face of all of this, what I discovered: that there was a centuries-long legacy of people whose laughter—and joy and movement and music and love and freedom—was not governed by the gong.

1

No Place in Babylon
The Maroon Impulse

> It is a wise Maroon Law that tells us never to cry over lost possessions, but to look steadfastly at what is ahead.
>
> —Vic Reid, *Nanny-Town*

On a bitterly cold winter night in the second semester of my freshman year at Columbia University, I was in an East Campus dorm room complaining to two friends about how school was keeping me from revolution. "I'm a hypocrite," I whined in a voice rising in both pitch and volume. "Our people are suffering right down the hill, and here I am basking in this academic jewel of white supremacy. We wasting our time. I'm 'bout to drop out. This my last semester." My friends, Diana and Elodi, were juniors. They listened as a slight smile of "We've heard this before" lay across their faces. Then, softly, as I looked out the window through Morningside Park and down to Harlem, Elodi interjected, "You don't want to drop out. You just need to step away. You should leave the country."

It threw my rhythm off. A few weeks earlier, I had downloaded several Fred Hampton speeches from Limewire. It was the early—and legally dubious—days of digital audio file sharing. Until this point in the conversation, I was trying to match Chairman Fred's oratorical cadence, but Elodi's words made me lose my way. The contrast between her tone and her suggestion stopped me in my tracks.

"Wait . . . what you mean?" As hard as I tried, I couldn't hide my ignorance, and I certainly hadn't expected anyone to call my bluff.

"Summer study abroad," Diana responded. "Go and see if you feel the same after you come back." Outside of a few soccer tournaments in

Montreal, I had never been out of the country. My curiosity was immediately piqued, and as I sat there searching for a response, the path opened itself in front of me so clearly that it was as if it had always been there. The excitement bursting inside, however, was belied by my quiet response. I could only muster a humble "Okay."

A few months later, I was on a plane to a rainforest in Brazil. The following summer, I would find my way to Cuba before splitting my junior year between Ghana and Brazil again. I would return to New York right after Hurricane Katrina struck the Gulf Coast to finish my senior year, then I would head back to Brazil in a series of Atlantic crossings that ushered me from my late teens into my early twenties and imbibed in me a sense of clarity and purpose. Carrying a weathered copy of Frantz Fanon's *Wretched of the Earth* (1963) with me every step of the way as an amulet of insurgence, I committed to fulfilling the generational mission I was identifying out of the obscurity of early-twenty-first-century life.[1] I was searching for—or perhaps responding to—what I at first thought was revolution: an African Diasporic uprising to topple the emerging techno-imperialism ossifying global power structures. My travels, thinkings, wanderings, writings, reflections, organizing efforts, friendships, and aspirations, however, were motivated by something else—something that has spanned generations and continents and continues to serve as a wellspring of inspiration. I've come to identify this something as a *maroon impulse*. In this chapter I explore how my early travels were shaped by this maroon impulse and informed my understanding of marronage as an African Diasporic cultural process and practice.

The term *impulse* here means a driving force. It is marked by a sudden and unreflective urge to take action. It is not desire, however. Desire is merely wanting without the push to action. Impulse speaks to being impelled; moved forward by a force that acts briefly yet is powerful enough to alter trajectory. It is both spontaneous and without forethought. This impulse is visceral, not logical. It strikes and incites a response, then leaves physics to do its work. The *maroon* of *maroon impulse* reflects a collective drive toward a cultural practice spanning centuries. It has afforded African people the space to create, imagine, breathe, build, heal, rest, plot, plan, and reload. While this maroon impulse often includes removing one's self from adversarial social, political, and economic relationships, it is always proactive, motivated more by pursuit than by escape.

It is exceedingly difficult to speak definitively of marronage with any sweeping generalizations. This is due to its very nature, its evasiveness, its amorphousness. Any attempts to pin it down are immediately frustrated by substantial historical evidence that at once affirms and dismisses any such claims. The amorphous nature of marronage is its most effective characteristic. It is what it is needed to be at any given moment, and capable of transforming itself, should the circumstance require it. Similarly, it is also whatever its observer desires it to be. Even more slippery still, as one maroon shared, it is the running river: what you are seeing is no longer that which it was, though it looks the same. This has led to countless pages of interpretation and analysis, bending and twisting the practice into foils of political intent. I cannot say I am exempt from this intention or from the naïveté required to believe that such a mission as identifying a theory of marronage is attainable. Still, I find it vital to resist the urge to commodify concepts through neat packaging. For our purposes here, I understand marronage as the practices and processes through which African people pursue autonomous community. It entails disengagement, flight, and reengagement. Marronage is inherently messy and does not readily lend itself to definition or capture. It is neither easy nor practical. How could it be?

To complicate things a bit further, I would like to separate marronage from the maroon communities with which it is most often associated. Marronage is the process of disengagement, flight, and reengagement. Maroon formations (communities/societies) are *a* product of marronage, but not necessarily the *only* product. It is, perhaps, expedient to examine seemingly well-defined historical examples of marronage like Palmares in the northeast of Brazil (R. N. Anderson 1996; Carneiro 1958; Funari and de Carvalho 1995; Kent 1996), but these expressions are neither exhaustive nor wholly representative. Furthermore, by focusing on these examples of maroon formations separately from the process that created them, we risk misunderstanding marronage as a phenomenon relegated to the past and the unique heritage of a specific group of people whom we now refer to as "maroon descendants." This nuance is crucial for refocusing our vision in ways that may reveal new insights into the dynamism of African liberatory praxes. Marronage is a global African cultural practice that is rooted in the past but not restricted to it, and it revolves around the pursuit of autonomous community. The maroon impulse, then, is the spark that ignites the journey of marronage.

These sketches of a definition of marronage are necessarily broad, as they must account for the dynamism and shape-shifting needed for it to maintain effectiveness. A maroon impulse impelled me to venture throughout the African Diaspora. It also greeted me every step of the way. It provided wings to scale language barriers. It offered shelter and company in the midst of unanticipated torrents. It supplied answers to questions I did not yet know to ask. My goal in this chapter is to explore a broadened concept of marronage that is processual, transtemporal, and an active force in cultural expressions throughout the Diaspora. By *transtemporal*, I am referring to marronage's utility and appearance across space and time. As Imani Owens writes, it is the ongoing and "recursive work of forging new collectives" (Owens 2023, 163). To approach marronage in this way, I jump through geography and epoch in order to highlight elements that, together, may form a working tapestry of marronage. While I draw on some specific examples from the vast history of marronage, I also call attention to some of its contemporary imaginings.

Meeting the Maroons

The study-abroad program Diana and Elodi were talking about was a five-week earth science course, and while I can't say that I remember much about the things I learned in class, I do remember the way the sun flickered off the golden-brown cover of Richard Price's *Maroon Societies: Rebel Slave Communities in the Americas* (1979) as it lay on a table in the research center's library. The defiant image of the Nèg Mawon seemed to rise off the paper stock and call directly to me. I picked the book up and didn't put it down until I'd read every word it contained. I was absorbed in the stories of African people who escaped the plantation to establish autonomous communities outside of the purview of the plantation complex.[2] This signaled to me that our destinies were not to be wholly defined by the enslaving order. While not all maroon efforts resulted in San Lorenzo de los Negros or San Basílio or Nanny Town (Meléndez Guadarrama 2009; Reiter 2015)—generally characterized as *grand marronage,* or massive settlements spanning extended periods of time—each expression provided lessons that may be relevant to what I understood as our contemporary struggle. I was loosely familiar with the maroons at that point, and I understood them not as the oxymoronic "rebel slaves" of Price's description but as African people who cherished freedom above all else. The oxymoron here is that if they escaped the plantation they were not "slaves." The suggestion that they could still be referred to as such even after having escaped or, in some cases, having *never* been enslaved speaks to an investment in a false ontological equation. That is, slave = Black and Black = slave, even if that Black was never a "slave." Slave, in this equation, is not a state of bondage but rather a state of being and the natural state of "Black." Price is not the only one guilty of this elision. In fact, it is disturbingly common in literature on marronage, where terms like "escaped slaves" or "fugitive slaves" are too commonly used to describe the maroons. How does one cease to be a slave if escape is not enough?

During an internship the summer before college, I shared a desk with a Jamaican man whose father was a maroon. This is why, he would say, he couldn't "take no shit from white people." I believe I first heard of the maroons, however, through reggae and the teachings of Rastafari. A few years prior, I was introduced to the philosophy and culture through the music of Bob Marley and Buju Banton. In my quest for truth and understanding as I struggled through an all-male, all-white Catholic high school, I sought to distance myself as much as I could from my environment—if not physically, then certainly culturally. The teachings of Rastafari opened a door for me. I would spend whatever weekends I could visiting my aunt Precious in East Flatbush, Brooklyn. She would march me up and down Church Avenue, introducing me to her friends who discussed Rastafari philosophy and theology with me. We would talk into the night on street corners as dollar vans raced by with red, gold, and green flags dangling from their rear-view mirrors. They zoomed up and down Utica, Nostrand, Clarendon, Flatbush, and Kings Highway. Voices from Guyana, Jamaica, Trinidad and Tobago, Barbados, or Grenada climbed over calypso, soca, and reggae and rolled out of sliding side doors that were pulled open and shut by tattered ropes. I could hum along to this music that Precious had introduced me to in her third-floor apartment. She would play the sounds of Dennis Brown, Freddie McGreggor, and Garnett Silk.

> I saw Zion in a vision.
> Jah was there amidst everyone
> Stretching forth his right hand.
> It's like a family reunion. (Silk 1993)

I would close my eyes and feel the music move me from the inside, far away from the forsaken halls of my private school to somewhere else. On the fringes of my own closed-eye vision, I could make out its shapes and shadows. Gregory Isaacs's voice guided me: "I'm'a leaving out of this here land. / This place could never be my home" (Isaacs 2006).

Precious is my mother's youngest sister. She is the only one of my mother's siblings born in the United States. My mother was born in Liberia. Her oldest sister, Florence, was also born there, but grew up in Ghana. My father is from North Carolina. From early, I understood the United States to be *a* place, but never the only place in the world. Black people were everywhere, and with my developing social and political consciousness, I heard Isaacs: "Africa, we want to go." While it would be a few more years until I touched the African continent for the first time, the maroon impulse present in the rhythms of Lee Perry and the Upsetters or Sly and Robbie animated my imagination and illuminated a path forward for me. Precious also introduced me to the poetry of Mutabaruka. His words, whether a cappella or accompanied by heavy bass lines rumbling through her shag carpet, were a masterful blend of insight, wordplay, and humor. His voice would boom through the speakers with a sobering honesty: "It nuh good to stay in a white man country too long!" (Mutabaruka 1996). We would laugh as we listened to his "The People's Court" where European imperialism would finally be put on trial, including that dastard Christopher Columbus—whom he referred to, appropriately, as Christopher Come-Bus'-Us. In time, I would recognize Mutabaruka as Shango, a rebel in Haile Gerima's *Sankofa* (1993).

Marronage as Pursuit

Set on a southern plantation in the United States during the height of chattel enslavement, *Sankofa* includes a secret society composed of field hands and house servants from neighboring plantations as well as "free folks from up in the hills" who sneak off into the caves to meet. At these meetings, participants plot rebellions, take inventory of armaments, and conduct spiritual ceremonies. There is an overlap between those who have permanently left the plantation and live free in the hills and those who, like Shango—the name of the Orisha of justice and thunder—still labor on the plantation yet retreat to the caves when they deem fit. This practice of temporary escape, known as *petit marronage,* takes on a significantly different tone in *Sankofa* than it does in Price's description of "repetitive or periodic truancy with temporary goals such as visiting a relative or lover on a neighboring plantation" (1996, 3). The rather flippant and perhaps even paternalistic use of the term "truancy" dismisses the significant potential that Gerima illuminates. Stephanie Camp's formulation of truancy, however, centralizes the autonomy of enslaved Africans: "Through absenteeism enslaved people established a form of spatial knowledge that granted them room and time for themselves" (2002, 3).

At one of the secret meetings in the caves, a maroon leader explains, "We come to talk with you, get you together to take you away to the hills one by one. . . . This thing is not to be known 'cause we are one people. We take you one by one until we all get together in the hills where you are free. Everybody free." The temporary escape employed by those who still reside on the plantation is more than merely "playing hooky," as Price's words may have us believe. Instead, the maroon leader's speech is met with applause, and the scene cuts to Nunu, a leader working from the plantation, bearing a torch as she chants in Akan and leads the Africans out of the caves and into battle. The film's narrator explains, "That time, the soldiers came to put down the rebellion and armed overseers from neighboring plantations and the sky *stayed* red hot. Smoke was everywhere. Acres of cane lain in ashes" (Gerima 1993). These covert meetings of the enslaved, *petit marronage,* took place in preparation for major revolts throughout the Americas, among which are the Haitian Revolution, the uprising of the Malês, the rebellions of Nat Turner and Gabriel Prosser, and numerous others, both known and unknown.[3] Of course, *petit marronage* does not always culminate in rebellion. Sometimes it serves the purposes of a temporary respite from the demands and terror of the plantation, an opportunity for enslaved Africans to commune with one another on their own terms (see Camp 2002).

Gerima is offering an understanding of the complex relationships that African people navigated in our individual and collective quests for freedom. This complexity is reflected in the work of Sylviane Diouf (2014), who discusses the overlapping relationships—familial, economic, social—between maroons and those Africans on the plantation. Her research contributes greatly to the vast yet underrepresented history of maroon presences in what would become the continental United States and further underscores the ubiquity of marronage as an African freedom practice.

Gerima's depiction, in conversation with Diouf's findings, illustrates the nonlinearity of freedom. These categories of *grand* and *petit marronage,* while consistent throughout the literature and useful for tracing a general sketch, are a bit too rigid for our purposes and must be expanded. As Gerima's depiction demonstrates, there are more nuances that cannot be accounted for in cut-and-dried binaries or categorizations.

One significant shortcoming in maroon literature is its insistence on relegating marronage to the past. For many scholars, the practice and process is inextricably linked to chattel enslavement, whose only application to the present is through metaphor. The end of chattel enslavement, it would follow, eliminated the need for marronage and its abject disengagement. This evinces the belief that marronage was rooted in a critique of the shortcomings of political society and not an outright refusal of its very terms. That is to say that the violation which motivated maroons to take flight was the denial of their humanity, coterminous in liberal language as their being barred from citizenship. They were, in Orlando Patterson's formulation, "socially dead" (2018), incapable of knowing social life. Marronage in these terms, then, becomes a means for the "slave" to experience freedom. In so doing, as Neil Roberts (2015) argues, their marooning expands understandings of liberal notions of freedom as found in the liminal space of flight. For Roberts, it seems, it is not a question of the foundational legitimacy of liberalism and political society. Rather, it is a matter of making legible the presence of these errant "slaves" whose daring expressions of humanity can reinforce the validity of such a liberalism by simply expanding its borders in an evolved display of inclusion.

Brazilian sociologist Clóvis Moura approaches this through a Marxist analysis and argues that the *quilombo,* or maroon formation, appears as a "unit of protest and social experience of resistance and a reworking of the [enslaved's] social and cultural values" (2001, 103; my translation). In so doing, Moura is establishing marronage as what Edison Carneiro calls a "dialectical synthesis" (2001, 18). By the very act of escape, the enslaved, as the physical and ideological currency upon which the plantation complex exists, undermines said system through its negation. Moura takes this a step further by proclaiming that "the interior of the *quilombola*[4] had, for this reason . . . the desire to preserve the freedom gained when he/she objectively and subjectively denied the slave order" (2001, 104).

For Moura, the maroon's very reason for being/of being is the negation of the order of its creation.

Moura's analysis offers much by way of contextualizing the impact of marronage on the plantation complex. I am concerned, however, that it uses the plantation as a pivot point and thus an anchor from which there is no untethering. In this sense, the shortcomings of both liberal ideas of freedom and Moura's Marxist dialectics falsely interpret the ultimate impetus for marronage as that of escaping enslavement. What insights may we gain from an approach that emphasizes *pursuit* instead of *escape*? What could we learn about marronage as a cultural practice by framing it as a pursuit of freedom—understood not as participation/aspiration within liberal democracy, but as the creation and maintenance of autonomous community? This suggests much about marronage's viability as a continuing liberatory praxis that centers the values, experiences, and desires of those marooning.

More than a separation from the plantation complex, marronage allows for grounds upon which participants can effectively exercise autonomy through a process of both escape and arrival. As Cedric Robinson writes, "Away from the plantations, in the security of mountain retreats, on the continent toward the up-country sources of the great rivers that emptied into the ocean at the coasts, Black communities could be reestablished" (2000, 310). Mountains, hills, swamps, caves, and even urban centers: these were and are some of the locales where marooning Africans found/find the space to secure what Robinson calls "ontological totality." The invocation of the historical maroons—and their forged landscapes continues to figure prominently throughout the African Diaspora and serves as an expression of and inspiration for this maroon impulse.

Hill and Mountain

I arrived in Havana in the summer of 2004 to study how hip-hop artists in the city were contributing to a diasporic conversation on identity and revolution. As I ducked off of the propjet and descended the stairs onto the tarmac at José Martí International Airport, I was swallowed by an unrelenting sun. I shaded my eyes and got lost in the staccato rhythm of Spanish words dancing out of the African mouths all around me. Eventually, I found my way to the studio of Pablo Herrera, the island's biggest hip-hop producer. I knocked on the door and was relieved when a cloud of air-conditioned coolness picked me up and carried me inside. Pablo greeted me: "Yo, bro, what's good? Welcome to Cuba!" His English held no trace of a Caribbean-Spanish accent, even though he was born and raised on the island and had spent most of his life there. Over the next few weeks he would introduce me to the artists whose music had reached me in New York in the years prior. I was particularly eager to meet Anónimo Consejo. This duo, composed of rappers Kokino (Adeyeme) and Sekou Umoja, was among the island's more popular artists. Their lyrics were a seamless blend of incisive wit and political commentary that resonated with crowds and drew both admiration and concern from the Cuban government. Like many of the city's rappers, they participated in workshops held at the house of New Afrikan political exile Nehanda Abiodun. Born and raised in Harlem in the 1950s, Mama Nehanda, as she was known, joined the Black Power movement and arrived on the island in 1990 after going underground for nearly a decade. Shortly thereafter, she began hosting political education workshops with rappers, teaching them about global radical struggles and placing these young artists within a larger context of revolutionary art. Many rappers, including Anónimo Consejo, refined their pro-Black ideologies during their time with Mama Nehanda, who became known as the "Godmother of Cuban Hip-Hop."[5]

The group combined this global consciousness with their knowledge of a national history of struggle in songs like "Afrocubano Soy Yo," which is about the Cuban Army's 1912 massacre of thousands of Afro-Cubans, including members of El Partido Independiente de Color. Opening with a Yoruba-styled roll call of ancestors, Anónimo Consejo place themselves within the lineage of these revolutionaries and call for Black Cuban listeners to "open the eyes" and "open the mind" to this shared identity. In "Loma y Machete" they take this further by inviting listeners to escape Babylon and head to the hills. The song's chorus states,

> Loma y machete
> No somos esclavos ya.
> Loma y machete
> Ya no hay grillete más.
> Qué Iyalochas van
> Pa'los montes [Palo Monte].

Qué Babalochas van
Pa'los montes [Palo Monte].

Hill and machete
We're no longer slaves.
Hill and machete
There are no longer shackles.
The Iyalochas go
To the mountain [Palo Monte].
The Babalochas go
To the mountain [Palo Monte].[6]

In keeping with Cedric Robinson's observation, the rappers find their freedom in the hills, where a spiritual community—made evident by the song's explicit references to both Palo Monte and Santería—serves as the grounds upon which all else is built. This is confirmed not only in their call for Iyalochas and Babalochas[7] to go but in the double entendre "Pa'los montes [Palo Monte]." Cuban Spanish is known to abbreviate and drop the "s" sound from the ends of words, thus "Para los montes" ("for/to the mountains") becomes abbreviated as "Pa'lo monte." Pronounced as such, it becomes indistinguishable from Palo Monte, an African spiritual system brought to the island by Africans captured from central-west Africa. They will leave their shackles behind to head for the isolation of the mountains, where a spiritual community under armed protection can thrive.

Kokino jumps into the song's final verse with a fiery call to action:

Cimarrón, arriba!
Lucha por tu vida.
No dejes que grilletes sofoquen tu energía
¿Qué pasa?
No te detengas camina.
Se acercan los perros.
La lucha es por vida.
En la loma esta tu casa.
. . . .
Fuera a palenque

Es sólo por grillete.
No más esclavos.
Loma y machete!

Maroon arise!
Fight for your life.
Don't allow the shackles to suffocate your energy.
What's happening?
Don't keep yourself from your path.
The dogs are closing in.
The fight is for life.
Your house is in the hills.
. . . .
Outside of the *palenque*
Is only for the shackle.
Slaves no more.
Hill and machete![8]

The world outside of the *palenque,* or maroon community, is one of enslavement. Though subtle, Kokino is expressing a significant philosophical stance when he says "Don't keep yourself from your path." This could also be interpreted as "Don't stop yourself. Walk." Though humbly disguised in poetry, this expression evinces the belief that ultimately "death or victory is an internal affair" (C. J. Robinson 2000, 168–69). Both this verse and "Loma y Machete" as a whole affirm an approach to marronage as pursuit. Yes, the dogs are closing in. They are only chasing us, however, because we left to *pursue* freedom: "The fight is for life." Further still, the song's title contains an entire story in three words: "Hill and Machete." It tells us where we are going and what we need to bring.

The statue that graced the cover of the edition of Price's *Maroon Societies* that I read in Brazil, the *Nèg Mawon* or *Le Marron Unconnu,* is located in front of the National Palace in Port-au-Prince, Haiti. The figure kneels on his right knee as his left leg stretches behind him. His head is leaned back and he is blowing into the *lambi*—conch shell—which has been used as a communication device due to its ability to produce a clear and distinguishable sound that travels for miles over hills and valleys (see Banton 1997). There is a shackle with a broken chain on his left ankle—*no hay griellete más*. In his right hand, which supports his body, is a machete. The 2010 earthquake that shook Port-au-Prince crumbled the National Palace. The *Nèg Mawon* was unscathed. The machete, commonplace throughout the Caribbean, is at once a tool and a weapon capable of both building and destroying. It is what Vic Reid (1983) calls a "friend and protector." It is Ogun's instrument of choice. While most often characterized as the Yoruba Orisha of iron and war, Ogun is also the clearer of paths. In this sense, the machete serves as an effective symbol of marronage: a weapon to break the chains and fight off those who dare try to enslave, a tool to open a way toward a free community, and an instrument to cultivate the sustenance of that community—disengagement, flight, and reengagement.

It is difficult to consider historical maroons without accounting for the animating axes of African cosmologies expressed through spiritual systems laden with ways of being and knowing that predate and exceed modernity. These worldviews constitute the very grounds upon which Moura's dialectical synthesis could play out. The maroons had recourse to a cultural matrix that could find neither affirmation nor accommodation within the plantation complex. As such, they sought something beyond it that would allow them to "consciously reconstitute a group identity" that "was no less a legacy from Africa" (Wynter n.d., 72–73). To view marronage as anything less than an expression of an African cultural continuum is to misread marronage. Of course, Anónimo Consejo would weave Santería and Palo Monte into their lyrics, for these systems form the tapestry of their Afro-Cuban worldview.

I am hesitant to apply the term *religion* to these spiritual systems precisely because they emanate from cultural contexts that do not separate the sacred from the profane. Instead, they view life—in all its sacredness and profanity—as part of an integrated whole. "Loma y Machete" makes explicit references to African spiritual traditions. More than a recitation, however, the song's message embodies the thrust of these spiritual systems: full and abundant life—ontological totality—for the community, here and now.

Land and Bone

Sylvia Wynter brings together these concepts of African spirituality/ "religion" and community through a discussion of land among maroons. In speaking of the maroons of Jamaica, she alludes to their flexibility of expression in both size and location. While geography and topography shaped their forms, the ancestral traditions of the maroons informed their cultural values and thus how they maneuvered in their environment. More specifically, "the religious concept of the earth as the base of the community is essentially a philosophical and political ideology" that stands in contrast to the plantation system, "in which the material base, the earth, is seen as the private property of individuals" (n.d., 72). Land is the foundation for the sustenance of a spiritual community populated by living and nonliving members. It allows for the cultivation of the provision grounds and medicine fields that sustain them. It is where their ancestors are buried, thus leaving unbroken the spirocycle of time. It is also where those accompanying Anónimo Consejo could encounter the chance for a life on their own terms.

The embattled nature of marronage, however, made it difficult for historical maroons to establish lasting and stable relationships with land. We do find histories of long-standing communities in places like Brazil, Dominica, Jamaica, and Suriname, where maroons could raise generations of children unobstructed by European incursion. Still, these communities had to remain on guard and ready to move at a moment's notice. Palmares's history included a ceaseless war with Dutch and Portuguese armies. French colonialists did not largely bother the maroons of Dominica, but war commenced when the British took over the island (Honychurch 2017). Maroons in Suriname and Jamaica were able to fight European forces to a standstill and sign treaties securing their independence. This independence would be challenged by shifting global political and economic interests over the course of the twentieth century and into the twenty-first. Regardless of the duration of these formations, however, the community was, as Wynter points out, the "overarching concept." We also find resonance of this in Moura, who writes: "The status of prestige . . . was granted collectively to those who accepted the mandate of community: to defend it, organize it, and protect it" (2001, 104; my translation). Communal well-being was paramount. It was the primary consideration when determining where maroons would settle and for how long.

Vic Reid's novel *Nanny-Town* (1983) offers a fictional reading of the great maroon leader Grandy Nanny that speaks to the primacy of community. Believed to have been an Akan woman born in what is now Ghana,

Queen Nanny led her Windward Maroons of Jamaica to victory as they defeated the British over the course of the first half of the eighteenth century, eventually signing a treaty that granted them land and independence. In the novel, Reid tells the story of the unification of the island's Windward and Leeward Maroons, led by Queen Nanny and Cudjoe, respectively. Laced with philosophical and pedagogical majesty, the novel is truly a gift. For our purposes, I would like to explore what Reid refers to as the "sling-shot town" and its implications for the inherent and necessary mobility of marronage.

After maroon scouts discover British plans to attack Nanny-Town, Queen Nanny decides it's time to leave. She addresses her people:

> Do not be sad, you mothers and daughters at leaving Nanny-Town. There shall be a new Nanny-Town, for, like the turtle, we Maroons carry our refuge on our backs and live longer than other creatures. As Maroons, you have always known that when the story comes to *bump*, our town is as much a weapon as the musket or the machete. Our town is a stone in a sling and the time has come to hurl it at the enemy. Anywhere we go in the mountains, there will be logs, vines, thatch and stones to build new homes. There will be earth, and seeds to plant, streams and rivers for fishing, moon-shine nights for old story time and laughter. (1983, 56)

While this choice to leave sacred ground may at first seem to be at odds with the spiritual understandings of land that Wynter offers, I read Queen Nanny's words as affirming Wynter. The maroons have to leave the particular land that they have come to know, and this is a potential point of sadness as this has become home to the bones of ancestors and communal memories. Queen Nanny reminds them, however, that the Earth will continue to provide for them no matter where they find themselves, confirming the reciprocal relationship of the cosmic whole in which the person—*muntu*—and the Earth are one. This allows for an advantageous flexibility whereby maroons, who carry their refuge on their back, may always find shelter and sustenance.

Before breaking into a war dance that both captivates and inspires, Queen Nanny assures her people that "it is always more beautiful where you are going than where you are coming from" (56). The narrator was one of the adolescents chosen to prepare the evacuated Nanny-Town.

The villagers were moved to a temporary settlement at an obscure location. The adolescents remained behind to gather wood while the warriors cut holes in the back of huts and placed boiling pots around the village's center. As the British soldiers—the Red Ants—arrived, they found what appeared to be a village caught off guard. They saw silhouettes in the huts, heard chatter, and found cooking pots alight. They fired their canons on the town, but not before the warriors, masquerading as unsuspecting villagers relaxing in their homes for the evening, were able to exit through the back of the huts and wait in the bush. Once the Red Ants stormed into the village center chanting and celebrating, the hidden adolescents slung rocks from the surrounding trees, bursting the oil-filled cooking pots that erupted into flames and consumed the Red Ants. The warriors unleashed gunshots, spears, and arrows and defeated, once again, the militarily inferior British. The Abeng, or war horn, sounded, and Nanny called her children home.

I agree with Wynter that the maroons were drawing on historical and cultural precedents. While their environments in the Western Hemisphere may have been new, their cultural technology was not. The British, unable to accept the reality of continuing defeat as reflected in their historical record and archives, spread propaganda that painted Queen Nanny as a supernatural murderer. They generated the myth that she possessed the ability to catch bullets in her buttocks and fire them back at the attacking soldiers. This is the inspiration behind Reid's use of the oil pots, for the British said that Queen Nanny would cook and eat her captives.[9] "Into Nanny cook-pot" (76), yelled the maroon soldiers as "all the houses in our Town pointed brightly burning fingers at our British visitors" (75). The town itself, the land, was converted into a weapon—a slingshot—to defend the community of maroons. In her speech, Queen Nanny could have said that they carry their *home* on their back. She chose the word *refuge*. Just as a home is more than a house, a refuge is more than a home. It is at once shelter and a place that removes one from danger. To carry refuge on one's back is to always have access to safety and room to grow. It is also to be in a position to weaponize one's environment in order to preserve freedom. Location is never as central as freedom. As such, movement becomes an extension of a freedom praxis. Marronage is a processual unfolding. There is no arrival, only arriving in ways that mandate all settlements temporary. Settlement increases vulnerability. Continuous mobility, though, exhausts. Marronage necessitates a dynamic interchange between the two. They build what they can where and with whom they find themselves, knowing that when the time comes they will depart not as fugitives—for fugitives are escaping—but as perpetual seekers who carry their refuge every step of the way.

The examples in my discussion—Gerima's cave encounters, Anónimo Conejo's hill and machete, and Reid's Nanny-Town—are contemporary readings of a maroon past. We continue to see the maroon impulse, however, as an ongoing animus in the lives of African people. Precious's listening sessions and street-corner reasonings were some of my early recognitions of it. But it was also embodied in her mother, my grandmother, whom we also call Nanny. She left Liberia with her daughter—my mother—for 1960s New York. There they settled into a Brooklyn enclave of migrants from all over the African world, seeking what they may have called a "better life." I, a product of that life, would set out to find my own version of better and, in the process, encounter that maroon impulse as that which both drove and welcomed me. My grandmother, her neighbors, the people I would encounter in New Orleans, and I had this in common. This maroon impulse is an animating force of diasporic cultural expression. It is neither relegated to the past nor limited to political superstructures. Marronage exists outside the political. While traces of it may be found therein, the political is not its source, nor is it hospitable soil for its blossoming. It grows in people and communities that bend, morph, and shift in pursuit of a shared world. It is rooted in the past, but persists in, shapes, and is shaped by the present.

When I arrived in New Orleans, I entered into a city on the move. The geological, political, economic, and demographic landscape was shifting. And while there was a lot of newness being introduced, I was also witnessing the cultivation and continuation of legacies. I was first drawn toward the possibilities of marronage through the efforts of a workers' cooperative attempting to intervene in the city's housing crisis. I showed up looking for it, uncertain of the shape it may take. I would learn, however, that the maroon impulse was already all around in the places where and people with whom I spent my time, imagined, and worked. It was and is, at all times, everywhere, even if not always acted upon. Fortunately for me, I had moved into a community of people who heard its call.

2

West Bank Is the Best Bank

Algiers and the Unseen Presence as Landscape

Everything you love about New Orleans is because of Black people.

—Mynameisphlegm

Algiers is the only New Orleans neighborhood located on the west bank of the Mississippi River. Often referred to as "'cross the river," it sits perfectly across from the French Quarter and is about five miles from the city's Central Business District, making it closer to downtown than some other parts of the city. The cultural chasm between the two sides, however, is greater than the distance. In my time living there it was common to hear things like "Aww, I ain't goin 'cross the river for that" or "Damn, why you live all the way out there 'cross the river for?" In addition to two ferries, the banks sit about two thousand feet apart and are connected by the Crescent City Connection, twin structures passing 1/4 feet above the Mississippi. Despite their proximity, the idea of crossing the river is often communicated as a harrowing journey into the unknown, belying distance and suggesting an inconvenience not worth its reward. Some on the east bank view Algiers as their country cousin. Others view it as existing in their shadow. Those from Algiers, however, see the relationship quite differently, speaking of their neighborhood with an unshakable pride.

This was on display one night in 2010 when a group of poets hosted an event on Holiday Drive. It was a special night. It wasn't common to see so many of the city's big-name poets in one place, let alone in Algiers. There was a palpable sense of love and excitement in the air. This must be what emboldened Phil Coolidge to take the stage unannounced. Phil wasn't a poet. He and his brothers ran a cultural center in Algiers that their father founded, and with liquor in his hand and a slur in his speech, he barked into the mic, "You know I had to say somethin' real quick. I *had* to say somethin' with ya'll all up in *my* house. I know ya'll be tryna play us, or whatever. But look where y'all at. The West Bank! Ya'll know, just like I do, the West Bank the best bank! The West Bank the best bank!" The crowd of friends was laughing and, in typical New Orleans fashion, talking right back: "Say now, get off the stage, Kanye Coolidge!" It was a lighthearted exchange, and the Kanye nickname stuck for a while, but Phil was speaking to a larger, complicated reality of proximal distance that characterizes the relationship between the two sides of the river and extends back several centuries to the city's very founding. This chapter explores how the geographical location of BlackStar Books and Caffé was itself shaped by an unseen presence. It excavates the soil that fertilized the seeds of a maroon impulse that found expression through the BlackStar community.

What would become Algiers was settled in 1719, a year after New Orleans was established and the same year that two ships introduced 451 enslaved Africans into the would-be city. While the intentions for the settlement on the east bank as a commercial center were clear, this was not the case for the river's west bank, which was mostly undeveloped swampland until the Company of the West, which held a monopoly charter to French settlements in North America, established a plantation there.[1] The Company Plantation, as it came to be known, was used as a lumber mill and depot providing goods to the larger colony. Its farms produced rice, indigo, tobacco, and sugarcane. Its primary function, however, was as "a place to receive the African slaves brought in by the company for sale to the French colonists and for use in its various construction projects" (Wilson 1990, 163). They were Bambara, Mandingo, Kongo, Hausa, Fulbe, Igbo, Wolof, Fon, Makwa, Yoruba, Chamba. They came from the Senegambia, the Bight of Benin, and West-Central and Southeast Africa. Throughout the 1720s, upwards of thirty cabins were built to house this influx of Africans. Upon arrival on the Company Plantation, they were "seasoned" before being sent across the river to be sold in the parks, private residences, or street corners of New Orleans. By 1731 there were 224 enslaved Africans on the Company Plantation, making up an overwhelming majority of the West Bank population. That number would nearly double every Sunday when Africans from across the river would arrive in small boats and gather to dance, drum, and assemble (Campanella 2020; Le Page du Pratz 2015). As per the Code Noir established by Louis XIV in 1685 and amended by Philippe II in 1724, enslaved Africans throughout the French empire were entitled to Sundays and holidays off.[2] This led to gatherings where Africans could play music, reconvene with friends and lovers, barter, trade, and steal away.

The Company Plantation went bankrupt in 1731 and the settlement was returned to the French Crown, becoming King's Plantation and placed under the leadership of Jean-Baptiste Le Moyne, Sieur de Bienville. In addition to being a former governor, Bienville was also the founder of New Orleans and did little to maintain the economic viability of the settlement of the West Bank. Upon his retirement, new leadership rebuilt the decaying buildings, culminating in the construction of twenty-five new cabins for enslaved Africans. It wasn't until the Spanish took over New Orleans, however, that Algiers would become residential. France formally ceded control of the city to Spain in the Treaty of Fontainebleau (1762). It was a contested forty-year possession, with citizens never relinquishing their allegiances to France and French culture that were cultivated over the previous forty-five years of French possession. Still, the mark of Spanish influence remains through the present. After fires ravaged the French Quarter in 1788 and again in 1794, for instance, the area was rebuilt. The French Quarter we know today is a Spanish architectural style—not French—replete with passageways and hidden rear gardens. Despite this physical presence, however, Spanish authority faced continual opposition. A massive influx of French-speaking people—both enslaved and enslaving—fleeing the Haitian Revolution further challenged Spanish authority.[3] In Algiers, Spain began subdividing King's Plantation and selling to colonists, thus opening up the settlement for greater access to private ownership. Over the next four decades, the development of villages and neighborhoods would begin to take shape.

Maroons in the Bayou

When the Spanish took over New Orleans, they inherited a problem that plagued the French but with which they too were familiar due to its ubiquity in all of their holdings: marronage. Before this, however, the Company of the Indies (formerly Company of the West) hired architect and writer Antoine-Simon Le Page du Pratz to manage a major tobacco expansion on the Company Plantation in 1726. Le Page was a self-proclaimed expert in the "governing of Negroes" and confidently took the job, knowing that a large importation of Africans would be required. His self-assuredness came in handy a few years later when, according to him, it enabled him to unearth a plot of rebellion on the King's Plantation and arrest its conspirators. While Samuel Wilson (1990) notes there is no evidence of Le Page's involvement in this case in colonial records, Le Page reports that it began when a French soldier violently struck an African woman and she warned that "the French should not long insult negroes."[4] Le Page was not so quick to dismiss the retort as a harmless threat hurled in the heat of the moment, and explored its validity by sneaking "from hut to hut" whereupon he heard some people talking. One of the plot's leaders was an African named Samba, who was Le Page's *commandeur*, or plantation foreman.[5] Eight people were arrested and tortured with burns, but none spoke. Finally, they confessed and were condemned to be "broke alive on the wheel." The aggrieved woman who first spoke was hanged.

In accordance with Le Page's suspicion of Black assembly, he was antagonistic toward the Sunday gatherings. In the penultimate paragraph of his *History of Louisiana* (2015), he writes:

> In a word, nothing is more to be dreaded than to see the negroes assemble together on Sundays, since, under pretence of Calinda or the dance, they sometimes get together to the number of three or four hundred, and make a kind of Sabbath, which it is always prudent to avoid; for it is in those tumultuous meetings that they sell what they have stolen to one another, and commit many crimes. In these likewise they plot their rebellions.

Le Page banned gatherings after it was reported that some Africans from the west bank were heading across the river to rob people. This cross-river movement couldn't be entirely restricted, however. Enslaved Africans conducted much of the day-to-day business in early New Orleans, from managing hotels and taverns to constructing levees and canals. The comings and goings of Africans across the river and throughout the region formed a network expanding across the colony (J. M. Johnson 2020). This was particularly true on the Company Plantation. Charged with the development of Louisiana, the Company of the Indies was constantly engaged in construction, transportation, and the building of fortifications. Instead of paying exorbitant fees associated with white skilled labor, the company apprenticed enslaved Africans to learn the trades of shipmaking, sailing, blacksmithing, and carpentry—if they had not already brought such skills with them from Africa. These skilled laborers would regularly travel throughout the colony to complete their forced labor. Those who worked on the plantation would grow the food that sustained those traveling (Hall 1992).

In the midst of this movement—clandestine or otherwise—absconsion was pervasive, as the swamps and marshes proved beyond the reach of European comfort and convenience (Hosbey and Roane 2021). Marronage existed during French rule, but after the Spanish took over, larger numbers of Africans took flight. They would form settlements in the cypress swamps, either deep into the marshes or close to the fringes of plantations. They produced goods such as baskets and woven articles. They cultivated crops like corn, squash, rice, and herbs. They hunted, fished, and made trips to New Orleans to sell or trade their offerings, and moved freely through a series of paths and networks connecting the bayous. They socialized with, married, and often worked for Africans living on the plantation. Most remarkably, this clandestine network extended over miles of inhospitable terrain (Diouf 2014; Hall 1992).

There is perhaps no maroon in Louisiana more famous than Jean St. Malo, or Juan San Maló. His story demonstrates, among other things, the fluidity of marronage in the colonial era and embodies many of the unique characteristics of marronage in southeastern Louisiana. St. Malo is believed to have escaped from the D'Arensbourg plantation on the German Coast, which sits on the west bank upriver from New Orleans in today's neighboring St. Charles Parish. There is little known of him, except that he was French-speaking. There has been speculation about his name—was it of French, Spanish, or Bambara origin?[6] Despite his vague biography, however, it is clear that St. Malo was a distinguished leader who coordinated a federation of settlements in both remote and local environs. His network spanned uninhabitable swamps in the lower river region known as Bas du Fleuve. These settlements required entrance through secret passageways with water up to the chest. Some of the maroons' more permanent settlements occurred between the Mississippi River and Lake Borgne, which sits roughly thirty miles east of New Orleans.

Their principal strongholds were Terre Gaillarde to the south of Lake Borgne and Chef Menteur to the northwest. They also occupied the Rigolets, near today's Slidell, at the entry to Lake Pontchartrain and into the marshes further south at Bayou Terre Aux Boeufs. St. Malo and the maroons are known to have moved regularly between these places and further west onto the plantations surrounding the city of New Orleans.

St. Malo's vast network spread over southeastern Louisiana like a blanket. Beginning with the rise of the cypress industry in the mid-eighteenth century, plantation owners would purchase vast swaths of property, the boundaries of which extended far into the swamps. Enslaved Africans would be tasked with laboring in these impenetrable forests. As familiarity with these hostile environments grew, some would begin settling in the swamps with their families and an embattled freedom. Communities of maroons would emerge, as they forged pathways facilitating movement throughout the swamps. They maintained relationships with those still on the plantation, trading food, crafts, and labor. Maroons were so common that in some instances they even established business relationships with plantation owners who hired them to cut and transport cypress wood. The maroons were also armed for self-defense and sustenance. By the time St. Malo came to the attention of Spanish authorities in the 1780s, the maroon landscape was highly developed and far reaching.

St. Malo and the maroons of southeastern Louisiana are somewhat unique within the history of marronage in that they had an unusually large number of women and children. As Gwendolyn M. Hall points out, they left the plantations in families (1992, 203). Parents with adult children and even grandchildren would disappear into the swamp, where they would encounter other families as well as single adults. This allowed for some semblance of stability. The maroons maintained regular contact with Africans on the plantations, sometimes settling close by for months or years at a time. They would work and often eat together in the forests. A common practice was for those on the plantation to drive cattle toward the outskirts of the forest for the maroons to capture and slaughter. In exchange, the maroons would perform chores for them (Din 1980). They would also sustain themselves by raiding plantation stock houses for staples such as rice, sugar, flour, alcohol, gunpowder, and ammunition.

The Spanish began spreading propaganda about bloodthirsty maroons seeking to overthrow the plantocracy through murder and pillage in an attempt to drum up support for their capture and execution. In truth, the violence with which they were associated was largely self-defense. For instance, four maroons were lured into a gun trade by a group of Americans. As they arrived at the point of exchange, more men with guns emerged and held them captive, tying them up in a canoe bound for New Orleans. When the kidnappers stopped to cook dinner, the maroons were left in the boats with a single guard. St. Malo emerged and untied his comrades. He passed a hatchet to Joli Coeur, who proceeded to smash the skull of their captor before regaining freedom (Hall 1992; Diouf 2014). The Spanish dedicated significant resources to the neutralization of St. Malo, but often had difficulties securing sufficient numbers for the campaigns. Many of the would-be Black militiamen had preexisting relationships with the maroons. Even with the promise of their own freedom, they were hesitant to involve themselves out of fear of inciting retaliation or vengeance from their families or social networks on the plantation. The murder of whites, whether Spanish or not—even in self-defense—served as sufficient justification for the Spanish to raise their efforts. After several failed attempts over the course of two years, the Spanish finally captured St. Malo in a raid that required two hundred soldiers to guard the exit of Terre Gaillarde (Hall 1992). In all, more than one hundred maroons were captured, including St. Malo, who was hanged at what is now Jackson Square.

The case of St. Malo and his maroons is helpful because many of the maroons captured gave testimonies. Two interconnected themes throughout those testimonies are that of justice and gratuitous violence. It was violence, whether committed against an individual or a relative of the individual, that served as impetus for flight. This, of course, precedes St. Malo. Hall cites a case from 1763—right as the Spanish were taking over—in which fourteen Africans took to the swamps in a collective decision to maroon after the plantation owner violated their rights under the Code Noir. We find this, too, in Le Page's account of the soldier who struck the African woman. The threat in her response indicates a collective boiling point that sought insurrection. This exposes the maroon impulse present as an urge to pursue. While they were escaping the violence of the plantation, they were, more centrally, *pursuing* the dignity available in the freedom of the swamp. When St. Malo arrives at Terre Guillarde, strikes his axe in a tree, and proclaims "Woe betide the white man who crosses these bounds," he is proclaiming the realization of that maroon impulse.

This is *their* land, where they can live on their own terms. They have arrived and are willing to defend it—whatever the cost. After his death, St. Malo would take on a mythic presence in New Orleans. The invocation of his name either struck fear or pride, depending on one's position (D. Allen 2022; Hosbey and Roane 2021). St. Malo and his maroons represent a tradition of marronage and an expression of a maroon impulse still present in the region today.

The Oldest Black Neighborhood?

I frequently heard it mentioned in passing that Algiers was home to the oldest Black neighborhood in the United States. This was a challenge to the historic Faubourg Tremé, on the east bank, which more popularly holds this title. Founded in the 1810s, Tremé was home to a mixed neighborhood including "free people of color." It is considered by many the birthplace of jazz and a center for New Orleans culture. Tremé is where Congo Square, a historical gathering place for enslaved Africans sometimes numbering as many as six hundred, is located. While I have not come across any documents explicitly naming Algiers as the rightful owner of the title that Tremé holds, the anecdotal ubiquity of this claim presents some worthy questions in a discussion of the unseen presence. I have devised two possible explanations. The first is rather straightforward yet inconclusive, while the second requires some exploration.

John McDonogh has a strong legacy in New Orleans. At one time, thirty schools in the city bore his name, even more than a century and a half after he arrived in New Orleans. Born in Baltimore, McDonogh was a plantation owner and recluse who purchased a large swath of land stretching from Algiers into current-day Gretna.[7] This area would become known as McDonoghville. As early as 1815 he began selling land to "free people of color," which included some of his formerly enslaved (Campanella 2020; Swanson 2004). The section in which they settled would become known as "Freetown." The Black settlement in McDonoghville was founded around the same time as Tremé's indistinct "1810s" founding. While Tremé itself was established in 1812, the emergence of its Black population into what would become known as a "neighborhood" is unclear. It does seem that Freetown was primarily Black, while Tremé was mixed. This historical ambiguity opens up the possibility for Algiers to make its claim.

The second explanation relies less on a technicality and more on conceptual excavation. Nearly a century before either Tremé or McDonoghville, Le Page undertook major construction projects on the Company Plantation. This included a compound of up to 154 enslaved Africans housed in thirty-two cabins located behind what is now the Algiers Courthouse. As Richard Campanella notes, this was "the largest concentration of African people in early Louisiana" (2020, 202). While it was simultaneously both a permanent and a transient population, in that some Africans were held there before being either sold across or up the river or remained on the Company Plantation, is it possible to read this early and steady presence as a proto-neighborhood? Allow me pause to acknowledge the seeming absurdity of suggesting that a plantation of enslaved Africans could qualify as a "neighborhood." I am doing so, however, to open up a discussion that reframes the landscape of legitimacy. What constitutes a neighborhood? It is not, wholly, an intentional community, but is rather formed by necessity (safety, affordability, proximity to family, work, etc.). Black neighborhoods in the United States, in particular, have often been determined by where they have been "allowed" to live (Purifoy and Seamster 2021). In the case of larger plantations, such as the Company Plantation, Black people were the overwhelming majority. As we see in colonial New Orleans, the boundaries of these plantations were less than fixed.

When Darius Scott (2021) and Katherine McKittrick (2011) talk about noncartographic mapping, they are speaking of places "unseen" but still there. How do you map the liminal landscape of the swamp and marsh? There is an unseen presence in them where social lives of Black people—kinship, friendship, friction, faction, and grievance—abound. The plantation is a complex of violence and terror, but it is never totalizing. The fourteen Africans who collectively escaped the wanton violence of the plantation owner argued that they had not, in fact, run away, since they remained on the plantation the entire time. They were merely out of sight and reach of the landowner (Hall 1992). They went noncartographic. A concept of Black place is one that is shaped by and shapes the violence of the plantation (Purifoy 2021; McKittrick 2011), but it is not restricted to it. It would be inaccurate to view the plantation as wholly devoid of agency. Instead, it is composed of what Stephanie Camp refers to as rival geographies, or "alternative ways of knowing and using plantation space that were inconsistent with the planter's requirements" (2002, 3). Whereas the plantation geography is fixed, the rival geography is characterized by motion, moving through and beyond the structures and boundaries of the plantation. The relationships between those Africans living on and off of the plantation provide an example of this. Maroons established semi-permanent settlements on the fringes of the plantation and maintained ongoing, familial, fraternal, and working relationships with the enslaved in a way that complicates lines of status. Even the use of term "enslaved" is troubled, since it is known that many of those residing on the plantation regularly engaged rival geographies through practices such as *petit marronage*. This language runs the risk of flattening their experiences and the rival geographies they inhabited.

If a convincing argument can be made for the plantation's rival geography as the site of a neighborhood, it would be difficult to conclusively designate the Company Plantation as the first. In the developing landscape of continental North America, large plantations inhabited by a majority of African people were common (though many of them were privately and not corporately owned). However, my discussion here is less about which community is the oldest and more about how we recognize such communities. What are their criteria for constitution/recognition/visibility? Tremé and Freetown were home to a group of free Blacks who were able to purchase their land. The Africans on the Company Plantation were enslaved on land they worked for no pay. Does land ownership alone constitute belonging or legitimate claim? If so, how many Black neighborhoods in the contemporary era would we need to dismiss?[8] Furthermore, is ownership—by deed and title—the sole determinant of commitment and therefore claim to that land?

Louis Congo was an African enslaved on the Company Plantation. He gained his freedom in exchange for serving as the Crown's executioner. He would spend nearly twelve years killing those who violated the law—white, Black, or Indigenous—in the most gruesome fashions: flogging, hanging, breaking on the wheel, or burning alive. Among other things he requested before taking this job, Congo asked for the freedom of his wife, also of the Company Plantation, and a plot of land. His first request was denied, as it was viewed as too costly for the company to lose two of their enslaved. His second request, however, was granted. His wife would join him on the land and be relieved of her labor duties, though maintain her legal status as enslaved. As Jessica Marie Johnson observes, "Louis's request to be given the plot of land he labored on suggested something of the ownership Africans felt over the physical land itself—even if it was land they worked as slaves" (2020, 145), underscoring the discussion in chapter 1 on the significance of land for African people.

At Kamali Academy we were cautious about "Black firsts," limiting their use to self-esteem-boosting devices for small children. My discussion of Algiers and Tremé is aimed at raising questions about legitimacy and space claims. Recognized by whom? Why do we take for granted and leave unquestioned colonial claims of ownership or legitimacy made on the hot potato that was early America? The rival geography of Africans laboring and moving on, between, through, around, and away from plantations sketches a map that leads us to different conclusions.

New Orleans West

Spanish rule came to an end in 1803, when the settlement was ceded back to France. The French, suffering devastating loses during the Haitian Revolution, turned around less than three weeks later and sold New Orleans and another 828,000 square miles of land to the United States as part of the Louisiana Purchase. Algiers's uncertain and at times contentious relationship with New Orleans continued. It remained unincorporated when New Orleans received its municipal charter in 1805. Over the next seven decades, Algiers's status was a hopscotch of local and state governance. It was at one time or another part of Orleans Parish and/or the short-lived Orleans County. After 1840 it was run by a police jury through which jurors "passed ordinances and oversaw everything from policing and leasing to education, improvements, and taxation" (Campanella 2019). Industry flourished as Algiers's economy boasted of shipyards, stockyards, iron foundries, slaughterhouses, and monocrop plantations. The settlement's economic success drew the attention of New Orleans, which was seeking to expand its control over the area. By 1858 there were three ferries with regular service to Algiers and other points on the west bank. The right side of the river, with its sparse population, was seen as a refreshing reprieve from the east bank's crowdedness. As the city desired expansion, it recognized what the people of Algiers had known all along: New Orleans had much more to gain from Algiers than Algiers had to gain from New Orleans. It had a bustling economy, high real estate values, a longer riverfront, and more direct access to the growing wealth of Texas.

As New Orleans sought annexation, Algiers sought to maintain its distance, fearing that annexation would raise taxes, drain wealth, and rob it of its autonomy.

The desire for annexation was not motivated by economics alone. Reconstruction created a new political landscape throughout the country, especially in the larger urban centers of the South. The annexation of Algiers, with its sizable Black population, would incorporate presumed Republican voters to balance out recent, heavily Democratic acquisitions. In 1870, Algiers became a part of New Orleans as its only neighborhood on the west bank of the Mississippi River. The insider/outsider relationship between the two banks, however, was not resolved by annexation. Two hundred and thirty-five years after being settled, both sides would be connected via bridge, with the Gretna New Orleans Bridge opening in

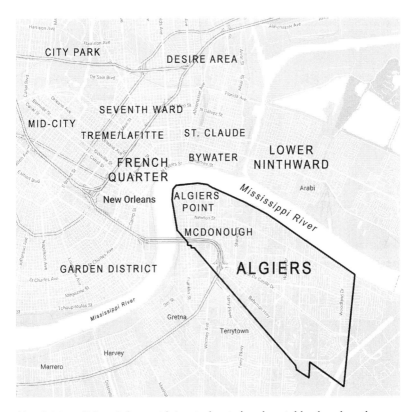

Map 1. Map of New Orleans. Algiers is the city's only neighborhood on the west bank of the Mississippi River.

1954 as the longest cantilever bridge in the world. The second bridge would open in 1988, and both would be dubbed the Crescent City Connection a year later. By that time, cultural divisions and independent identities had solidified which persist, in many ways, into the present. Even as recently as 2015, state representative Jeff Arnold proposed HB744, which sought to incorporate Algiers as a separate municipality in Orleans Parish (Ballard 2015).

Representative Arnold cites the lack of city services available to Algiers, referring to the neighborhood as the "red-headed stepsister of New Orleans."[9] While his sentiment is clear, Arnold's metaphor falls short of the racialized realities of New Orleans in a way that affirms the unseen presence of Black Algiers. Colonial Algiers was considered, according to Malik Rahim, "the land of the Wild Congo Niggas" (Chenier 2020). Le Page warned whites "never to suffer [Negroes] to come near your children, who, exclusive of the bad smell, can learn nothing good from them, either as to morals, education, or language" (Le Page du Pratz 2015). It was, for the duration of its early settlement through the twentieth century, majority Black. With the enacting of civil rights legislation in the mid-twentieth century, white flight set in and white residents sprinted out of New Orleans and into the suburbs, including St. Bernard and Jefferson Parishes.[10] Algiers Point has historically had a large white population, but developers needed to make room for those leaving the East Bank. They settled on Aurora Gardens in Algiers and Terrytown, just over the city line. By 1970 these neighborhoods were 97 and 98 percent white, respectively. For some, Algiers was still New Orleans, and New Orleans meant Black. Further into Jefferson Parish, the Timberlane opened in 1959 as the first private country club on the west bank, with an affluent community settling around the club in communities that would be gated in the future (Campanella 2020). This trend would continue over the next several decades.

Above Ground during Hurricane Katrina

When Hurricane Katrina ravaged the Gulf Coast in late August 2005, images of Black people wading through chest-high water or crowds of people corralled on overpasses began circulating at the same time as stories of "looting and violence." Television commentators were shocked by the level of poverty that the storm revealed, dumbfounded that such poverty could exist in the United States. Their commentary over the next few days would reflect their infuriating ignorance. I became aware of Katrina through an image of what was clearly a boy trudging through water. He held a twelve-pack of Pepsi in his right arm and a black trash bag trailing behind him in his left hand. His yellow-and-white striped shirt was soaked. The caption from the Associated Press reads, "A young man walks through chest deep flood water after looting a grocery store in New Orleans on Tuesday, Aug. 30, 2005" (Martin 2005). The AP would, on several other occasions, refer to Black survivors as "looters." This would be criticized and juxtaposed with a photo from Agence France-Presse/Getty Images of two white people walking through the water after "finding bread and soda from a local store" (Graythen 2005).

The destruction in the city, however, resulted less from the hurricane itself and more from the failing infrastructure of the levee system. For years leading up to the storm, researchers, journalists, and concerned citizens pointed out the flawed and inadequate design of the levee system. The flooding that consumed nearly 80 percent of the city found its way through overwhelmed or broken levees with gaps that reached up to a thousand feet long in some instances. Water levels rose higher than fifteen feet and when it was all said and done, nearly fifteen hundred people in the area lost their lives. This does not include the corpses that were left to decay in the sun or float in the floodwaters until they were beyond recognition. Hurricane Katrina is a horror story all the more terrifying because it was never beyond the realm of possibility.

In the midst of all of the tragedy playing out on TV screens around the world, Algiers did not receive much attention. This is understandable. First, the general public doesn't know about Algiers in a way that would allow it to be called to attention as the French Quarter would, for instance, with its idiosyncratic identity. Second, Algiers, like most of the West Bank, is largely above sea level, so did not suffer from devastating flooding to nearly the same degree as the East Bank did. This was supported by the fact that the levees guarding the river's west bank did not break. Still, the right side of the river occupied a precarious position in the Katrina story as "part victim, part witness, part bystander, part beneficiary, part casualty" (Campanella 2020, 236). Within a few weeks, the lights were back on and stores were open. This is not to say, though, that the residents didn't suffer any hardship or casualty in the aftermath of the storm. They certainly did. The source of such hardship, however, was of a different nature.

White Terror on the Point

As night fell in New Orleans, survivors—tired, thirsty, hungry, and terrified—could look out across the river and see lights in the distance. Somewhere on the West Bank—Algiers, Gretna, Harvey, Marrero, Westwego?—there were signs of potential shelter. They made their way through the water toward the twin bridges and out of the flood. When they arrived, they met a blockade of armed officers from the Gretna Police Department and Jefferson Parish Sheriff's Department. Gretna is in Jefferson Parish and is Algiers's immediate neighbor. The police decided to set up a barricade to prevent "any Superdomes" from happening there, a reference to rumors of widespread violence and lawlessness taking place in the football stadium turned shelter. For the next several days, thousands of people—mostly Black—would be turned away by officers protecting a majority-white municipality. The racial implications were immediately apparent. Patryce Jenkins, a Black resident of Gretna working as a 911 operator for the New Orleans Police Department, was stuck on the East Bank during the storm. After a grueling two days, she made it to the bridge, where she encountered officers with "huge guns like they have in Iraq" (Witt 2008). She was told to turn back, despite showing her ID confirming her address. "These police didn't even look at my ID," she said. "I was called racist names." At one point a police officer fired a warning shot above the heads of six survivors seeking to cross the bridge in an incident that became known as "The Bridge to Gretna."[11] In another occurrence, police used the wind from a helicopter to force people off the bridge and back into the floodwaters.

It is important to note that the bridges are maintained by the Louisiana Department of Transportation; that is, they belong to the state, not a particular municipality. Furthermore, the first exit on the other side of the bridge is 9B: Louisiana 428 East or West, also known as General De Gaulle Drive in Algiers. This did not stop the Gretna police from stepping outside their jurisdiction and turning people back. Eventually, federal judges would find no wrongdoing on the part of the officers. Several civil suits would be brought and dismissed. The police officer who fired the warning shot and his chief would be hailed as heroes.

Black residents already on the West Bank, however, were not left unharmed. A. C. Thompson's groundbreaking article published in *The Nation* in December 2008 presents his findings from an eighteen-month investigation on white shootings of Black people in the days following the storm. All of the shootings Thompson investigated took place in Algiers Point. His article, "Katrina's Hidden Race War," features the story of Donnell Herrington, a Black man who survived a close-range attack by a vigilante with a shotgun. On September 1, 2005, Herrington, thirty-two, his seventeen-year-old cousin Marcel Alexander, and his eighteen-year-old friend Chris Collins were heading to the Algiers Ferry, which was operating as a National Guard–designated evacuation point. To do so, they had to pass through Algiers Point. On the way, Herrington was shot. He struggled to get up, but was shot again from behind. As Thompson reports, Alexander and Collins were also hit. "The buckshot peppered Alexander's back, arm, and buttocks" (Thompson 2008a). Herrington told his companions to run when he saw the three white men who had shot him. In his search for help, he stumbled up to a pickup truck. He pleaded for help, but the white men in the truck told him, "Get away from this truck, nigger. We're not gonna help you. We're liable to kill you ourselves." Finally, he made it to the house of a Black couple, and they rushed him to the nearest hospital. "According to the records," Thompson writes, "a doctor who reviewed the X-rays found 'metallic buckshot' scattered throughout his chest, arms, back and abdomen, as well as 'at least seven [pellets] in the right neck.'" Had Herrington not made it to the hospital when he did he would have surely died, for "he had a hole in his internal jugular vein." When Herrington returned to the Fourth District police station to check the status of his police report, he learned that there wasn't one. Officers at the time failed to file a report on the incident.

Thompson sketches a picture of white vigilantism in the days following the storm based on his interviews with "the shooters of Algiers Point, gunshot survivors and those who witnessed the bloodshed." He writes (2008a):

> Facing an influx of refugees, the residents of Algiers Point could have pulled together food, water and medical supplies for the flood victims. Instead, a group of white residents, convinced that crime would arrive with the human exodus, sought to seal off the area, blocking the roads in and out of the neighborhood by dragging lumber and downed trees into the streets. They stockpiled handguns, assault rifles, shotguns and at least one Uzi and began patrolling the streets in pickup trucks and SUVs.

What is revealing about Thompson's report and other sources detailing the exploits of these groups of vigilantes is that they were motivated by a deeper animus. This was, for them, a seized opportunity to act on a long-held desire to kill Black people. They were not defending. They were hunting.

The film *Welcome to New Orleans* (Holm 2006) chronicles the early days after the storm and its impact in Algiers. It focuses on Common Ground Relief, headed by Algiers Point resident Malik Rahim, as they sought to provide free medical care, food, and supplies to those in need. The film also includes interviews with some of the vigilantes Thompson writes about. One man, in a thick, white New Orleans accent admits, "If you want to call it 'vigilante,' yeah. We just looked out for everybody. . . . You had to do what you had to do. If you had to shoot somebody, you had to shoot somebody." In another scene, a gray-haired man is holding a beer and leaning on the front of a sedan parked near the levee in Algiers Point. He offers, "I never thought, eleven and a half months ago, I'd be walking down the streets of New Orleans with two .38's in my pocket and a shotgun over my shoulder. . . . It was great! It was like pheasant season in South Dakota. If it moved, you shot it." The woman sharing a seat on the hood laughs as the man exclaims, "We shot 'em!"

"They were looters," she interjects.

"We don't allow that around these parts. What happens in other parts of the state, I don't know about."

"We don't care about . . . In this neighborhood, we take care of our own."

"You know what?" he asks as he leans in. "Algiers Point is not a pussy community."

The transcript reads like a caricature of classic American racism, with its uncreative employment of stale tropes: "looters," "these parts," "our own." These terrorists hid behind rhetoric of self-defense to actively hunt, shoot, and kill Black people in Algiers in the days and weeks after the storm. The same person who compared that time period to pheasant season bragged to Thompson about keeping the bloody shirt of one of his victims as a trophy. Elsewhere, Thompson reports on an anonymous source whose uncle and cousins reveled in the moment. "My uncle was very excited that it was a free-for-all—white against black—that he could participate in. . . . For him, the opportunity to hunt black people was a joy" (A. C. Thompson 2008a). She goes on to speak of an email her cousin sent her in which he rejoiced that they were "shooting niggers." He attached a photo of himself posing next to a dead Black body, reminiscent of photos taken at lynchings throughout so much of the twentieth century.

In all, Thompson reports eleven cases of shootings in the Algiers Point neighborhood. This is a conservative number. The New Orleans Police Department did not keep many records, and the coroner's reports were incomplete, either failing to perform autopsies or leaving out key information, such as where and when the bodies were found, by whom, and so forth. Due in part to Thompson's article, a federal investigation was launched in Herrington's case, and on July 15, 2010, a federal court indicted Roland J. Bourgeois Jr. on conspiracy to commit a hate crime, committing a hate crime with a deadly weapon and with intent to kill, making false statements, and obstruction of justice (A. C. Thompson 2010b). Bourgeois pled not guilty. It is worth noting that federal investigators had to step in because local police would not. In late September 2011 a judge ruled Bourgeois mentally unfit for trial, and he was hospitalized under state supervision until he could be reevaluated, as he maintained that he had a fatal case of Hepatitis B (Stevens 2019). In February 2019, Bourgeois was sentenced to ten years in prison for the use of a firearm in a crime of violence and a hate crime. He died five days after his conviction (DeBerry 2019).

Algiers and the Unseen Presence

I have relied heavily on A. C. Thompson's work here because, in the years immediately following the storm, he was the only one writing publicly about this phenomenon. His research led to several federal investigations resulting in the convictions of both vigilantes and New Orleans police officers involved in the murder of Black residents of Algiers.[12] While his article title refers to a "race war," that war wasn't two-sided. Thompson describes an interaction with an older white man who is curious about what he is doing. Thompson offers a general response about looking into the untold stories of Hurricane Katrina. The man, without missing a beat, responds, "Oh. You mean the shootings. Yeah, there were a bunch of shootings" (2008a). In a time when the world's eyes were on New Orleans, Algiers remained invisible. So much so that Black people were being hunted with impunity and no one noticed. As I have illustrated, however, Katrina did not birth this invisibility. It was there since the dawn of the west bank's settlement, as several hundred Africans were forcibly imported into what would become one of the most booming markets in the history of the Western world. While building a city for others, they also built a world for themselves—in the shadows, the cabins, the swamps, the marshes, the fields.

When I moved to New Orleans in the summer of 2009, the ghost of Katrina was everywhere. It was kind of like when a friend's loved one passes away. You don't really know what to say. Do they want to talk about it? Do they want to not talk about it? Either way, it was impossible to ignore. Red or black X's were scrawled across the fronts of houses in the Bywater and the Marigny.[13] Gentilly had FEMA trailers. The Lower Ninth Ward was quiet and still and dotted with stairs that didn't lead to porches. In Algiers, I moved into a three-bedroom house in a mixed neighborhood with my friend Samori. He grew up in the Fisher Projects

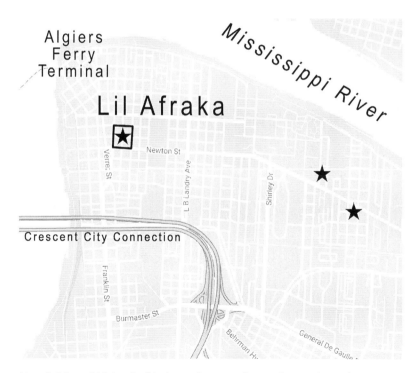

Map 2. Map of Algiers highlighting the constellation that made up the BlackStar community.

right at the foot of the Crescent City Connection. Algiers was his home. His mother lived in Marrero as part of the increased Black population in Jefferson Parish since the storm. We lived on a quiet block with paved white asphalt. Nearly four years after the storm, several houses on the street remained abandoned. Busted windows, hanging downspouts, and overgrown lawns caught the eye. Other than that, though, life moved on as the populations on both sides of the river increased by the day.

 I had never heard of Algiers before meeting Samori, and after my first visit I saw it as a suburb of the city. Eventually, it became the center of my world, and I ventured across the bridge only for work, music, or the occasional restaurant. What I did not see at first was the seedlings of a community sprouting in the above-sea-level soil of Algiers on the west bank of the Mississippi. One could view these communities—the Africans enslaved on and around the Company Plantation, the maroons, BlackStar—as existing on the margins of a marginalized part of New Orleans. In so doing, though, one would be missing that these communities are and have been central to their own world, whether through rival geography or disengagement and flight. This is what Phil Coolidge was trying to tell everyone that night. It is in what the outside world sees as its margins that this group of people finds the freedom to create for themselves a productive and protective unseen presence.

3

Black Star, Keep Shining

Invisibility as Cloak

Welcome Black home.

—Greeting at BlackStar Books and Caffé

If you were to enter BlackStar Books and Caffé in the Algiers section of New Orleans around 2010 or 2011, you would be greeted with a call: "Welcome to BlackStar." If it was your first time, this nicety wouldn't necessarily strike you as abnormal, but as a warm welcome to a local business. You might be startled, however, when every person in the café took a moment away from whatever they were doing to look up and respond: "You know who we are!" The "are" would be drawn out for flavor. The first time you'd be delightfully confused, but you'd catch on quickly. By the time you finished your sandwich, you'd have joined the chorus, contributing your harmony to this communal melody each time a new guest entered. This call-and-response started out as something done in fun, but each time the greeting was repeated it grew into an incantation summoning a collective affirmation.

The first thing to catch your eye when you walk in is a five-foot-tall wooden carving of the African continent. TIA—written in bold, white letters—stretched from Cameroon to Kenya. You are no longer in New Orleans. This Is Africa.[1] The walls are covered in earth tones. The sputtering window air-conditioning falls a few cubic feet too short, so humidity hangs in the air along with the art of local painters and coffee mug light fixtures. Music from around the Diaspora blasts through the sound system. Nag Champa and fresh brew dance into nostrils. A life-size painting of Malcolm X, Marcus Garvey, and Elijah Muhammad peers down from the back wall. The conversation, which guests jump into and out of like Double Dutch, moves from politics to history to celebrity gossip to speculations on the "new" New Orleans. And while there is no apparent logic to the conversation's flow, it all blends perfectly.[2] Handshakes, hugs, and smiles are the currency, and, for the duration of your stay at least, BlackStar—tucked into an often-overlooked corner of a rapidly changing city that uses Black people but never sees them—is a little piece of Black heaven.

This chapter explores what I call the *unseen presence* and the creative potential of invisibility through the ethnographic case of BlackStar Books and Caffé. The unseen presence refers to the strategic use of invisibility and clandestine measures to create and maintain community in the midst of a hostile society. In this sense, it is an outward shield allowing for an unrestrained mobility under the cloak of this invisibility. While many writers view this invisibility—and its perceived attendant marginalization—as cause for recourse and amelioration, I argue that communities such as BlackStar have managed to leverage this invisibility to pursue an autonomy and freedom otherwise impossible within the context and confines of mainstream American society.[3] The image of the black star itself has long stood as a symbol of hope and liberation across Africa and its Diaspora. In this chapter I explore another layer of its significance: the luminous world hiding within its darkness. I will demonstrate that the black star's nature as an unseen presence represents a point of potential for communities seeking autonomy in the midst of an adversarial social, political, and cultural order. Furthermore, BlackStar Books and Caffé can help us understand how this unseen presence may translate into an expression of a maroon impulse that offers us an opportunity to "come Black home."[4]

Birth of the BlackStar

Baakir Tyehimba founded BlackStar Books and Caffé along with a team that included his then girlfriend Efua, Samori Camara, Baba El, and me. Initially, it was intended to provide financial support for a home-based educational initiative run by Baakir and Samori. We had underestimated, however, the time it would take to get up and running. When the café opened, it opened to a community of supporters. I use the term *community* intentionally, as even before BlackStar opened for business, people invested their time, skills, and money to get the place in order. This included massive renovations to the space, which had been a hair salon before Hurricane Katrina damaged the property.

Roughly a year before this, Baakir and Samori began making plans for a homeschool cooperative that would offer Black students a culturally relevant, quality education that was less concerned with test scores—in many ways the hallmark of a charter education in New Orleans[5]—and more concerned with developing students who would use their studies and their skills to serve their communities. The two had met when Baakir was a substitute teacher for Samori's class at Edna Karr High School in Algiers, and they maintained a friendship over the years. Part of their vision was a coffee shop that would supplement the financial needs of the school, which would be called the BlackStar Educational Cooperative. The café would be BlackStar Books and Caffé. They just needed a space.

In the spring of 2009, Baakir and Samori were walking on General Meyer Avenue when a man standing outside a laundromat called to Baakir.

"What you say there, Baak?"

"Wazam, Bull! Look, you know this Quack's son?"

Quack was Samori's father, and from what I could gather, every Black person in Algiers over the age of thirty knew him.[6] He had passed away when Samori was young, so Baakir felt it was his duty to show Quack's son off to the neighborhood. Bull had recently gotten home from a two-decade bid at the infamous Louisiana State Penitentiary, known more commonly as Angola Prison—the largest maximum-security prison in the United States. Sitting on eighteen thousand acres, the former plantation—which is still used for agriculture and pays inmates as little as two cents an hour—was once known as the "bloodiest prison in the south." While twenty years in prison is a long time, it is on the shorter end of the sentences held by those incarcerated at Angola, where nearly 65 percent of inmates are serving life. Bull knew both Quack and Baakir's stepfather, and after Baakir explained what they were up to he offered his full support. It just so happened that they were talking outside of Bull's laundromat, which shared a parking lot with a defunct beauty salon. It needed quite a bit of work, so he agreed when Baakir proposed to transform the space into a bookstore and café. They settled on "six months no rent for renovation. Then incrementally brought the rent up to like $500 or so."[7]

Baakir, a lifelong New Orleanian who reps Algiers as hard as he does Africa, is somewhat of a local celebrity in the New Orleans cultural community. He's spent a large portion of his life moving through various religious, political, and philosophical circles, and as such he has created a large network of people who hold him in high regard. Always full of warm greetings and big smiles, he is a visionary whose sight sometimes runs a bit too far in front of the people. Still, he maintains a perplexing optimism that keeps him in pursuit of his ideals. This persistence paid off. Now, he had a physical space to manifest his vision. Here, in the skeleton of an abandoned beauty salon, we first draped the walls with our imagination. We planned and debated the best way this place could serve us. It would be more of a community center than a café, and we wanted people there all times of night and day: chess clubs, poetry readings, martial arts classes, and whatever else. This would work in tandem with a curriculum that would train students to practice self-determination and not just theorize about it. We now had a physical space to house anything we could think of. Most of all, we wanted it to feel like we were somewhere else, somewhere that belonged to *us*—not just those participating in its renovation, but to all of Black New Orleans.

A little less than a year later, on February 13, 2010, BlackStar held a soft opening during the NOMTOC[8] Mardi Gras parade, which passed right in front of the shop's newly opened doors. Family, friends, and passersby could be seen dancing through the storefront window, on which was painted the shop's original logo: a mug emblazoned with a Black Star of Africa resting atop a book. We didn't have much to offer in the way of material products. The coffee was nothing to write home about; the muffins were store-bought; and the books were tattered second- or third-hands from our respective libraries. Still, this initial stage contributed to the solidification of the BlackStar community. People came from around the city, crossing the bridge in many instances, to support the latest addition to a constellation of Black cultural institutions in New Orleans.[9] They donated labor, laughter, and conversation as we got the bookstore on its feet, creating in the process a sense of collective ownership that influenced the shape and tone of the venue.

BlackStar quickly became a meeting place for intellectuals, artists, activists, and "cats from 'round the way." On any given evening one could encounter laughter and debate late into the night. The café's location on a busy street attracted regular foot traffic. Study groups, book clubs, movie nights, community meetings, and vegan brunches populated the calendar. The shop's earliest claim to fame, however, was its weekly open-mic event, Liberation Lounge, which attracted musicians and poets from around the city and, eventually, the country.[10] It was clear to all involved that the intention of BlackStar Books and Caffé extended beyond business plans. In many ways, the business aspect was the least of its concerns. It was to be a liberated territory, a patch of Black independence in the midst of a turbulent sea of speculators and real estate developers. In the years immediately following Hurricane Katrina, New Orleans was the Wild West. Institutions like education and housing were being forcibly reconfigured in a way that excluded many Black New Orleanians. A tent city emerged under the I-10 overpass that stretched for miles and drew national attention. When I began frequenting the city in 2007, two years after the storm, FEMA trailers still languished in neighborhoods, and electricity had not been fully restored. By the summer of 2009, when I moved to the Crescent City full time, the scramble for the *new* New Orleans was fully underway.

In Plain Sight

BlackStar's architectural structure embraced the invisibility embedded in its name. It looked like a shotgun house with a two-car garage in the back of the parking lot it shared with the laundromat. A residential-looking home on a commercial corridor would have made it stand out were it not for the tan paint job that blended it into the surrounding environment. The parking lot was often filled with the cars of people cleaning their clothes, leaving the building further obscured from those driving by. Beyond this, the building did not sit perfectly parallel to General Meyer, so those approaching from the east would only see a long, nondescript exterior wall of clapboard and brick. Those approaching from the west wouldn't see BlackStar until they'd driven past the neighboring strip mall that was home to a dentist and pharmacy. Then, a colorful mural done by Joe Parker on the shop's front might catch the eye. It was a collection of scenes: Black children dressed in blue with their fists raised, men and women cultivating coffee beans, the faces of Baakir's children, and rolling hills that billowed under a blue sky. I say that the mural *might* have caught the eye, because we regularly received calls from first-time visitors who were having trouble locating us. When they finally made it, many had driven by several times without noticing.[11] What would otherwise be a business owner's worst nightmare turned out to serve the larger mission of BlackStar. It required intentionality to arrive there. When guests did, they were acknowledged immediately by a shop full of people who sang out at their arrival.

While the image of the black star is prominent across Africa and its Diaspora, there were three primary influences for its use as a symbol for the educational cooperative and café: Marcus Garvey's Black Star Line, Kwame Nkrumah's Pan-Africanism, and the teachings of Elijah Muhammad.[12] These inspirations left an indelible mark on the ideological landscape of the café. BlackStar—in its educational and entrepreneurial efforts—maintained an African-centered orientation, which, as Kwasi Konadu offers, "conceptualizes reality and situates Africans within their cosmological, symbolic, and pragmatic universe. Such an unambiguous approach not only affirms African agency and serves their best interests, but also authenticates the notion of an African cultural-historical continuum" (2004, 34). This orientation was reflected in the iconography and lexicon of the space. It was common to see guests in lapas, Ankara head wraps, mud cloth, and dashikis. Local jewelers would sell necklaces, earrings, and other adornments made from copper, stone, and cowry shells. Guests used the term "Afrikan"[13] to refer to one another, speaking to a larger belief that Africa was both our lineage and our aspiration. This place—New Orleans; America—was not our home, and we had recourse to something outside of it. There was also a strong emphasis on Black self-determination, as both the café and the school sought to encourage the creation of a community that exchanged goods and services not solely mediated by the monetary. Consequently, it created an environment that promoted the trading of ideas and ideals. All of this was done while avoiding any dependence on governmental or nongovernmental agencies. BlackStar sought no grants, small-business loans, or anything that would attach it to what we identified as inimical forces.

It may be tempting for some to dismiss BlackStar's expression as an obsolete "cultural nationalism," but to do so would be to overlook its salience. Both the so-called cultural and revolutionary nationalisms of the 1960s and 1970s undoubtedly played a pivotal role in the development of the institution's identity. The notion of a collective African heritage was held alongside the belief that Black people should strive toward self-determination, particularly through the development of autonomous institutions. BlackStar believed that we could never be—nor should we aspire to be—American citizens in the sense of possessing full access to the spoils of Americanism.[14] Instead, we understood Black people to constitute a colonized population with no access to the benefits and resources that citizenship affords.[15] While this nation-within-a-nation formulation is largely considered passé and seems to have been left in the 1970s, for the BlackStar community this was as contemporary a reality as ever. Some of the people who walked through the doors were the same people who, just a few years prior, had been abandoned on rooftops or separated from family and scattered around the country with no information as to where they were being taken or for how long. Some of them remained in the city where they had to gather water for bathing and cooking from puddles in parking lots. They braved the sweltering August and September heat during the day and had to lie low at night while gunshots rang out in a darkness unpenetrated by streetlight. Exclusion and abandonment, then, were no abstractions. While not all members of the BlackStar community shared the same sense of urgency for building self-determining communities, there were very few for whom the notion and need was unfathomable.

 This led to ongoing exchanges, challenges, and debates that encouraged wider patterns of thought. Anyone who felt so empowered could organize an event or meeting in the space. I use this phrase "so empowered" because strong voices and personalities emerged that alienated others who, consequently, may not have felt invited to take ownership within the space. BlackStar was welcoming, but it was also a place where debates could get heated. This never escalated beyond words, but did occasionally result in people not returning. Baakir's personality was essential in mitigating any larger conflict. His amiable and attentive disposition attracted people. His manner of disagreeing was rarely off-putting, and his friendliness brought people to the café who otherwise may not have come. He had a way of articulating his vision that inspired and drew others in. Still, this was not enough for everyone—particularly those who found BlackStar's brand of militant Black pride extreme. Some potential patrons outwardly disagreed with the overt agenda of the space—claiming it was "too Black"—and kept their distance as a result.

In many ways, though, it was this overt agenda that allowed BlackStar to be effective. An often-quoted proverb at BlackStar is, "One who sits on the fence gets shot down from both sides." BlackStar could not accomplish its mission of creating a self-determining Black community if it did not take an intentional stance on the path to doing so. BlackStar was concerned less with building a business than building a nation, and nations are built on communities and institutions. Business licenses and zoning clearances were less a priority than providing people with what they desired: a space we run, offering products, services, and experiences specifically and explicitly for us. It is important to note, however, that the "us" was not enveloped in some mythological and universal Blackness. BlackStar sought neither to be everything to everybody nor to proselytize people into joining some cause. Instead, it consisted of a community of people who held a broadly shared set of values and aspirations: self-determination and freedom for ourselves, our families, and our people. While the specific understandings of these ideas were always up for debate, the grounds upon which they stood never were. In both form and expression, BlackStar sought to live up to its ultimate ideals.

What Is the Black Star?

My interest here is not with painting an idealized picture of an unflawed community nestled in a corner of the West Bank. Like any human community, there were strengths and weaknesses, accomplishments and shortcoming, all of which are worthy of exploration and critique. Instead, I am concerned with what this intentional community brought to light in its pursuit of autonomy and how so much of it was occurring in the dark, under the radar, or outside of the surveilling eye of city officials and government agencies. In this sense, BlackStar was not particularly unique. It falls in line with an extensive tradition of underground gathering spaces that offered—and continue to offer—room for community building on their own terms.[16] While their political, economic, social, material, and geographic expression may vary, Black survival in this part of the world has meant clandestine organization. Building and maintaining communities that meet individual and collective needs for sustenance, safety, productivity, and joy has necessarily meant reducing visibility—that is, embracing the dark.[17]

In "Plotting the Black Commons," J. T. Roane addresses this reduced visibility by identifying "black holes," which "represent strategic blurring, aphasia, and unaccounted-for space by which and within which enslaved and post emancipation Black communities created and perpetuated underground social life" (2018, 244). BlackStar operated according to its own logic, with all of the liberties and drawbacks that entailed. For instance, the hours of operation were loose guidelines. The 11 a.m. opening time listed on the front door did not guarantee that the shop would, in fact, be open at 11 a.m. Baakir called it Afrikan Standard Time—a reclamation of the pejorative CP (Colored People's) Time. This was often a point of frustration for customers. Was this an attempt to push us to rethink our concept of space and time, or simply to validate tardiness? There were certainly more than a few of us who believed the latter—and they were perhaps justified—but I would also like to leave room for the possibility of the former.[18] Black holes tear "openings into the artifice of master time wherein enslaved and post-emancipation communities created affirmative collective identities" (252). There is no liberation in the master time of the plantation. Rival geographies necessarily extend into the temporal, itself a fourth dimension of the spatial. This bending of time, indeed its materiality, also operated inside the café. One immediately felt a shift in tempo and rhythm when stepping through the door and away from the hustle and bustle of General Meyer. Once inside, time moved like the incense smoke dancing and dissipating in the air. It was hard to hold on to. A "quick stop" would end with the sun suddenly descending, or what felt like a "long conversation" would only last the duration of a song.

Roane's black holes speak to an unseen presence. They name a "strategic invisibility or hiddenness" (2018, 249) that Black communities have used to create independent, if not autonomous, space. Black holes emerge after the collapse of a star, causing a breach in space-time due to its infinite density, which creates a gravitational pull so strong it eliminates any surface area, preventing even light from escaping. Black stars, on the other hand, are theoretical alternatives to black holes, and *would* have a surface area. Although they would emit light, that light would be also trapped by gravity, rendering it unperceived on the black canvas of space. It is there but not seen. Within its even horizon, those of BlackStar could shine invisible to the outside world and were free to build a community of autonomy. Inside the café, they tried on new names, explored new talents and interests, and experimented with new ideas. Regulars welcomed first-timers and helped them find the beat. It was a familiar yet varying cadence that allowed them to dance out of master time and into the brilliance of something else.

I am cautious here of a slippery tongue that speaks of autonomy yet leaves unquestioned the hegemonic seer for whom this community would be invisible. In my formulation of the "unseen presence," it would seem that I am in fact privileging the visual capacity (or lack thereof) of someone outside this community and thus undermining any argument for autonomy. Unseen by whom? This is a tension also present in the work of Black geographies, which acknowledges the role of power in naming and demarcating space and place while also recognizing the simultaneous practices of Black communities doing the same.[19] All geography is contested. Katherine McKittrick writes that "the relationship between Black populations and geography—and here I am referring to geography as space, place, and location in their physical materiality and imaginative configurations—allows us to engage with a narrative that locates and draws on Black histories and Black subjects in order to make visible social lives which are often displaced, rendered ungeographic" (2006, x). There are two points here worthy of exploration. The first is this expanded idea of geography that includes both the material and imaginative configurations of space. This allows us to account for the immaterial impact that locations have on us—and we on them—and challenges the relationship between space and time. BlackStar, for instance, was shaped by the people who frequented it as much as by its physical structure. As such, its resonance can extend beyond the limits of its physical existence. The second point returns to the tension I am addressing: the suggestion that the function of Black geographies is, at least in part, to "make visible" often displaced social lives. What assumptions are at play by suggesting they are not visible and must be made visible? Again, to whom? Furthermore, what do these social lives stand to lose and gain by being made visible? What might be the creative potential of *in*visibility?

Seeing the Invisible Man

Ralph Ellison's *Invisible Man* ([1952] 1995) offers a manuscript-length treatment of invisibility that proves useful to this conversation. The book opens in the cellar of a whites-only apartment building somewhere near Harlem. The narrator begins by identifying himself as an invisible man because "simply people refuse to see me" (3). In his quest for a place in society, he discovers that the only place for him is the place that he makes for himself, so he forges a home in his basement, a "hole in the ground" illuminated by lights covering every inch of the ceiling and part of the walls. In the safety and sanctity of his hole, the invisible man takes shape. It is here that our protagonist feels his "vital aliveness." He finds that his "world has become one of infinite possibilities" (576) since accepting the potential power of his invisibility—a "fact of Blackness" (Fanon 1994) with which invisibility seems synonymous. How is this possible? Is not invisibility indicative of marginalization, social exclusion, and social death? How can such a destitute designation denote anything short of the unrelenting misery of nonbeing? His vitality grows from his understanding that he can shape his world. Once he dispenses with the ideals and aspirations of his former life, once he steps inside the time of his new world, he discovers himself and the life all around him: "I myself, after living some twenty years, did not become alive until I discovered my invisibility" (7). This is no reactionary self-identity nor the self-consolation of a losing team in a perpetual game of power, privilege, and history. Rather, it is an ontological condition transcending the plastic borders of perceptibility. While this invisible man had to be chased into the darkness due to his sociological Blackness, once there, he realizes it was what he was searching for all along: chaos and creativity, potential and possibility. This is, in many ways, consistent with Simone Browne's *dark sousveillance*, which includes practices of both undersight and invisibility as "an imaginative place from which to mobilize a critique of racializing surveillance . . . [and] plots imaginaries that are oppositional and that are hopeful for another way of being" (2015, 21). It requires tactics that render one's *self* out of sight, a tactic of which BlackStar made regular use. Through his decision to retreat to a hole in the ground, our invisible man's world was made anew.

This is an important pivot point. Invisibility cannot be productive so long as the emphasis is on what is not seen—or that which must, in McKittrick's formulation, be made visible. Once there is a shift in perception to that of what one can be or do by virtue of not being seen—become unknowable, unobservable, unmeasurable, undeterminable, undetectable—one is thrust into the realm of infinite possibility.[20] For we cannot forgo the question of whether or not Black people in Black bodies should even *want* to be rendered visible, recognized, seen, or acknowledged by a white society. Considering the long history of what white recognition of Black bodies has done to Black people, this invisibility or unseeability can offer not only a space of refuge but a way out.

I agree with Toni Morrison, who poses a familiar question that challenges this premise of Ellison's novel: Invisible to whom? (Greenfield-Sanders 2019). Despite insisting on a keen sense of sight, the narrator overlooks one crucial element of a thriving and sustainable invisibility: community within its cloak. He sees the potential of his invisibility, but still mourns his exclusion. He explains, "You ache with the need to convince yourself that you do exist in the real world, that you're a part of all the sound and anguish, and you strike out with your fists, you curse and you swear to make them recognize you. And, alas, it's seldom successful" (Ellison [1952] 1995, 3–4). A Black world is a real world, and dark faces in the dark are free. They are alive and they are plentiful. There is no need for living with the oxymoron of an isolated freedom, no mandate to strategize from the solitude of an over-illuminated basement. As the invisible man himself, observes: "Step outside the narrow borders of what men call reality and you step into chaos . . . or imagination" (576). We are not invisible to one another, as is made evident in the abundance of variations of the colloquial expressions of "I see you" or "get your shine on" heard across languages throughout the Diaspora. Liberatory potential lies in the embrace of invisibility, for in the absence of light—stage light, stadium light, spot light, camera light, flashing light—Black people become unrecognizable to those external forces that threaten to extinguish them. There are endless worlds in the darkness, and the cloak of invisibility offers possibilities of cover, sustenance, and expression through this chaos and imagination.[21] As Jayna Brown observes, "Unburdened by investments in belonging to a system created to exclude us in the first place, we develop marvelous modes of being in and perceiving the universe" (2021, 7). It is chaos/imagination. It is the black star.

The 2019 film *Queen & Slim* offers a different take on invisibility. It, too, makes use of clandestinity and escape, but does so in a way that affirms a *community* of invisibles. The film follows an ill-fated couple who, after a lukewarm first date, end up killing a police officer in self-defense. Seeing no way out, they take flight. New Orleans comes to the rescue when Queen suggests they drive through the night in search of her uncle, who can give them temporary shelter. When they arrive, Queen's uncle takes them in and reluctantly agrees to give them new clothes and a car: a turquoise Pontiac Catalina.

"I don't know how low-key we gonna be riding around in a turquoise Catalina," Slim offers.

"That's the whole point," Queen replies. "We'd be hiding in plain sight."

Queen is invoking the unseen presence. By this point, their faces are being broadcast on news programs across the country. Instead of retreating from the light, they move toward it in a calculated attempt at transcendence. Slim throws on a blood-red velour track suit, and Queen jumps into a tiger-print dress with knee-high snakeskin boots. They embrace their invisibility by moving against a logic of visibility: shinin, stuntin, flexin, and so forth.

A particularly demonstrative example of the unseen presence and a communal embracing of invisibility that *Invisible Man* overlooks comes when the two pull off the road to go dancing. As they enter, Little Freddie King is onstage performing an up-tempo blues shuffle. Faded green paint coats the cinder-block walls. Red and tungsten lights illuminate a dance floor full of people moving in shared rhythm. When Queen expresses that she's nervous, Slim scans the room, a slight smile tucked into the corner of his mouth, and responds: "Ain't nobody out here thinkin' 'bout us." They are afforded an anonymity among their fellow partygoers. Tension arises when the woman behind the bar recognizes Slim but is eased when she clasps his hands and says, "Don't worry. You're safe here." Later, while dancing, Queen catches eyes with a woman on the floor who very deliberately salutes her. Couples dance. Queen cradles Slim's head, their curves and bends fitting together like puzzle pieces. Little Freddie King wails on. They are all here, each of them in their own world together.

This scene plays with a breathtaking beauty. The colors, the pace, the subtleties in the acting all work together to create a viewing experience that captures the power and potential of the unseen presence for opening a space of refuge and community. Queen and Slim came here to replenish their energies. The bartender, the fellow dancer, and presumably others knew who they were and draped them in the cloak of invisibility. None of them knew the particular details surrounding the interaction with that police officer, but perhaps they could, through their lived experience, find room to justify the outcome. So, they welcomed Queen and Slim by leaving them alone. That is to say, ain't nobody out here thinkin' 'bout them, choosing instead to express their support from afar as they sought their own respite.

The unseen presence acknowledges the coexistence of "ungeographic" social lives—Black people—and the forces that have rendered them ungeographic. Instead of centering the latter and bequeathing it the power to define, the unseen presence embraces the possibility contained in the amorphousness of the former. It is a purposeful invisibility precisely because that invisibility—that remaining unseen by predatory forces—allows for the proliferation of those social lives. What the people in Queen and Slim's juke joint knew that the invisible man didn't is that freedom is found in the dark, in the unseen, in the worlds that we build for ourselves. As Jared Sexton observes, "Black life is not lived in the world that the world lives in, but it is lived underground, in outer space" (2012). BlackStar Books and Caffé did not want to live in the world that the world lives in. Like many other communities of Black people in the city and beyond, BlackStar understood the limits of life in that world. Instead, it sought to create its own world where it could operate unencumbered by the world that the world lives in. That which is at stake here is the difference between perceiving the site of New Orleans as only an extension of the emotional repression of the movie theater—wait until the gong sounds to laugh at the film—and understanding the city as an arena for place-making.

Several years after my grandfather experienced the gong, my father, in what seems to have been a rite of passage in the Jim Crow South, would frequent the balcony of a segregated movie theater outside Greensboro, North Carolina. He and his friends would purchase tickets, enter through a door in the alley, and find their way upstairs where they would join friends and sweethearts. The movie was never as central to the experience as the company of other young people, unsupervised by parents, teachers, or the specter of authority. They talked and laughed and held hands with their dates. They threw popcorn down on the white boys who had scowled at them at the concession stand. For the duration of the film—whatever it may have been—they experienced a collective joy in the dimly lit upstairs of a segregated south. A few miles away, students at North Carolina A&T were staging sit-ins at the Woolworth's near campus.

The protests would reverberate throughout the nation and further catalyze the civil rights movement. Desegregation slowly crawled through Dixie and eventually found its way to my father's movie theater. In keeping with federal law, the theater began allowing all patrons to share the downstairs section and so closed the balcony. The Black patrons, barred from their elevated dark haven, stopped going altogether.

I was most likely in high school when my father first told me about his preteen moviegoing experiences. I asked him what growing up in the segregated South was like. At that time, my own early teenage days were consumed by a seething rage traversing my spirit as I began reading about the horrors of our history in this land, which highlighted the misery of deprivation and exclusion. My father's story was perplexing in this regard. On a macro level, I envisioned the calculated terror of racial violence so synonymous with the United States. I saw billy clubs and fire hoses and dogs sicced on youth who would have been my father's peers. But a macro view does not attend to the "warm data"[22] present in my father's telling of his boyhood in the balcony. This is what McKittrick is referring to when she writes, "We produce space, we produce its meanings, and we work very hard to make geography what it is" (2006, i). It is possible for both of these histories—the macro and the warm data micro—to share cartographic coordinates, but their dimensions are worlds apart. This is the unseen presence. It is the joy my father experienced with his friends in the very space carved out for his humiliation. It is the intimacy of Queen and Slim's dance in a hall full of heroes. It is the material base that BlackStar offered for a community of people to redirect their trajectory. It is the creative use of invisibility as a tool for world-making.

On the Corner of Power and Freedom

BlackStar leveraged invisibility as an avenue to autonomy by intervening in the lives of its community in ways that other institutions did not. During the afternoons, schoolchildren would hang out on computers, read, or play board games as they waited for their parents. These parents knew the café to be a safe and affirming environment. They knew their children would be fed and attended to until they could pick them up. In its early days, BlackStar housed the educational cooperative, which provided an alternative to the public charter school system dominating the city. Baakir and Samori helped adults study for their GED. The café also became a space for conflict resolution and intervention that allowed us to avoid police involvement. Sunday mornings were reserved for vegan brunches that promoted healthy eating and living. On Sunday nights, everyone from nervous diary poets to seasoned musicians would share a stage. While other places may have addressed these needs individually, BlackStar serviced them all and did so from outside of the direct dictates or awareness of the city, state, or federal government.

In the fall of 2012, BlackStar relocated to a quiet block deeper in Algiers. Roughly two miles from the original location, this new neighborhood was markedly different from the bustling thoroughfare of General Meyer, sitting instead across from a school and surrounded by manicured lawns. This would become the home of Little Afraka Street Festivals and Marcus Garvey celebrations.[23] Like the old spot, students would find their way to the café to study and hang out. Neighbors would stop in for sandwiches and conversation. It was, in many ways, both a continuation and a culmination of the work started on General Meyer. This is, perhaps, best illustrated by its coordinates. The new BlackStar was at the corner of Nguvu and Uhuru—Power and Freedom—in the heart of what it dubbed Little

Figure 2. These street signs at the intersection of Nguvu and Uhuru—Power and Freedom—were erected and maintained by the BlackStar community. Photograph by author.

Afraka. The street signs were erected by members of the community and consisted of fat letters in black marker flanked by red, black, and green stripes that stood in stark contrast to their woodgrain background. They hung above the city's street signs underneath them that read "Slidell" and "Belleville" in reflective blue-on-gray. The city, in several attempts to preserve the "rightful" names of the intersection (Slidell had been a Confederate ambassador to France), would remove the unofficial signs, only to find that new ones had been mounted in the shining darkness of night.[24]

This was a claiming. The people of BlackStar were creating space in a city that had none for us. It was not a *re*claiming. BlackStar did not "take back" anything. Instead, we moved on what we believed already belonged to us. We didn't look to take down the city's street signs. Those markers had no significance to us. This was neither debate nor contest. There was no desire to enter into dialogue with the city. The process of doing so would entail a necessary sacrifice of power, a tacit acceptance of the legitimacy of the illegitimate organizing logic of "ways and means" and thus an acquiescence to the city's rules of engagement.[25] The marking of this intersection was a claiming in that BlackStar was speaking to its people: those who found solace under the cloak of invisibility. Nguvu and Uhuru do not exist on any official city map,[26] but in the clandestine cartography of invisibility this intersection continues as a site of power and freedom and serves as a landmark for the possibilities of autonomous community in New Orleans. This unseen presence is animated by a maroon impulse in an attempt to realize a collective potential. Its clandestine cartography demonstrates the blind spots and dimensional limitations of a political world that cannot account for—indeed, must necessarily negate—the coexistence of multiple worlds. BlackStar stood at the intersection of Power and Freedom in Little Afraka, not Slidell and Belleville in Algiers. The claims of the latter have no impact on the conceptualization and existence of the former.[27] The difference is a matter of the invisible man accepting the intended marginalization of his designation or embracing a self-defined identity. BlackStar was a brick-and-mortar business location with a social media presence and burgeoning reputation. It was discoverable, but not "officially recognized" by city agencies. Instead, it worked to build a community by providing a space to gather. And when that space no longer served the community, it sought another one that would, always doing so on its own terms.

If You Know, You Know

In languages such as Portuguese, Spanish, or French there is a nuance to the verb "to know" that is not present in English. The Portuguese *saber* is to know in the sense of factual knowledge, in the way that one would know one's birth date or street address. *Conheçer*, on the other hand, is familiar knowledge, like knowing a person or a place. It is qualitative in nature. BlackStar's greeting was a recognition of our individual and collective selves. You know who we are. You *know* who we are, because you are part of our we. We are the unseen presence. We are the unsaid heard. Our presence bespeaks our potential. Our mutual acknowledgement affirms our shared existence. The black star, as the eponymous rap duo explains, is "commonplace and different / Intimate and distant / Fresher than a infant" (Black Star 1998). It is an oxymoron with a breathtakingly simple logic. It is what happens when Black people step outside of the narrow borders of reality and into the chaos of imagination. You know who we are: those who shine bright enough for the right eyes to see. If you know—if you find shelter under the cloak of invisibility—then you know.[28]

BlackStar Books and Caffé shone from the West Bank, washing Black New Orleans in its glow. It was a cultural refuge in the midst of the storm of gentrification and displacement ravaging the city. The vacancies left by the denied right to return for evacuated residents, combined with governmental incentives for "redevelopment," left decreasing amounts of autonomous spaces and institutions for Black communities in the historically Black city. Still, the café was able to create its own opportunities by pursuing the potential of its luminous moniker through an unseen presence, which leveraged invisibility in order to foster its community. By embracing, rather than running away from, an invisibility inherent in the disaster landscape of New Orleans and the United States more broadly, BlackStar Books and Caffé offered us a reason and a chance to come Black home.[29]

4

"They Ain't Talkin' 'bout Nothin', Y'heardme?"

Fugitivity and the Educational Landscape

> We know this place . . .
> for we have glanced more times than we'd like to share
> into eyes that stare with nothing there behind them but an
> Unfulfilled wish
>
> —Sunni Patterson, *We Know This Place*

They flung their bodies over the fence—Black faces in bright orange polo shirts. Behind them were the high, windowless walls of Roberts High School, one of New Orleans's many public charter schools. In front of them were the quiet side streets of Algiers. Daily, I witnessed them make their escape well before the final bell rang. I saw them from my front porch or through my window or out of my side door. Their faces were a blend of focus and joy as they sprinted out of sight. The way they tossed their bags before scaling the fence in a single, fluid motion reminded me of an anti-drug commercial that aired during my childhood in the early 1990s: "To Kevin Scott and all the other kids taking the long way home: we hear you. Don't give up." Kevin was running for his life. He was ducking through alleys to avoid the drug dealers who would surely pull him off of the straight and narrow and introduce great peril into his burgeoning life. A solitary, staccato piano punctuated his movements. As a child, I wondered: Who are the "we" that heard Kevin? Could I be counted among them? And who were the others? Did being heard save them from the threats of their environment? What became of Kevin? Every time that commercial aired, I stopped what I was doing and held my breath as I watched. Maybe my attention would secure his safe passage. And just as I found myself rooting for Kevin, so, too, was I rooting for these young people who were cutting school, as I watched them hit corners and disappear.

In both instances, we see acts of fugitivity at play. Kevin Scott was escaping from the tentacles of street life. The fleeing high school students were seeking refuge from the enclosure of public charter education. I am looking here to the work of Damian Sojoyner and Tina Campt. For Sojoyner, enclosures consist of more than physical barriers (walls, fences, those things that limit freedom of movement).[1] The youth were evading an institution socializing them into marginalized roles in society. Kevin was fighting against the social pressures of his environment—even if their state-sanctioned roots were not immediately known to him. Both Kevin's and the youths' actions display what Sojoyner calls Black fugitivity, which is based on "the disavowal and disengagement from state-governed projects" (2017, 516). For Campt, fugitivity hinges on a refusal, "a rejection of the status quo as livable and the creation of possibility in the face of negation . . . using negation as a generative and creative source of disorderly power to embrace the possibility of living otherwise" (2019, 83). Fugitivity and its refusal become portals to generative and creative expression. They come to function not as resistance but as foundational disengagement. This is not to say that they, in and of themselves, can "save" the fugitive. They do, however, shake up the grounds of power. This brings to mind Tony, the rebellious African who in 1675 was involved in a plot to kill all the whites on the island of Barbados. As he stood waiting to be burned at the stake, he unflinchingly announced, "If you roast me today, you cannot roast me tomorrow."[2] The relevance of my childhood question remains: Can being heard save Kevin? Can my silent well-wishes for safety protect those young people? Tony's pronouncement did not save him from the flames. Does that even matter? Fugitivity factors into our discussion of a maroon impulse, but on its own remains incomplete. In this chapter I aim to do two things: first, provide a wider view of the context of the BlackStar community's emergence, with particular focus on the educational landscape through an ethnographic sketch of my time teaching at a New Orleans charter school; and second, explore the powerful yet limited potential of fugitivity as a liberatory practice.

Figure 3. The fence surrounding Roberts High School. Photograph by author.

The Charter Takeover

At the end of the summer of 2009, a friend called me to ask if I would be interested in teaching Spanish at an all-boys charter school in New Orleans East named Henson Academy. Except for one Vietnamese student, all the students were Black, and the school served grades six, seven, nine, and ten.[3] Curious, I took the interview. My friend greeted me as I pulled up to a cluster of trailers that housed Henson and another school. Four years after Hurricane Katrina, these modular classrooms were common throughout the city, as nearly 110 of the city's 126 school buildings had sustained significant damage, and 44 had been completely destroyed. I was ushered into a conference room where, after some time, I was joined by the principals of the high school and junior high school. The junior high school principal was a Black woman who appeared to be in her late thirties and had a heavy Arkansas accent. The high school principal was a Black man of around the same age who mentioned he was from Detroit. Together, they founded the school the year before with a focus on business, technology, and mathematics.

In the interview, they asked me a bit about myself and began to talk about the school's literacy levels. "We have a student population that is behind in reading. Many of them lost a few years of school because they were displaced by the storm. We need someone to work with our students who are struggling the most. Over this school year, we want them to improve by two grade levels." I was a little slow on the uptake. I was waiting for them to tell me about the position I was there for. Instead, they were going into detail about how these students were struggling to read. Eventually, when I asked about Spanish, they looked confused, then said: "Oh, oh. No, we need a literacy specialist. That's more urgent at the moment."

In 2019 New Orleans became the first major American city to have a school district made up entirely of charter schools. It was the culmination of a fourteen-year trend set in motion in 2005 by the devastation caused by the storm. The city, with no means to redress the widespread destruction, appealed to the state, which earmarked $20.9 million for the creation of charter schools. Two months after Katrina, the legislature passed a bill transferring 112 Orleans Parish School Board schools to the state-run Recovery School District (RSD). New Orleans's schools would now be split between the RSD, the Orleans Parish School Board, the Louisiana Department of Education, and the Board of Elementary and Secondary Education. The RSD immediately began offering contracts to local and national nonprofits in an attempt to resurrect a long-underperforming public education system. These events prompted Secretary of Education Arne Duncan to make the crass remark that Hurricane Katrina was "the best thing that could have happened for education in New Orleans" (Heitz 2010).[4] By the spring of 2007 more than half of the public schools in the city were public charters. In Algiers, Roberts High School was one of the eight schools run by the Algiers Charter School Association.

The city's charter school movement was unique in that it was composed of mostly Type 5 charters, which are those that take over preexisting public schools. Consequently, it was difficult to make a distinction between "public" and "charter" education. Since George W. Bush's No Child Left Behind Act of 2001, there had been an increased focus on test scores nationwide. This trend was exacerbated in Louisiana, as standardized test scores were used to determine much of the funding for the charter schools. The Louisiana Educational Assessment Program (LEAP) was administered at the end of fourth and eighth grades and determined whether a student was prepared to advance to the next grade. The Graduation Exit Exam (GEE), administered at the end of tenth and eleventh grades, determined whether students would receive a standard Louisiana diploma. Consequently, these tests created a high-stress environment not only for students but also for teachers, whose jobs were largely dependent on successful scores.

While there was overwhelming support for charter schools from state and federal government, public opinion was divided. The schools receive both public and private money and differ from public schools in that they are not subject to the same regulations and oversight. They operate with greater autonomy but have an accountability system in which they must produce results as negotiated with the state. Critiques of the charter school movement in New Orleans centered on a lack of qualified and invested teachers, harsh disciplinary tactics, and an overemphasis on testing. Furthermore, concerned parents and activists claimed it to be undemocratic, as these schools maintained no public accountability.[5] Teacher training and hiring was largely outsourced to national teaching organizations such as Teach for America, which provided the city with inexperienced teachers who did not, on the whole, share sociopolitical, economic, and/or racial backgrounds with the students they were teaching. On average, teachers made a two-year commitment, and concerned residents questioned the long-term investment of these teachers. The reorganization of the school system following Hurricane Katrina was crucial to the reconstruction of the city.[6] The result was a system of education that undermined the citizen autonomy it professed to provide. Charter schools promoted the concept of "school choice," which was said to offer parents and communities greater options than the traditional public school system by allowing them to choose schools beyond their neighborhoods. In practice, however, limited seats and elaborate busing routes that often transported students across the city severely reduced those options. This led to further marginalization by forcing students into schools with which they had no connection.[7] For many, this turn to charter education represented the privatization of public education, where only a select few were left to profit.

This was the case at Henson. The principals were graduates of New Schools for New Orleans, a leadership training program through which many of the city's charter recipients passed. Both principals made $100,000 per year, making them the thirteenth-highest-paid school leaders in the city. The boom in education investment after the storm rose the median salary for principals by more than $30,000 between the 2004–5 and

2008–9 school years. The majority of Henson's faculty and staff was divided between Teach for America teachers (white, Black, and one Asian), family members of the central administrators (brothers, sisters, cousins, and in-laws), and friends brought from their previous work in a different state (all Black). Students attended from around the city, including Algiers. The commute all the way across town to the school in New Orleans East meant they would have to set out before sunrise. Henson did provide buses. A few years later, both principals would be fined $5,000 for issuing a busing contract to the company owned by the junior high school principal's brother.

Henson Academy

Despite the initial confusion about my role, I was excited for the opportunity to work at the school. The Friday before I started, I attended a training meeting where I was given a stack of workbooks. My job was to work with small pull-out groups composed of students who were reading below grade level. I was told in my interview that most of these students were two to three grade levels behind. In actuality, the majority of them fell further below than that. In some cases, they were struggling with fundamental phonics, word structure, and letter recognition. In keeping with the charter school's emphasis on statistical data collection, part of my job was to assess my students' reading levels once per quarter. I was young and somewhat naive, and my relaxed teaching style, exemplified by my request to be called "Brother Johnson" instead of "Mister Johnson," won me favor among my students, who saw me as a stark contrast to the strict authoritarianism of their other teachers. While this certainly came with its disadvantages and drawbacks, it also removed some barriers and led some students to share with me their frustrations with both the school's administration and its structure. I didn't have a steady classroom like most traditional teachers, so I maintained the flexibility to move around the school and gain a better understanding of the Henson environment. I was also able to form relationships with students outside of my assigned groups. As I walked the trailer halls, it was common to hear someone yell "Yo, what's good, son?" from a classroom in an attempt to imitate my thick New Jersey accent. In the spring, I joined the track team as the hurdling coach. This position, in addition to friendships with some of the teachers, also led to further insight about the charter school system.

In my mind, I was going to be the cool, young teacher who effortlessly performed miracles and set students up for a lifetime of academic success. I wanted to help them crack the code to reading comprehension and critical thinking, leaving the administration scratching their heads in awe. This didn't happen. My nonchalance worked against me about as much as it worked for me. The ninth and tenth graders with whom I worked were often disengaged and used their time with me as an opportunity to zone out. Their level of need, even in small groups, exceeded what one—especially one untrained—"specialist" could provide. This isn't to say that there wasn't any progress. I did see improvement in some of their reading abilities, even if their quarterly assessment scores were inconsistent. The sixth and seventh graders were struggling with issues that extended far beyond the trailer walls of Henson Academy. On a day when they were particularly unresponsive, I stopped class to discuss their lack of engagement. In what seemed to be a series of non sequiturs, they ultimately led me into a conversation about their experiences after Katrina. They would have been six to eight years old at the time of the storm. They offered stories of being stuck in attics, viewing dead bodies, and being evacuated to different cities on buses, speaking in a manner that was as mundane as describing what they watched on television the previous night. I remember the detail with which one student described seeing his father's gun—its shiny chrome glinting in the late-morning sun. It made him feel safe, he said, while he clung to his father's side as they waded through water that would have been up to his neck had his father not been carrying him. Many of them had spent over a year out of school, and while they may not have made the explicit connection, it became clear that the weight of their experiences severely affected their desire to engage in school. These children would have been better served by a therapist to help process the unaddressed traumas they were still living with than by a reading specialist barking at them about phonemes and diphthongs.

But the Henson environment offered no space for these wounds. The school valued disciplinary excellence over academic performance or emotional well-being. The students were corralled from one place to the other. The lunchroom was reminiscent of a scene from *Lean on Me* (1989), where Joe Clark ("Crazy Joe" or "Batman," played by Morgan Freeman) demanded absolute silence and no movement from each and every person in the cafeteria. When Mr. Darnell, the English teacher and assistant football coach, went to retrieve a piece of trash from the floor, Joe Clark immediately scolded him and sent him to the principal's office, much to his embarrassment. This was the spirit of the cafeteria at Henson. Both students and faculty were expected to abide by the rules. This did not have a positive impact on the school's academic achievement. Despite Joe Clark's declaration in the film that "discipline is not the enemy of enthusiasm," it appeared as if Henson's administration was most enthusiastic about discipline. The faculty, on the other hand, often took a different approach. Teachers, in some instances, displayed the same disengagement as the students. As I entered different classrooms to gather my identified students, I noticed with eerie consistency how little learning was taking place. Time after time, I would find teachers reading magazines with their feet on the desk as students thumbed through cell phones or held boisterous conversations. There was one teacher in particular who, when I asked for a student, would respond, "Take as many as you want. Matter of fact, take them all." I do not want to give the impression that all teachers worked this way, however. In fact, there were several who shared deep-seated frustrations with the structural demands imposed by the school's administration. One teacher maintained a notebook detailing all of her grievances, including hostile superiors and unethical practices. Sometime near the end of the school year, she left the notebook in her classroom filing cabinet. Somehow, the administration knew where to find it, confiscated it, and fired her on the spot.

    I wasn't the only one suspicious of the school's inability to live up to its mission to "educate urban males, prepare them for college, and instill in them virtues such as critical thinking, responsible citizenry, and positive community leadership, while promoting a structured learning environment." Mama Tamieka, whose fifteen-year-old son, Kamal, was a sophomore at the school, shared, "Okay, when I first initially went to the meeting, they were telling me how they're gonna teach them structure, but when I went to the school, they did not have that structure. They told me in reference to their academic level, it would increase. It didn't seem as if it was increasing."[8] I saw Kamal around campus, but I really got to know him in the spring, when he was one of my hurdling athletes. Kamal was dissatisfied with the level of education offered at Henson. He described the place as "basically an environment where I would just basically sit down in the class, they'll throw work at you, and the teachers would go sit down. They wouldn't explain how the work is. They'd just put on a slide show and just flip through different slides, and if you didn't get it, you wouldn't learn about it."[9] His mother agreed with him and added that she never got a sense of what he was learning—or if he was learning anything at all. She was often surprised when the grades he received on his report card were incongruent with the low level of work he was putting in. Kamal echoed this sentiment: "Most times, I'd just sit back and do nothing and then I'll keep getting C's over and over and over and I'd be like, 'How am I getting these grades and I didn't do anything?' And then when I tried, I still—I got C's and a B, showing that I improved a little bit, instead of actually doing a lot. I mean, I actually tested that theory for myself."[10] After noticing that minimal effort would earn passing grades but that greater effort did not improve them much, Kamal chose not to expend energy on something that would go unrewarded.

Kamal's response to not seeing the results of his labor is similar to something I noticed with my students and their reading assessments. One quarter, a student may have demonstrated a two-level increase. The next quarter, however, his reading may have fallen below his original level. By the third assessment, several students expressed frustration with having to read the same stories over again. This in itself reflected a level of reading retention. Months later, they could recall familiar stories. Still, the students who voiced these protests, coincidentally enough, suffered decreased reading levels. It was not that they were incapable of matching their previous performances, but that, similar to Kamal, they perceived their efforts to be in vain. They had read the same stories several times and, whether they demonstrated any improvement or not, would be asked to read them again. Having seen no apparent transformation in their grades or academic standing, they limited their participation. Kamal suggested that these seemingly predetermined outcomes were a structural phenomenon.

> KAMAL: I started noticing they was changing grades and stuff.
> AUTHOR: What you mean?
> KAMAL: The teachers were—every time you sit down with the teachers and talk with the teachers and everything, every single teacher would

be like, "Yeah, but it's strange how I send the grades out one way and they come back another way." Because, I know [one teacher]. He didn't even really care about what he taught anymore because they would change the grades so much. . . . And you also had [another teacher],[11] with the glasses and everything. He said he thought he was gonna be going there to teach students and everything and inspire them to reach new levels and stuff like that, but he said as soon as he got there, it just wasn't all the things he was promised.[12]

Funding for charter schools was based on head count at the beginning of the year and test scores at the end of the year. Over the course of my year at Henson, I noticed that students, particularly my students, were disappearing in a trickle—whether through suspension or expulsion. At the end of the year, however, that trickle became a torrent. Kamal confirmed that "[the principal of the high school] would either be like, 'You know what? I'ma suspend you for doing thus and so.' Like, we would all be talking for a while and everything at lunch, and then he'd be like, 'You talking too loud. Go to the office. . . . I'm not playing with ya'll. As soon as ya'll do one thing and ya'll go into my office, ya'll going home.'"[13] Kamal said this would always happen around LEAP time. Suspension and expulsion were not the only methods used.

> KAMAL: They would tell certain students, like, they would tell them not to show up for the LEAP, or they would just come out of nowhere and suspend them for no apparent reason. . . . Yeah, they would tell kids not to come to school and everything. They skipped school and then wouldn't count it against them.
> AUTHOR: Who would tell them this?
> KAMAL: Oh, the principal. The principal and the coaches would tell them.[14]

Henson Academy administrators were actively telling low-performing students not to show up on the days of state examinations. That is, of course, if they had not already been suspended or expelled. This would presumably result in a higher percentage of passing test scores, which would then translate to more funding the following year. Several of my reading students confirmed that they had been asked not to show up.

The principals of Henson Academy would go on to face scrutiny at the local and state level for some of their dubious practices, including cheating allegations and nepotism. They would leave the city in 2012, but scandal would follow. Henson Academy was never able to escape its poor performance and controversy, and its doors closed in 2015.

Educational Landscape

State and local funds were being distributed to private organizations that provided compulsory education in the city of New Orleans free of state and local oversight. While I have been discussing the particular transgressions of Henson Academy, these issues were endemic to the city, including Roberts High School. A report published in the spring of 2010 details the elevated rates of suspension, expulsion, and school-based arrests throughout the RSD, as well as the RSD's underreporting and data distortion. The study also details legally questionable acts, such as schools failing to provide resources to students with special needs or denying them access entirely.[15] To be clear, I am not making a comparison between the effectiveness of public versus charter models of education. They are, in this case, an extension of one another.[16] I am, instead, highlighting the educational landscape of the city during the time that the BlackStar community was forming. It was a time of dramatic reorganization, but not so much that it disrupted the foundational power structures in the city. It ultimately solidified a neoliberal turn and granted private organizations access to the spoils of generations of poverty and neglect through real estate and education.[17] The Obama administration was a staunch advocate of charter education and looked to New Orleans as a potential model for reform across the country. This is very much in line with Clyde Woods's argument (1998) that New Orleans holds the key to understanding the nation's past, present, and future. The blatant contradictions and exaggerations that proponents of charter education were engaging in did not go unnoticed by parents forced to make difficult decisions about the education of their children. Students were also aware of these inconsistencies. For many, there was no marked difference in terms of the quality of education or psychological injury before or after the storm.

But what if, like Kevin Scott, the young people hopping the fence were running for their lives? What if there was more at stake than an abstract "educational success"? What if their escape or captivity was more significant than simply skipping school? For parents in the BlackStar community, psychological well-being was more important than reading, writing, and arithmetic. These parents' experiences made the city's schools unacceptable options. Mama Afivi was a mother of two students and a teacher at Kamali Academy. She joined Kamali after noticing drastic changes in the behavior of her children. Her seven-year-old son, Kwame, had completely shut down. "It turned into such a challenge," she says, "that he actually internalized that, 'Okay, I must be bad because I'm always in trouble. . . .' And this was during the point he was actually talking, right before he just stopped talking. My son didn't speak for a while. He would come in and just be in his room and cry—don't talk to anyone. Also, at school, he would sit in the corner behind the desk and pile things in front of him as if he was isolating himself from whatever was out there in his school environment." Mama Afivi says the response of her fourteen-year-old daughter, Ayana, to school was slightly different from that of her son but equally detrimental. "In my experience," she shared, "I think mainly girls will work to adapt to their social conditions and accept that 'this is how I should be, obviously, because this is what they're saying I should be. So maybe I shouldn't write this poem . . . it's stupid.' You know, that kind of thing with her. . . . My daughter would—she sews, she knits, she did all of these things, but she stopped drastically."[18] Ayana had many talents: writing, painting, acting, and singing. She even won a spot on the television show *America's Got Talent* as a stilt-walking rapper. She refused to participate, however, because of what she said was her shyness.[19]

In the 1990s television commercial we hear Kevin's voice: "My teacher tells us all we gotta do is just say no. And the other day, a policeman came to our class, talkin' 'bout 'say no,' too. Well, my teacher doesn't have to walk home through this neighborhood. And maybe the dealers are scared of the police, but they're not scared of me. And they sure don't take no for an answer." Here, Kevin is acknowledging that the rather dismissive simplicity of the advice his teacher offers—"all you gotta do"—is out of touch with his reality. The police officer who extends the same advice and should presumably know better is equally disconnected. So, too, was Nancy Reagan's national "Just Say No" campaign, given what we now know about Ronald Regan's role in the creation and proliferation of the "War on Drugs" that targeted real-life Kevins and their neighborhoods.

We find similar reflexive refrains in educational discourse: stay in school; get your education, for no one can take that from you. These statements do not interrogate what happens in those schools and why staying is viewed as the only option worth considering. The concept of "education" is often discussed as if it were some singular talisman that could open doors, put food on the table, and ward off hardship. There is significantly less discussion about the role of education as a process of socialization whereby students are introduced to and prepared for their respective roles in society. This is what Mwalimu Shujaa refers to as "schooling," which is distinct from "education" in that it is "a process *intended* to perpetuate and maintain the society's existing power relations and the institutional structures that support those arrangements" (1998, 15). In the case of Henson Academy, we saw the reproduction of mainstream power structures whereby these Black students were exploited for economic gain and socialized into submission to an omnipotent administrative power that can single-handedly, and whimsically, decide their fate. And while the school's practices may have been on the more egregious end of the spectrum, they were not aberrations.

This is not—at least not fundamentally—about underperforming schools, nor is it about the carceral implications of the enclosures Sojoyner (2016) addresses. There are greater stakes best summed up by a grandfather in the community who, when speaking about his grandson's experiences in school, offered, "You know, you give him something one day and then, like, you know, he goes to school the next day like all the spirit done went out of him."[20] Elsewhere in the city, children as young as six years old were being handcuffed to chairs or suspended for being unable to walk in a straight line due to a broken limb. The journalist Jordan Flaherty provides one example of a charter school in the city that suspended 20 percent of its senior class for "singing."[21] Whatever the contents of the book bag that Kevin Scott tossed over the rotting wooden fence he was scaling, it could not teach him how to save himself; it could not preserve his spirit. More alarming is the dismissiveness with which his concerns were met by those authorities around him. Despite what we want to believe, "education" alone, in all of its myth and abstraction, is no singular way out. Perhaps it buys time, or better yet, comfort, but the finite resources necessary for human survival guarantee there is no collective access in a system based on accumulation. What are we to do when we come to the realization that we are in the midst of a society that must knock the spirit out of us in order to function most optimally? It would seem that the only way out is out.

These are the true stakes and the reason why it may not be hyperbole to suggest that those hopping the fence may have indeed been running for their lives. These institutions—Henson, Roberts, charter schools in the age of education reform in New Orleans, America—have spirit-crushing consequences for which there is no redress. Who will, after all, pay reparations on my soul?[22] This is the problem space that fugitivity comes to occupy. Redress is an impossibility. Escape is a release into uncertainty, or as Stephen Best and Saidiya Hartman offer, "the interval between the no longer and the not yet, between the destruction of the old world and the awaited hour of deliverance " (2005, 3). Sojoyner, Campt, and others offer powerful insights into fugitivity as a means by which Black people may intervene in the forces acting upon their lives. I am sympathetic to the heroism of the fugitive. Their courage and disengagement are sources of hope for those of us grappling with our commitments to the comforts of—and simultaneous distaste for the discontents of—political society. Fantasies of tossing our phones and unplugging abound. Dreams of stealing away in the dark of night occupy our imaginings. The students of Roberts possessed the boldness and courage to hop the fence in broad daylight. And perhaps they arouse in me a sense that we have not completely lost, that the game is not yet over. The youth are still in rebellion. I am sympathetic to the heroism of the fugitive, but what becomes of it? What becomes of Kevin?

The concept of Black fugitivity is useful for understanding both the how and why of Black disengagement—whether it takes the form of students hopping the fence or zoning out during reading assessments. Disengagement contains the potential for positive communal transformation in that these young people are removing themselves from the educational institutions and systems facilitating their oppression. In so doing, they create the possibility for an engagement with culturally reaffirming institutions that empower Black youth and communities. Why, we must ask, should Black people *want* to be engaged in mainstream society—understanding as we do society's extractive relationship with Black people? Fugitivity, as both refusal and removal, gives us a conceptual language to articulate these realities. It provides us with a framework for understanding disengagement and flight. It falls short, however, in that it does not allow us anything beyond escape. That is, it does not offer insight into a direction fugitives may move. What happens once people disengage? Where do they go? With whom? As Sojoyner observes, Black fugitivity establishes "spaces (sometimes momentarily) of freedom" (2017, 527). At best, it offers a passing freedom—a freedom that is unsustainable.

Fugitivity strikes a balance between metaphor and description. It is a tool for theorizing the lives of enslaved Africans and the lived experiences of African people in what we call the world—the two being separated only by chronology. The psychological and emotional needs of my junior high readers were overlooked for disciplinary excellence. They were ignored and left to their own devices to meet those needs. The escaping students of Roberts High School also had needs. They pursued them as I watched them—several times per day—sprinting into the back streets of Algiers and out of sight. What became of them? They certainly did not, despite our fantasies, run off into the sunset. Disengagement from the system vis-à-vis school too often leads to a reengagement into the system vis-à-vis prison, with New Orleans leading the state with one of the world's highest incarceration rates. On more than one occasion, my students at Henson would go missing for weeks at a time. I would later find out that they had been locked up.[23] Whether these students were forced out of school through questionable attendance practices on the part of the Henson administration or chose not to show up on their own accord, the options available to them were limited.

I am not attempting to dismiss fugitivity. It is a practice with great liberatory potential. This potential is the heart of the issue: it cannot be realized through fugitivity alone, for fugitivity—as disengagement and flight—does not, in and of itself, lead to a reengagement into an affirming community. Marronage, as disengagement, flight, and reengagement, is the blossoming of fugitivity, offering at once both direction and fulfillment. Fugitivity gets us out of bondage. Marronage brings us "home." This movement from fugitivity to marronage is the transition from the escaping African—the misnamed "runaway slave"—to the maroon, part of a larger group of people practicing, experiencing, forging, and creating life together.

On some days, the chosen path of the fleeing youth would lead them right past my gate. One such afternoon, I was finishing lunch with my roommate, Samori, who called out to the passing student.

"Say, bruh, why you cuttin' school?"

"Man, it's borin' in there. They ain't talkin' 'bout nothin', y'heardme?"

He didn't slow down as he said it. He barely took his eyes off of his path. We didn't know his name. We didn't know where he was going or what would become of him. We never saw him again.

But we did hear him.

5

The Seed of Our Ancestors
Kamali Academy and Navigating the Impulse

One who learns, teaches.

—Ethiopian proverb

"Who *are* you?" a voice calls out, disturbing the birdsong. A solitary car meanders across General Meyer, the main street at the end of the block.

"I am the seed of my Ancestors," the students respond in rehearsed unison. "I am the hope of today. I am the builder for those unborn. I am the promoter of our Afrikan Way." Their voices ricochet off the high walls of Roberts High School, speed back towards them, then soar over the one-story homes that line their side of the street.

"What is your purpose?"

"To use my personal skills and talents for the benefit of my community. To think of others first and build Umoja—Afrikan unity."

The morning air is cool, but holds a humid bite that will certainly turn hot before noon.

"Where are you from?"

"Mama Afrika is my home. Liberation is my song. You can't steer me wrong. I'm Afrikan to the bone. Birth is not the beginning and death is not the end. I am because we are. Together we shall win."[1]

Their instructor leads them through the daily ritual with a puzzlingly effective balance of sternness and humor. They pour libations to their ancestors, pledge allegiance to the red, black, and green Liberation flag, and sing the first verse of "Lift Every Voice and Sing." On the verse's last line—"Let us march on till victory is won"—the students throw their fists in the air, repeat the line, and give an exaggerated march back into the three-bedroom house. This is how each morning began at Kamali Academy, an African-centered, systematic homeschool operating out of a three-bedroom house I shared with my roommate and friend, Samori Camara.[2] It was a small school with no more than nineteen students at any given time and a curricular approach that revolved around loosely structured classes in various subject areas. Kamali's mission was to build "a self-determining (kujichagulia) community of Afrikan people equipped with self-love, self-awareness, and a commitment to the resolution of our collective problems" (Kamali Academy 2011). We used primary and secondary education as our entry point.

Kamali began in 2010 in a house across the street from Roberts High School. We held our morning meetings, lunch, and outdoor activities in our front yard, which had an unobstructed view of the charter school. On particularly lovely days, we would play sports or hold class under a tree in Roberts's yard. While close in proximity, Roberts and Kamali were worlds apart. Roberts was one of a growing number of charter schools, reflecting the city's neoliberal turn in education in the wake of Hurricane Katrina, which promoted and adopted "new" ideas through a corporate model that often equated students with dollars—head count at the beginning of the year and test scores at the end. Kamali was a collective of community members seeking to educate Black youth in a culturally affirming environment. It identified with a legacy of Black educational institutions intent on nation building for independence and self-determination. While on one level this may appear to be a matter of school choice, I argue that it speaks to a maroon impulse for community autonomy through educational control.

A "homeschool collective" was still a foreign idea in this New Orleans neighborhood when Kamali opened, and it represented a dramatically different approach to education in several ways. First, Kamali's one-room-schoolhouse model prioritized students and not test scores. The small student body allowed for stronger relationships between faculty, students, and parents and promoted a communal approach to education wherein the school and the students' homes became extensions of one another. Second, Kamali maintained an explicit identification with African-centered and Pan-African traditions, infusing them into the school's practices and curriculum. This was attractive to parents seeking a more holistic education tailored to the cultural identities of their children. Third, the flexibility afforded the school through its in-home format allowed for greater attention to the academic and personal needs of the students, including the opportunity to discern and pursue interest-based learning in a guided manner. Relatedly, a fourth way in which Kamali employed a different approach to education was through its centralization of care. Kamali Academy provided a culturally empowering education in a safe, supportive, nurturing, and attentive environment. While there were certainly caring and loving teachers in the charter schools throughout the city, their structures—predicated as they are on a business model of quantification—held no room for such a governing ethic. That is, while individual teachers may offer care, they are overshadowed by the limiting structures of their institution.

In this chapter I pick up where the previous chapter left off by exploring what lies beyond fugitivity. I've argued that a challenge to fugitivity as a liberating practice is tied to its inability to usher in reengagement into a community of people sharing similar values and aspirations. In part, the amorphousness of marronage means that there is an inherent messiness that accompanies an undefined and constantly adjusting shape. The transition into Kamali was much the same. Teachers, parents, and students were experimenting with needs and desires. While we were attempting to move away from the system, it was our only frame of reference. As Kamali staff, we were confronted by the practical limitations of our Black nationalism. Kamali families had to revisit their relationship to the educational system/process. In order to create something new, we all had to try on different things to get a sense for what fit best and felt right. As such, the journey was one of incongruence, coincidence, and discovery. Each day, we were learning more about ourselves, each other, and what we wanted. We had never done this before. Samori, the school's founder and director, was a historian and teacher. He possessed a rare combination of theoretical astuteness and pragmatism. From a pedagogical and even logical standpoint, we were confident the school could be a success. Still, we could not account for or fully appreciate the challenge parents must have gone through when deciding to send their children to Kamali. It would require them to move away from the certainty of a long-standing institution—albeit a harmful one—and step into something new and untested. Will I mess my child up? Will they fall behind their peers? Is this the right thing to do? The families of Kamali possessed a courageousness that emboldened them to try. That doesn't mean their fears or uncertainties subsided. Ours certainly did not. This journey of responding to a maroon impulse is not binary. Fear and courage coexist. It includes back and forth, contradiction, and instability. This chapter explores some of the trials and triumphs of that journey through the world-making efforts of Kamali Academy.

The Development of Kamali Academy

New Orleans's summer sky is a quilt of clouds. The sun doesn't exactly shine, and the humidity wraps its arms around you like an overly affectionate lover. So it was when I arrived at the three-bedroom house in Algiers. Samori's two nephews were jumping from the sassafras tree in the front yard. When he came out to greet me, his first words were, "Shoulda came down in September. These summers ain't nothing nice." It was the middle of July in 2009. He had moved back from Austin in early June and hit the ground running, working with Baakir Tyehimba in preparation for the coming school year when they would be opening the Black-Star Educational Cooperative. Samori wanted to start a school after he quit his job teaching seventh grade English at a school in Baton Rouge three years earlier. Dissatisfied with what he viewed as the ineffectiveness of public education in the city, he decided to run for school board as a twenty-four-year-old Independent candidate. When canvassing, he happened upon an older woman sitting on her porch. She invited him to take a seat, and they began talking. Samori expounded upon the ills of the current school system: overcrowded classrooms, under-resourced teachers, and the criminal absence of a culturally relevant curriculum. When he was finished, the woman told him, "I have two grandbabies in those schools. I'm not gonna vote for you. I don't vote. But I like what you're saying. You got good talk." Then, easy as the sun setting just on the horizon, she told him, "But until you have *your* school, I gotta send my babies to them white folks in the morning."

Although he didn't win a seat on the school board, the experience had an impact on him. When Samori returned to New Orleans three years later, he did so in the midst of a changing tide in public education. There was money and opportunity available to those willing to brave the

Figure 4. Samori pouring libations at the Second Annual Little Afraka Street Festival. Photograph by Jafar M. Pierre.

uncertainty and difficulty of rebuilding infrastructure. The same friend who invited me to work at Henson Academy also encouraged Samori to apply for a charter. She was in the advanced stages of doing so herself and had the legal and human resources to position him favorably. He declined, referring to one of his favorite proverbs: "He who butters your bread has an effect on your stomach." Samori believed that independent education—free from the mandates and politics of public, charter, and public charter schools—was the only way to provide Black people with an education for liberation. So, he teamed up with his friend Baakir, a former substitute teacher. They both studied the teachings and methods of Elijah Muhammad and the Nation of Islam. "Fishing" was a means by which the Nation of Islam recruited new members. They identified the most downtrodden and alienated members of society and provided them with spiritual and ideological resources that could assist them in returning to their "true selves."

To recruit students, the two headed to the housing projects and sought out disengaged youth.

"Say, bruh, we got a school."

"It's gonna put me in my right grade?"

Several people were interested in attending BlackStar, but when the school year began only two students enrolled: DeAndré, a fourteen-year-old boy from the housing development where Samori grew up; and Akil, a thirteen-year-old boy whose aunt attended college with Samori. Their parents would register them with the state as homeschool students and send them to BlackStar for "tutoring." The school opened in early September 2009 and was held in our house. The walls were army green and brown. The smell of Zatarain's and incense settled in couches crowded with books bearing folded paperback covers. None of the electrical outlets on an entire side of the building worked, so bright orange extension cords snaked across the hallway and provided power to the kitchen and living room, where classes were held. The teachers would split the days of the week, Samori teaching English and ourstory[3] and Baakir teaching math and science. Baakir, who had carpentry skills, had taken on the responsibility of renovating what would soon be BlackStar Books and Caffé, which would fund the school. Due to limited resources, however, renovations were taking longer than expected. This left the school to depend solely on the $150 (in cash or kind) tuition and community support. Some of Samori's contacts in Baton Rouge donated book bags, notebooks, pens, and pencils. His mother provided old workbooks. I would print out worksheets from Henson. They also sold T-shirts online to generate some revenue. It still wasn't enough. On top of this, at the end of two months Baakir's tasks at the café limited his time for teaching and the two decided it would be best for Samori to take over full-time. DeAndré, who was often in trouble with the law, eventually stopped coming.

Around April of 2010, Baakir's mother—a social worker—referred two younger students: a brother and sister, ten and eight, respectively. The two were under the guardianship of their grandmother, and because the charter lottery system had not placed them, neither had been in school all year. To help with the vast age gap between Akil and the new students, Samori enlisted the help of sister Tosin, who was a regular at the café and expressed interest in working at the school. As the year drew to a close, the BlackStar Educational Cooperative had three students and two teachers.

None of the students would return after the first year, however. While their parents were extremely satisfied with BlackStar, they felt it had done a great job of preparing their children for a return to public schools. It was a year of hard lessons in what ultimately proved to be an unsustainable model. The café was up and running but barely making ends meet, so there was no money to support the school. Samori, who was completing his dissertation, used the summer to clarify his vision and adjust his approach. Around the same time, I was ready for a change. My involvement with the educational cooperative was limited. I was working at Henson that year, which kept me away for the greater part of the day. While we had regular discussions about the school's philosophical and ideological aspirations, I did not have any direct participation beyond providing some reading workbooks from Henson and greeting the students when I saw them. By the close of the school year, however, I was looking for a healthier learning environment and was much more interested in the changes that were taking place under my roof. I approached Samori to offer my assistance.

"Can you teach English two days a week?"

I was the school's newest teacher, though this status wouldn't last long. Shortly thereafter, Mama Efua joined the team to teach reading. Sister Akosua, who learned about the school through the café, made the hour drive from Hammond, Louisiana, to teach mathematics. Her cousin Kumi also came to teach physical education. Sister Tosin was still on the staff, but her schedule did not permit as much flexibility as the previous year. Because we were all volunteers, we arranged a schedule whereby no one besides Samori, the lead teacher, would teach for more than four hours a week.

Whereas BlackStar sought to work with high school–age students, Kamali chose to focus on younger students in order to intervene at an earlier stage of academic, social, and emotional development. Mama Efua and Baakir had two of their daughters come to the school. Baba El sent his two children. Samori's mother recruited the son and niece of one of her friends. Kamal, my student from Henson, and his mother heard Samori speak at an event and signed up. Two other families also heard Samori speak and enrolled their children. A cousin of one of the girls came to orientation and decided she, too, wanted to attend the school. When her mother saw the environment, she also enrolled her four-year-old daughter. By the first day, we had eleven students—seven girls and four boys—and six teachers. The majority of the students had repeated at least one grade. All but two had attended public schools prior to coming to Kamali. We were honored that these families would entrust us with their children, and excited by the larger significance their presence came to represent: a group of people willing to navigate unchartered territories—pun intended—in pursuit of something more aligned with their vision for their lives. To reflect the new school, Samori chose a new name: Kamali, Shona for "the spirit that protects the youth from death." The students covered a wider age range (four to sixteen), and the tuition rose to two hundred dollars per month, but parents could supplement what they could not pay with volunteer hours or food donations. We reduced overhead costs by requiring the students to bring their own lunch. Fridays would be reserved for home economics, where we cooked together.[4]

Samori and I had moved into the house across from Roberts High School several months earlier. This bigger house included a large extension suitable for a classroom. The living room in the front of the house served as a perfect room for the younger students. We put out a call for support on our YouTube show and set up an online registry. Within days, we had donations coming from all across the country—pencils, toilet paper, printing paper and notebooks, wall maps, projectors, and computers. We also tapped into our social networks. Samori's mother provided old desks and filing cabinets from the school where she worked. Friends offered paper and copying services. Strangers offered monetary donations. There were also constant phone calls from word-of-mouth referrals. Although the school began as Samori's vision, he was responding to and in conversation with a larger need. Kamali was growing and incorporating the ideas, wants, and needs of those involved.

Self-Reliance and Self-Determination

Kamali Academy was part of a larger tradition of independent Black education. The school's immediate predecessor was Kuumba Academy, which offered African-centered home education in New Orleans East. Kuumba paused operations after Hurricane Katrina and was reorganizing when Kamali was starting. We also studied the philosophical and pedagogical approaches of schools that emerged during the Black Power movement, which formed in major urban centers and reflected a serious engagement with the slogan popularized by Amiri Baraka: "It's nation time!" This was a call to create institutions that would buttress the Black nation emerging from the shackles of white America and seizing its own destiny. For many within the movement—including Baraka—Africa became a source for a more robust cultural identity.[5] These institutions took the shape of private schools, Saturday schools, after-school programs, and community rites-of-passage processes.[6] Two of these formations—Ahidiana's Work/Study Center and The East's Uhuru Sasa Shule—had a direct impact on Kamali.[7] Ahidiana's Work/Study Center, founded in New Orleans's Lower Ninth Ward in November 1973, sought the development of politically progressive, socially advanced, academically excellent, and physically sound students. Fully funded by a community of supporters and refusing governmental assistance, the program stressed "both academic excellence and social responsibility" (Ahidiana n.d.). Uhuru Sasa Shule ("Freedom Now School") was founded in Brooklyn a few years before Ahidiana. The school's mission was "the development of the skills and thinking necessary for nationhood and liberation from the dominant political and cultural thought and behaviors" (Konadu 2009, 89). It sought to meet the needs of the students, families, and the broader community through high-quality, culturally relevant early childhood through adult education (Hotep 2001).

Similar to its Black Power predecessors, Kamali Academy was trying to do something that Black communities have been doing in this country, with varying levels of success, for several centuries: use education as a means of assuming control of their destiny. James D. Anderson qualifies this quest as a history marked by a "persistent struggle . . . that prefigured their liberation from peasantry" (1988, 3). From the dawn of the Civil War through the nadir of race relations, there were pockets of Black people who were agents in the design of their own educational systems. They saw a link between education and liberation, and Anderson's work on education from Reconstruction through the Great Depression explicates a larger history of struggle, not for integration and assimilation, but for independence and self-determination. "The ex-slaves struggled to develop a social and educational ideology singularly appropriate to their defense of emancipation and one that challenged the social power of the planter regime" (33). Education was a means of making sense of and equipping themselves to prosper in their new world.

W. E. B. Du Bois also unearths a legacy of Black schools working toward these ends. In the District of Columbia in 1818, for instance, "free colored families" were encouraged to support a Black school through subscription or by sending their children to attend. Between 1800 and 1861, Washington, D.C., had "no less than fifteen different schools" run and largely supported by Black people. In Cleveland in 1832, John Malvin, a Virginia-born "free colored preacher," sought to teach the children of a few Black families. Enough subscriptions were collected to guarantee a teacher's salary of twenty dollars per month. After three years of "indefatigable work," Malvin organized a convention in Columbus, Ohio, with the aim of devising "some way of increasing the means to educate their people."[8] Preceding Anderson's observation, Du Bois points out that "to the Negro slave, freedom meant schools first of all. Consequently, schools immediately sprang up after emancipation" (1907, 77). In Georgia, for instance, 191 day schools and 45 night schools were reported in 1867. Ninety-six of these were either wholly or partially supported by the freedmen and -women.

The extent to which African people were committed to their own education before and after the legal end to chattel slavery in the United States became clear with schools emerging all throughout the South and Midwest, even in places the Freedmen's Bureau hadn't reached. Anderson tells us that "many missionaries were astonished, and later chagrined, however, to discover that many ex-slaves had established their own educational collectives and associations, staffed schools entirely with black teachers, and were unwilling to allow their educational movement to be controlled by the 'civilized' Yankee" (1988, 6). There were several records of the newly emancipated preferring that their children be educated in Black private schools instead of the white-dominated free schools, even though the former were more expensive, suggesting that "self-help and self-determination underlay the ex-slaves' educational movement" (5).[9] As Heather Andrea Williams points out, Black people in the days following Emancipation were determined to get an education "on our own hook" (2005, 81). Throughout the Deep South, Black people would petition organizations such as the Freedmen's Bureau for resources but not for teachers. They would share what they had in order to form a composite of knowledge which they would then use to secure self-determination.[10]

The legacy of independent educational initiatives that Kamali inherited highlights an alternative reading of Black aspiration and its realization. It challenges the assumption that Black "progress" necessarily means advancement toward mainstream acceptance, pursuing instead the central values of self-reliance and self-determination.[11] In so doing, we were attempting to model—in form and content—that which we sought to cultivate in our students. At Kamali, Samori would often remind us that the teachers were the curriculum. Baba El agreed: "Kids hear what you saying. They listen to what's coming out your mouth, but they—80 percent of they vibe comes from what you do. How you walk, how you talk. So if everything is consistent with them, with seeing you just all the time, 'Okay, this must be a sound brother, a sound sister, a sound person . . . [because] he always like this.'"[12]

A New Culture

We often used the term *homeschool* when referring to ourselves. This, however, was incongruent with how the term is generally used, namely, home-based education in which parents teach their children directly. Homeschooling has seen a dramatic rise among Black families over the past two decades due to many factors, including what Cheryl Fields-Smith and Monica Wells Kisura identify as "resistance to institutionalized racism and ideological mismatches" (2013, 266). Families are pulling their children out of traditional schools and choosing instead to educate them directly and in a manner more congruent with their values and beliefs. We also used the term *homeschool collective* freely. This, too, is misaligned with the term's broader usage, which suggests a loose organization of homeschool families who participate in shared social and educational activities. Homeschool collectives are found in major cities and suburbs across the country, with many libraries, museums, and other educational institutions offering programming specifically for homeschoolers. Kamali didn't fit into either of these categories. We eventually settled on *systematic homeschool*, which reflected an approach organized around a central curriculum and set academic year. Similar to the BlackStar Educational Cooperative, our students were officially registered with the state as homeschoolers.

Fields-Smith and Kisura are accurate in identifying resisting racism and ideological mismatches as motivators for Black homeschoolers. This was only part of the story for Kamali leadership, however. While we shared views with many Black families in the growing homeschool movement, we found greater alignment with the legacy of independent Black schools seeking self-determination. The school was less focused on working against external forces—resisting—and more intent on cultivating and responding to an internal impetus, or what I am referring to as a maroon impulse. It was pursuit more than it was escape. This nuance speaks to a differentiation between social protest and institution building. Whereas the former is directed externally—namely, at symbols of authority—the latter is an intrinsic process centered on the group or community. Parents, teachers, and families were taking a proactive stance toward the education of their children rather than looking to the state or charter organizations to do so. As Joan Ratteray and Mwalimu Shujaa observe, social protest succeeds when the "desired outcome is 'granted' by the authorities." In this sense, its effectiveness is tied to the decisions of the external force. Institution building, on the other hand, is "an act of self-empowerment that may or may not have the indirect effect of changing power relationships" (1987, 42). Altering power relationships is important, but this can only be accomplished once a group has developed the internal power necessary to then shape their environment. While there were some discussions in the BlackStar community about the need to protest egregious practices and engage in direct action, these were often viewed as secondary options.[13] Our priority was to build a world for ourselves by developing our own institutions.

While there was often overlap between the ideals of Kamali and the aspirations of the families attending the school, they weren't always identical. We—Samori and the teachers—viewed Kamali as a nation-building initiative. The families valued the attention and care their students received, seeing the school as a safe and affirmative environment for their children. While they appreciated the role that a positive Black identity played in the curriculum, many could have taken or left the "nation talk." These varying emphases sometimes led to irritations and misunderstandings. Kamal's mother, Mama Tamieka, was disturbed by what she described as our inconsistency. "It seems as though things keep changing, even though you all put it down in your little pamphlet of what you all are going to offer the next year. It seems as though it's changing every so many months. With the volunteering work or the food thing, instead of having everything outlined in the beginning of the school year, 'This is how it's gonna be, nothing's gonna change.' I like consistency. It's not being consistent."[14] We were zealously pursuing our mission in a way that, at times, overlooked the immediate needs of our families. Our rapid growth meant things were constantly changing, opening up room for critiques of inconsistency. We were getting new students, new teachers, and new ideas. Mama Tamieka's critiques reveal that, in the midst of this, we weren't always tending to the fundamentals. This also became apparent in our teacher turnaround.

Over the course of my two years there was a total of ten teachers at Kamali. Some left due to schedule conflicts or work obligations, while others were asked to leave. Kumi, our physical education teacher, was released following an incident in which he stole a cell phone from one of the students. This was both a shock and an eye-opener for us, as we assumed that all who came to the school had positive intentions. We had safety precautions in place: generally, there were two teachers on duty at a time—a woman and a man. If one was not in the classroom, then he or she would be somewhere else in the house. No adults were alone with students behind closed doors. If a teacher needed to speak with a student privately, they would do so in the living room, which was located at the front of the house in direct line of sight from the classroom in the back. There was a lot of movement during the school day, however. Kumi came two days a week with his cousin Akosua. They drove over an hour to be there, so when they came they were there for the day. As other classes were taking place—perhaps outdoors as was regularly the case—Kumi took the opportunity to rummage through one child's belongings. When we discovered this, he was dismissed immediately. Next, Mama Efua was asked to leave the school after she failed to intervene in a fight between two of the students. We had noticed several changes in her teaching performance, including an antagonistic approach toward students. We attempted to speak with her about it on several occasions, but she declined. When she left, she took her two daughters with her. Around this time, all before the end of Kamali's first semester, Mama Afivi came to the school to teach reading. She brought her son and daughter with her. Mama Afivi, an artist and educator steeped in African-centered traditions and practices, brought a new energy and filled in many of the gaps that we were missing. She took on public relations, stepping into the role of liaison between the school and community by coordinating guests and field trips.

Kamali sought to be an incubator of community through an institutional model that revolved around its participants—students, faculty, parents, and neighbors—whether through the school's curricular content or community events such as the annual Kwanzaa celebration. Later on, Kamali would incorporate a biweekly enrichment period wherein people from the local community would come in and share their skills and talents through interactive workshops. It would be a way to expose the community to Kamali, and vice versa. Painters, scientists, storytellers, musicians, dancers, and many more would share their passions with the students. Parents would also be encouraged to lead workshops on topics such as health and nutrition, gardening, and crocheting. We wanted to have higher levels of parental participation for two reasons: first, it would foster a greater sense of community among the students, teachers, and parents by visually demonstrating a commitment to the educational well-being of all students at Kamali; and second, it would divide the labor of daily tasks over a greater number of people, allowing us to reduce overhead. This did not happen organically, however. Shortly after the start of the second academic year we implemented two mandatory volunteer hours per month. This is the change Mama Tamieka was unhappy with. Most parents did not meet this requirement with regularity. Admittedly, we were perhaps a bit naive in believing that our idealism could somewhat arbitrarily override the pervasive experiences that our students' parents had with the public education system, wherein they came to view the school's role as separate from their own. For some, school was an institution over which they felt they had little control, and it was the job of the teachers to teach, discipline, and watch over students in their care. Due to a number of factors—employment demands on their time, limited educational experience, or uncertainty about how they could contribute—Kamali parents were not always as present as we would have liked.

Building Relationships

This is not to say, however, that the parents did not find overlap between their home and the school. Mama Kia, who had several children at the school, explained, "It was important for my children to be in a learning situation that felt similar to home or similar to family, you know?"[15] This was reflected not only in the amount of time students spent at the house outside school hours (after school, weekends, etc.) but also in how Kamali seeped into the home culture of its students. One day, a student was sulking because his mother wouldn't allow him to eat pork at home. She said that since he couldn't do it at school, he couldn't do it in the house.[16] Mama Kia continues, "You know you can't go to school and act out because mama such and such talks to daddy every day, or we talk online, or whatever. So outside of school there is still another relationship. So those teachers or other parents may be involved in our personal lives outside of the school, which gives the children another respect for the adults."[17] Students stayed after school or would wait for their parents to pick them up from BlackStar, where the teachers spent much of their time. It would be common for me to pass Sunday night laughing with some of the Mamas and Babas at Liberation Lounge only to greet them a few hours later when they dropped their children off for morning meeting. Mama Afivi emphasized the centrality of relationships to the school's success: "Not only the relationship between the students themselves, but the relationships between the adults and the students. I think that makes a huge difference in the academic development of students, where they trust—like, there's a genuine trust. And not only them learning the academic material that is given to them, but also with personal challenges— just joys, you know. Things that are happy. Things that they can share. And that's very, very big at Kamali Academy, where I think the whole student is addressed."[18]

First with BlackStar and then with Kamali, we adopted the one-room-schoolhouse model that educated generations of Black students. Students across age sets and academic abilities could partake in the learning process together, bringing individual skills and experiences to the table in a manner that benefited all involved. Many of our students were part of the same underperforming school system as my students at Henson. They were struggling in at least one subject. The one-room approach mitigated any potential embarrassment or stigma associated with performing "below grade level." In fact, it promoted an unforeseen by-product whereby students developed an investment in the mutual success of their peers. They would offer support and encourage one another when it was clear that a student was having difficulty grasping a concept. For Yao, a fifteen-year-old student, this was very different from his previous school, where they didn't "teach us how to work together as a group. . . . But like, in Kamali, they teach you to help each other and not always be cruel to each other. But if you absolutely have differences with another warrior in the school, they try to teach us to learn how to solve our problems different ways instead of like in public schools—fighting and arguing, which is unnecessary."[19]

This took time to develop, and the school could never rid itself completely of the name-calling and taunting typical of students their age, but this teasing was rarely focused on a student's academic abilities.[20] Yao pointed out that "some students—I'm not the only one who's been pulled out of a public school system[21]—so I have to say that one of the biggest things is that some of us can let our old ways from being in public school affect how we treat each other."

Kamali offered standard subjects, such as math, language arts, reading, science, and foreign languages. It also offered ourstory, which emphasized and centralized the role of African people throughout world history. These "subjects," however, were approached in a way that did not allow for strict division. Rather, they were transdisciplinary. There was math and science in language arts, reading in math, science in ourstory, and so forth. Because we were not bound by state regulations and our curriculum was not dictated by state exams, we could work at our own pace. We knew that our students, as survivors of the schooling process, needed foundation building. We were free to address the specific issues and needs of our students; needs that would otherwise be ignored since they rested outside of the timeline of the state curriculum. This was clear to students, and they welcomed the contrast from their previous schools. Kwame, nine, observed that at Kamali "they teach you what you want to learn. Like, in public school, they'll teach you, but they'll only teach you what's on the LEAP test. They'll teach you, but at Kamali, they'll go back to it if you forgot. In public school, they will not go back."[22] His sister, Ayana, fourteen, agreed, pointing out that at public school "some of the teachers care for you, but some of them just don't. They just teach 'cause they get they money. The teachers here actually love you and take time to make sure you learning."[23]

Care, Attention, and Identity

Ayana's statement speaks to the thread that stitches school leadership, parents, and students together. We loved our students. And we didn't love them out of any sense of obligation—whether as stewards of the nation or because they were in our care. We loved them because at some point they stopped being students in a school we ran and started being children with whom our fate was tied. They were fellow passengers. Their success was our success. Their well-being was our well-being. We were present in their lives beyond the school walls, attending noncurricular events (athletic events, performances, etc.) and making occasional phone calls commending them on their progress. Parents were quick to inform Samori if their child had misbehaved and regularly asked that he get to the bottom of the situation. It was this love, expressed as deep care, that eased this transition into the unknown and alleviated familial anxieties about walking an unbeaten path. Parents were more concerned with the people and *space* of Kamali as a site of a holistic education than with curriculum or politics. Attention and identity were common themes in my conversations with parents. They felt that Kamali was a place where their children received the former and a strengthened sense of the latter. Attention was important because many of their children needed greater one-on-one interaction. Mama Jamila, whose grandson attended the school, noticed positive changes in him, noting, "I don't know if it is the [vegetarian and low-sugar] food. I think, really, it's the small group that, you know—and he have the attention. He get the attention that he need over there."[24]

Mama Kia, while underscoring the same point, speaks to a fundamental aspect of the Kamali educational model: "Just the ability and the willingness to be able to, I guess, accommodate each child is important to me. . . . That is important so children don't feel like they are being left behind or they're dumb because a lot of times, the way they're taught is not necessarily to their advantage."[25] This resonated with other parents who hoped their children's particular learning habits would be identified and catered to, as opposed to ignored and regulated. Samori is passionate on this point. He often remarked, "We don't need standardization. We need customization and Afrikanization," or the development of culturally appropriate approaches specific to the interests and learning styles of our students. At Kamali this meant discovering and developing the skills and talents of individual students with the expectation that those skills would be used for the improvement of their community. This falls in line with the second major theme that parents brought up in our conversations: identity.

Kamali was explicit in its African-centered identity and intention. We believed that Black people are an African people and that our ability to achieve freedom is directly tied to our connection to our culture—not as a fixed monolith but as a dynamic unfolding that operates on an alternative time-space continuum. While the majority of the parents may not have come from identical ideological standpoints, they did agree on the need for an environment in which their children's Black identities were affirmed, viewing it as an essential part of the educational process. Mama Naima, who had two daughters at the school, observed, "If you have a better love and understanding of self, then growing up as an adult, you won't be so confused about what it is you need to do—you know—what your purpose is here in life. . . . Learning about self and self-awareness, again, that helps with self-esteem, definitely. It gives you a sense of pride."[26]

Parents used phrases like "self-esteem" and "home-like environment" often. Mama Esi thought "it was good that it felt more like a family environment. They sat down to eat, washing dishes—I really liked that—everybody having to have some sort of responsibility instead of just, you know, sit around. I just liked the whole home-like environment."[27] Baba El was looking for a place where teachers were more than babysitters, a place where they not only took an interest in his children but set positive examples for them. Both he and Baba Ali expressed that they had found this in Kamali. Baba Ali was having a conversation with his son, Sadik, when Sadik told him, "Yeah. I'm getting my PhD like brother Samori." Baba Ali explained: "He says to himself, 'Here's this Black man with this degree. . . . Somebody who looks just like me is a doctor.' Doctors are hard to be, but when he sees you guys, you know, he's like, 'Oh, I'ma just be like them. I'ma do this. I'ma go to college for this. I'ma go to college for that.'"[28]

I would like to pause on this point. One could read Sadik's aspiration to pursue a PhD as further ensconcing himself in the very system we were claiming to want to move away from. Is there a contradiction in the fact that Samori started a school while finishing his PhD but was encouraging families—many of whom did not have the same access to educational opportunities—to disengage from the mainstream system? We would discuss this often. There were certainly those who attempted to use this as a means of detracting from the work we were doing. We viewed our proximity to and intimacy with the more "elite" aspects of "the system," however, as further support for the claims we were making. It was, for us, Ayi Kwei Armah's white road of death (Armah 2000). We had seen the inside and found that it had nothing to offer us except a life of deceptive comfort in exchange for extraction and isolation. Samori was always forthright in admitting that the reason he got a PhD was because he knew it would add weight to what he had to say. For better or worse, his educational pursuits proved to be a legitimizing factor among our people. At the very least, it opened up some of the parents' minds to what he had to offer.

Mama Kia pointed out what she felt was the vital role of Black male teachers: "I like the fact that there are a lot of male teachers. I think that that balance is important, you know. Especially for the young—well, not just for the young brothers, but it is good for the young brothers to see other brothers in situations where they are dealing with children that are not their own—you know, who are in a nurturing situation, in a teaching situation."[29] As a staff, we rarely had in-depth theoretical conversations about gender at Kamali. It was important for us to always model positive relationships between adults—which we displayed in how we addressed, considered, and supported one another in the school. Despite this, the staffing logistics of the school and the teaching positions that women and men filled played themselves out in ways that could appear to reflect more traditional, mainstream gender roles. While there were three primary teachers, there were also several volunteers. Men generally taught science and math classes, often deemed more valuable by the mainstream American educational value system.[30] In addition to arts, women tended to work with the younger children ("the babies"—ages sixteen months to five years). In other ways, though, we were complicating mainstream gender roles. Samori and I were working in a home environment in which we took on domestic responsibilities that would, perhaps in a mainstream context, be divided along gender lines. While this included instances of control or power, which would be congruent with ideas of men as "head of house" or even serving as principals in other educational contexts, we also maintained an emotional and affective presence that may often be attributed to maternal care. For us, our open expression of love for our students through knowing them, being consistent in their lives, and anticipating their needs was aligned with what we understood to be necessary for sustaining a community that had already responded to a maroon impulse. This wasn't unique to us as men, however. This was the approach that Kamali faculty and staff took toward the students. When teachers stepped outside of this care, they were asked to leave. The parents found value in this. In an educational space that was considered home-like, this praise may also have been a response to an overarching desire that parents, students, and teachers expressed in wanting to build Black homes and communities with the presence of positive and affirming gender relationships. As is often the case, however, the "celebration" of men as teachers and nurturers at Kamali sometimes overshadowed the crucial work that women were doing at the school.

A Place for Us

When the fleeing student in the previous chapter told us "They ain't talkin' 'bout nothin'," he was offering a critique of the school system. The school had nothing that he found relevant, interesting, or useful, so he wanted no part of it. When they could, he and his peers hopped the fence and went on to do things that could better hold their interests. In the case of my students at Henson, they found other forms of disengagement. Though outsiders may characterize these behaviors as irresponsible, counterproductive, or shortsighted, the impulse to leave is real. These youth, to a greater or lesser extent, understand what they are up against. They are told to stay in school, but they know that a high school diploma does not automatically open any more doors. In the city of New Orleans in particular, the most immediate avenue available to them is in the service industry, and the rapidly rising cost of living makes these forms of work untenable. Furthermore, it is likely not difficult for them to see that their presence in the schools is of greater benefit to their teachers and administrators, whose salaries, in many instances, are higher than a student's total household income (Thevenot 2009). As the parents of Kamali Academy students saw the ways the mainstream school system was marginalizing and alienating their children, they sought other options. Their decisions were a following through from disengagement to reengagement by tapping into an educational institution along with which a community could develop and flourish. They were making active decisions in search of a better education for their children. As I've outlined here, we faced difficulties and learned lessons along the way. It was a road paved with challenges and triumphs, shortcomings and discoveries. But I'm most interested in that maroon impulse that drove families to make such a foundational decision with what was most precious to them: their children. What does this tell us about the abject reality of the educational landscape? More importantly, what does it suggest about a possibility beyond the hegemonic order?

The idea of a systematic homeschool as an organized collective of children and families is something practiced by groups across the country.[31] Many were larger and older than Kamali, which never had more than nineteen students at a time. In this regard, the school was not doing anything particularly unique. So, what do a handful of Black children in an embattled city teach us about independent education and community formation? On the surface, Kamali appears to be just another group in the growing movement for culturally appropriate/inclusive education. If we look deeper, however, the school indicates something larger than its numbers would suggest. Samori observed: "What we find a lot of times is the people whose children are doing so-called 'okay' in the European system, they're comfortable with that and they are not gonna try to send them somewhere else. But we get the people who are like, 'The system ain't working for us anyway, you know? Go 'head on and take him. We can do a little experiment, I guess. See what happens.'" Kamali's growth indicates not only a dissatisfaction with the current system, but that people are actively searching for alternatives. It represents individuals assuming control of the educational lives of their children. The "see what happens" attitude is more of a willingness to pursue the unknown than an acceptance of defeat. For Kamali families, the "experiment" was placing their children in an environment that was intent on providing a positive socialization that emphasized both academic and character development, one in which their children would receive an education that placed them, as Black youth, at the center. By choosing Kamali, these families were responding to a maroon impulse and affirming this systematic homeschool as a viable model of specialized education.

But the experience of navigating that experiment was never seamless. The ideological vision of the school may have, at times, been incongruent with values in the home. Negotiating relationships between parents, students, and teachers proved difficult at times. Strengths and weaknesses across skill areas such as teaching and administration revealed themselves. These are, however, largely the types of hiccups one would expect with new organizations. The looming challenge was dealing with the consequence of responding to a maroon impulse and its attendant fear, doubt, and uncertainty. To do so is to step outside of the reliability and perceived comfort of the dominant apparatus—replete with infrastructure and resource. It is to defy the hegemonic cultural logic that validates and affirms said apparatus while simultaneously undermining and dismissing all else. The result is either the wholesale—at times, violent—rejection of anything outside of the established norm or the inability to conceptualize any such thing. Thus, parents enroll their students in schools that they ultimately find unsatisfactory because anything else would be either irresponsible or impossible. We saw this belief after the BlackStar Educational Cooperative's first year, when parents decided to send their children back to public schools. They praised Samori's efforts and were satisfied with the education their children had received. Nonetheless, they still viewed it as a temporary solution before returning to what they often referred to as "real school"—back to the very underperforming institutions that made the move to the homeschool necessary in the first place. Both of these beliefs—the irresponsibility and/or impossibility of a viable alternative—reveal a sense of resignation that is a reluctant abdication of power. The older woman in Baton Rouge with whom Samori spoke about the need for our own schools was not eager about sending her "grandbabies to them white folks." She simply felt she had no choice. This perceived lack of choice breeds disengagement. In the previous chapter, I shared the comments of one student's grandfather who noticed "all the spirit done went out of [his grandson]" when he had to go to his school. The boy's name was Kofi. He felt he didn't have any other options. He knew he had to go to school and was told he was supposed to "do well," but he didn't see how that was possible when there were fights every day and the teachers "didn't care about [the students]."[32] As such, he lost interest and, like so many other students, disengaged. Then he found Kamali.

So did Yaa. In the school's second year, a news crew from WDSU, New Orleans's NBC affiliate, came to do a story on Black homeschooling in the city. When they asked for potential students to interview, we recommended Yaa. She was nine years old and had a heart that was as expansive as her intellect. When the reporter asked Yaa what her favorite subject was, she responded: "My favorite subject is ourstory, because it teaches me about my culture, where I came from, and who I am. . . . It feels good because I finally get to know who I am instead of just being just a random person." We were shocked. Not that she said it—she was a brilliant student—but because it perfectly captured what we set out to do. Even the reporter had to take a second to get his bearings. We took

Yaa's statement about not being a random person as an affirmation. She was not a nondescript individual. She was a valuable member of our burgeoning Black nation. As I listen to her words again, however, I think we were misreading—at least partially—what she was saying. Yes, she was referring to having found a greater sense of self in a broader cultural identity. But I also believe she was communicating something about her needs. She was not a random person at Kamali. She felt cared for. She knew that she and all of her classmates were loved. She was engaging in a community of people concerned with and invested in her well-being, and that extended beyond the school's walls. The misreading of Yaa's statements reveals what I believe to be a larger misjudgment on what the concept of nation could do for us. The methods of nation building that Kamali inherited from our ideological predecessors are effective in advancing liberation. Constructing institutions and communities, forging collective identities, meeting shared needs, and centralizing care are avenues to generating communal power. I am not convinced, however, that the nation is the most effective vehicle for achieving that liberation. While they may have the same stated objective, the nation is, in many ways, at odds with marronage. The nation is fixed. It is rigid and bogged down with the weight of dogma and centralized bureaucracy. Marronage is flexible, amorphous, and dynamic. It bends, finding its way into the cracks and crevices that a bulky nation cannot.

Kamali Academy presents a potential beyond fugitivity. It is part of a process that *begins* as disengagement and moves *through* fugitivity but matures into a reengagement, not into the mainstream, but into a culturally affirming community. The students, parents, and teachers of Kamali, in this regard, partially left the "system" as individuals—fugitives—in search of positive institutions. I would like to say that once they reached Kamali they ceased to be fugitives, but perhaps that is forced poetry. Rather, they entered into a new phase. There was no arrival, for there is no arrival. Maroons never cease marooning. It is an ongoing process, replete with triumphs and setbacks, guided by an impulse that flickers, dims, and reignites. In this new phase beyond fugitivity, the families and teachers of Kamali Academy had each other—a community with whom they could work and explore and experiment, a community with whom they could keep going. The school saw its role as that of a central institution within this larger community. It sought to prepare students to fortify and serve that community through the development of their skills and talents. It was ambitious and difficult to quantify, for some trees takes several seasons to bear fruit. What the school *did* accomplish in those few years was to continue a process that started long before us. We responded to a shared impulse and sought to fashion a world for ourselves, one in which we could, together, protect the spirit of our children.

Samori and I were eating lunch on our front stoop. The students were playing dodgeball in the yard. It was a beautiful day in late spring. A layer of coolness coated the sun's bite. We saw him heading our way. Bright orange polo. Focus and excitement battling for control of his face—a face whose thick stubble distracted from the boy still peeking through his eyes. Feet tapping the pavement in rhythmic succession. Samori stood and called to him as he passed. He didn't stop. He didn't even look our way as he called back. He dipped around the corner. We watched him disappear. Our students—giggly and joyous—invited us to join the game.

6

Black in the Whirlwind
Hole in the Wall as Portal

Any place is better than here.

—Malcolm X

"Diamond in the back. / Sunroof top. / Diggin' the scene with a gangsta lean."[1]

The standing-room-only crowd packed itself into a beauty salon turned café the width of a shotgun house. They sang and yelled and shouted back, "OO, OOO," with chuckles and nostalgia. Some had closed eyes. Some nudged their neighbors. All swayed back and forth, dipping into their best gangsta lean—a unified mass of Black bodies. The vocalist, Nate "Suave" Cameron, called for the band to cut the music as the crowd sang on in their best shower voices, growing louder with each round. Outside, police cars rolled by on the desolate avenue. It was a quiet evening in Algiers. As New Orleans's only neighborhood located on the west bank of the Mississippi River, it was often derided for being "country" and not having much going on. This evening, however, just like all other Sunday nights, it was the place to be.

Liberation Lounge at BlackStar Books and Caffé was a weekly open mic that had grown into an underground experience being whispered about throughout the city. Poets, musicians, artisans, and art lovers would make their way from around New Orleans and, eventually, the country to participate in an improvised evening of communal expression. When the event ended, attendees would move to the parking lot, where conversations raged on until p.m. turned into a.m. Loud voices attempted to climb over the laughter. Lingering looks led to exchanged phone numbers and extended embraces. The ownership. The belonging. The pride. For a few hours each week we experienced a small piece of "Black heaven." While BlackStar aspired toward this Black heaven somewhere in the (hopefully not too distant) future, it was also rooted in a legacy of Black-owned performance and social venues that offered their clientele a liberatory experience in the midst of the confusion and uncertainty of American life. These locales—of which BlackStar Books and Caffé is one—are spaces of community formation occurring on their own terms and outside the gaze and intervention of mainstream society. While it is known by many names, here I focus on the hole in the wall—a descendant of the juke joint. At once seemingly vague yet culturally specific, the hole in the wall serves as a portal of Black potential where what Saidiya Hartman (2019) refers to as "beautiful experiments" result in underground cultural institutions that emerge throughout space and time. Beyond the invasive surveillance of a merciless and predatory society, the hole in the wall offers a chance of collective imagining and actualization through a maroon process of disengagement, flight, and reengagement.

In this chapter I explore these venues—the juke joint and the hole in the wall—as sites of agency as well as expressions of a maroon impulse. I sketch a nonlinear genealogy of some of the elements in their constellation and use Liberation Lounge as an entry point into a conversation about community autonomy and the possibilities of space and time travel through music. The hole in the wall functions as a portal into worlds both known and unknown.

BlackStar Rising

Although I was one of the cofounders of BlackStar Books and Caffé, working alongside a close group of people investing time, labor, and money to get the shop up and running, my largest contribution to the establishment was as the guitar player for the BlackStar Bangas, the house band for Liberation Lounge. What started out as a gathering of supportive friends on a summer evening in 2010 grew into a weekly event drawing talent and attendance from across the country. With time, my band would tour throughout the southern and northeastern United States accompanying a constellation of artists we met at Liberation Lounge. Partially by choice, the majority of our gigs were at venues similar to BlackStar: Black-owned spots catering to Black audiences in places that were stretched beyond the intended limits of their physical and psychic dimensions. It was the community center turned dance hall; the gymnasium used for a runway fashion show; the basement transformed into a bar; or the beauty salon converted into a concert hall. Some of these places were improvised, while others were more established. They did not always have official licensing from municipal governments or other such authorities. While the boundaries of legality inside were more elastic than outside of their doors, they were by no means lawless. They, like their juke-joint predecessors, maintained a strict code of conduct that best suited their collective needs, which came to be what defined the ongoing significance and relevance of these ad hoc venues. BlackStar Books and Caffé took the meeting of these needs as central to its institutional mission.

Music was foundational to the café. Whether its source was our improvised work songs or the home entertainment sound system we eventually purchased, the place was rarely silent. Hip-hop, jazz, Afrobeat, reggae, neo-soul—music from around the Black world pumped through the speakers. More than just consuming music, however, Baakir wanted us to create our own. He recruited me to start a band, Babatunde Omowale, and we began writing songs. At the same time, he introduced the idea for an open mic he wanted to call "Liberation Lounge." There was nothing unique about an open mic per se. It was New Orleans, after all. But Liberation Lounge would be so much more. A mix of live music, poetry, discussion, and political rally with plenty of laughter, Liberation Lounge's improvisatorial nature meant we never knew what we were going to get. We wanted it to be a mix of Philadelphia's Black Lily—the women-centered open mic responsible for so many artists of the neo-soul movement—and Fela Kuti's New Afrika Shrine. Our intention was to build a hotspot of African-centered cultural creation.

Liberation Lounge's 7 p.m. start time was a suggestion, and there was no designated end. Some nights would wrap up by 9:30 p.m., while others would flow on until well past midnight. Independent of whatever time the event ended, the last song was always the Liberation Lounge anthem, "BlackStar Rising." Baakir had written the lyrics and asked me to put music to them. After stumbling through some loose ideas, I managed to come up with a lick that struck at the heart of the blues: a blend of the minor and major scales. Jarred "Nation" Savwoir, our bass player, contributed something that echoed Charles Wright's "Express Yourself" and was accompanied by a Meters-style New Orleans funk rhythm. Baakir begins the song with a redemptive message from Marcus Garvey, who kept true to his words that we could "look for me in the whirlwind or the storm, look for me all around you, for, with God's grace, I shall come and bring with me countless millions of black slaves who have died in America and the West Indies and the millions in Africa to aid you in the fight for Liberty, Freedom, and Life" (Garvey 1986, 239). More than the inspiration behind BlackStar's name, the Honorable Garvey served as a patron ancestor whose lifework of self-determination and relentless struggle functioned as a guidepost. Significantly, the café was only a few miles from the New Orleans port where Garvey delivered his farewell address before being deported back to Jamaica in 1927. Many of us felt a duty to continue Garvey's legacy.

Baakir sings,

> I'm Black in the whirlwind
> Ready to begin again.
> Guess that means I'm continuing
> And I'm ready to win.
> Back in the Crescent,
> Where I was told to return no more.
> Chained my spirit to the port
> And I'm Black.

As the song reached its chorus, the crowd would erupt into a call-and-response that expanded Garvey's "One God, One Aim, One Destiny":

> And I'm still
> One God (*One motivation!*)
> One aim (*One destination!*)
> One people (*Afrikan Nation!*)
> Let's get it!

This last line would come out as a collective stutter: "Let's get it, g-get get it, g-get it, g-get get it, yeah!" The place was alive and would work itself into a frenzy once the song reached its vamp. This is when Baakir would feign overwhelm in his best James Brown impression. As he slurred his dance moves, he would drop to the floor. Someone from the audience would grab one of the many red, black, and green flags in the place and drape it over his shoulders. The assistant would guide Baakir's "feeble" frame offstage, but not before he would stand up straight with his right fist extended into the air and his left hand holding the flag aloft. He would then chant an embellishment of Garvey's words:

> Get up, you mighty nation,
> Accomplish what you will.
> Don't you be no race of cowards.
> Don't you be no imbeciles.

The crowd knew to expect these theatrics. We did it every week. Still, each Sunday it hit as if it were the first time. The laughter and shouts were loud enough to drown out the music. After the song ended and patrons exited to the parking lot, they continued singing and joking into the night as we began preparations for the following week.

In truth, BlackStar wasn't really a suitable concert venue. It was too narrow. The layout, with a bar jutting out past half of the building's width, didn't allow for any comfortable configuration of more than fifteen people, yet there were always significantly more in attendance.[2] The band—composed of bass, guitar, drums, keyboard, and percussion—had little room to situate itself. The drummer's back was flush against the foggy storefront window, and if horn players showed up they'd have to fit in where they could and try not to blow out the eardrums of crowd members. Still, every Sunday, Black people from around New Orleans made their way to Algiers to attend Liberation Lounge. They'd pack themselves into BlackStar twisting, stretching, and turning like an Ernie Barnes painting. Late into the night, they would sing and laugh and dance and joke, and in this small yet perfectly sized piece of Black heaven, they were free.

The Juke

The "unsuitability" of BlackStar's locale fits into what Katrina Hazzard-Gordon refers to as the "jook continuum," or those "institutions that appear exclusively in the black community and essentially underground, and thus they required practically no assistance from public officials in order to function" (1990, x). This would include formations such as the juke joint, honky-tonk, after-hours spot, rent parties, and, as we will explore shortly, the hole in the wall. While corporate performance venues like House of Blues make use of a juke-joint aesthetic replete with shiplap and southern cuisine, juke joints are rooted in an African martial tradition of clandestinity and were often dismissed and even persecuted as primitive dens of immorality and criminality. Hazzard-Gordon traces the juke's origins to the era of chattel enslavement. Because it was illegal for Africans to gather socially, slavery itself fostered "black social institutions that defied white control," which created a "recurrent pattern of covert social activity" (77). On a hemispheric scale we see similar expression in the myriad manifestations of marronage whereby African people created and maintained communities outside the purview and dominion of the plantation. More than an *escape from* the treacherous realities of white domination, these communities represent a *movement toward* a way of life centering African communal autonomy. In the United States this pattern would continue after Emancipation. The juke joint, as we would come to know it, took root during Reconstruction, as sharecroppers and others sought refuge in a time of heightened uncertainty and continuing white terrorism. It took many forms, as the physical structures of the space itself were always less important than the psychic space it enabled. While often accused of being a haven for illegal activity—drinking, gambling, or prostitution—and tied to a peasant class, the juke joint offered entertainment and an alternative economy to Black people otherwise excluded from the mainstream.

There are two points that come through here. First, the juke occupied a place outside of the mainstream moral economy. Its association with illicit activity was, therefore, unavoidable insofar as it fell at the nexus of marginalized race and class and emerged in response to a radically new concept: Black leisure.[3] As such, laws sought to regulate Black mobility in attempts to maintain the caste system that defined the social order. Any efforts made by Black people to provide for themselves outside of the restrictive avenues of sharecropping, domestic labor, and peonage would be met with violent repression. Second, the juke played a pivotal role in the expression of a collective Black agency. It was a means of circumventing societal barriers and providing for oneself—socially, culturally, and economically—and operated under a value system that was not governed by the tastes or mores of mainstream white society. The emerging class divisions among Black populations further stigmatized the juke. As Samuel Floyd observes, "Christianity's sacred-secular dichotomy and the frank atheism and amoralism of the jook crowd created a schism in the core culture" (Floyd 1996, 66–67) as the Black bourgeoisie attempted to distance themselves from the juke as a means of emulating white moral culture.[4]

While the juke may have been marginalized from mainstream society, it served its participants as a world unto itself where relationships were fostered and communities built—if only for a few hours at a time. Buried in the backwoods of the bayou or hiding down dirt roads in the Delta, they maintained autonomy, in part, because of their clandestine cover. These were not "official" establishments meeting the standards of zoning codes or the board of health. There were often no advertisements or street-side billboards. Instead, these establishments grew by word of mouth until they were institutionalized. We find this, too, in the case of BlackStar Books and Caffé. Marketing for Liberation Lounge, for instance, was sent out via text message. This allowed event organizers to curate who attended and set the tone for what the event would grow into, as well as guard against undesirable forces. Once the cultural character and social norms were established, the text messages ceased.

This unseen presence has played a central role in Black communal agency and survival through secret societies, maroon communities, alternative economies, twentieth-century political movements, and other forms of social organization. Secrecy, concealment, and deception have provided cover under which autonomy could be pursued. This, too, was BlackStar's pursuit. The café did not call attention to itself through things such as signage, advertising budgets, or any of the elements that businesses are encouraged to employ in order to thrive. Instead, it offered services to a clientele seeking cover, a clientele engaging in and working through incongruent conversations, rhythms, schedules, and spaces. BlackStar grew via word of mouth and quickly developed a network of clients and supporters that never extended beyond a few degrees of separation. There is significant overlap between the practices of BlackStar and the array of expressions of Hazzard-Gordon's "jook continuum," including the juke joints, honky-tonks, after-hours joints, rent parties, chitlin' struts, and Blue Monday affairs. While each of these has its own differences and nuances and is tied to specific time periods, I would like to turn to what I identify as a more contemporary descendant: the hole in the wall.

The Hole in the Wall

There are some songs that have a type of ubiquity that makes it difficult to discern their origin. When I was moving around New Orleans in the late aughts, one such song was Mel Waiters's "Hole in the Wall." Whether it was a bar on A P Tureaud, a car passing on Claiborne, or a front-porch radio in Holly Grove, this song blared out with a consistency that could only be described as culture. If you found yourself in the presence of the fifty-and-over crowd when this song came on, you would inevitably hear things like "Aww, this my *shit*!" or "What you know about this here!?" Younger audiences would chuckle at the song before they found themselves singing along. It was released in 1999. The tune opens with a guitar-matched bass line reminiscent of the Staple Singers' "I'll Take You There" with its familiar chord progression accompanied by a clap track. Waiters begins with the song's chorus, an invitation to the hole in the wall. As he enters the first verse, he explains that it's 3 a.m., all of the clubs are closed, and he finds himself somewhere he "didn't want anyone to know." Reflecting the judgment of and condescension toward the juke joint that Floyd, Hazzard-Gordon, and others describe, Waiters explains,

> I walked into the room
> Had my nose in the air
> It's 7 in the morning
> And I'm still in there

Having had such a good time, he returns the following night with his "high-class woman." As they arrive and she realizes where they are, she refuses to get out of the car. He convinces her to do so, and with a clever twist of the pre-chorus, it is she who is still there at 7 a.m.

The song's bridge describes the ambience:

> Smoke filled room
> Whiskey and chicken wings
> People dancin' and drinkin'
> And no one wants to leave

Like many classic songs, its power is not found in its mastery of harmony and rhythm alone. The production style of contemporary blues/soul often lacks the heightened processing and polish of mainstream pop. Waiters's voice, with its sing-talk intimacy, is more reminiscent of a talented uncle than a world-class crooner. This familiarity, I would argue, is where the song's true power lies: in its ability to tap into a collective experience. We don't know the particular hole in the wall Waiters is singing about, but we all know one (or a few) like it.

BlackStar was one, yes, but my band would encounter them all over as we ventured beyond the city limits. These were small places in Houston and Austin, Texas; Gulfport, Mississippi; or Mobile, Alabama—bars, basements, gymnasiums, community halls—often without a stage. We learned to travel with our own sound system, since these "venues" usually had little more than a cleared space in a corner for us. The DJ blasted music—sometimes through *our* equipment—as patrons filed in to these places with very few windows. Neon lights and disco balls bounced off of the smoke in the air, casting a red-and-blue haze over people who danced and caressed with a daring disregard that would have forced onlookers to avert their eyes were they not occupied themselves. The bartenders' unbothered fluidity met the needs of first-name-basis patrons looking to spend money or accrue credit. Loud voices raced each other across the room. When it was showtime, these crowds maintained an aesthetic standard far more demanding than our performances on New Orleans street corners, where eager tourists gladly tossed bills into a hat in exchange for the "real NOLA experience." The hole in the wall expected precision, style, and performative flare, sometimes so emboldened as to ask the band to stop and start again in order to "get it right this time." I began packing a twenty-five-foot guitar cable so I could walk out into the crowd during my solos and borrow loosely from the Jimi Hendrix playbook by strumming behind my head, picking with my teeth, or straddling my guitar in a way that would surely embarrass my mother. Hendrix, of course, had learned his ways from his years as a no-name hired gun touring the Chitlin' Circuit, where showmanship often rivaled musical prowess for highest importance. These venues, in some instances the very ones in which we found ourselves, were holes in the wall, dotting the country as oases of free Black expression where a maroon impulse preceded their gathering.

As "Hole in the Wall" fades, we hear Waiters belt out the refrain with a tinge of frustration: "I had my best time, ya'll!" Part of it is an attempt to effectively communicate the renewing joy and revelation he experienced in this place. But as he ramps down with "aww yeah" and into a relaxed "at the hole in the wall," he perhaps realizes that he doesn't need to strain. He can rely on the comprehension of shared experience, which he acknowledges earlier in the song: "I know ya'll—a lot of ya'll—heard of that before." Overcoming his limiting beliefs of propriety and respectability, Waiters allowed himself to experience the hole in the wall's darkness and could then bask in its luminance. As he shares, "You can hang out all night long." There, under the protection of night—a cloak of invisibility—he and those with him could shine and "have [their] best time."

Waiters is describing a cultural tradition of community autonomy that is rooted in a maroon impulse. The hole in the wall and maroon formations share defining qualities of amorphousness, guided by alternate value systems operating under the cover of clandestinity to serve communal agency. What is perhaps most important is that, drawing on Hazzard-Gordon's concept of the continuum, we consider the processual nature of both marronage and the hole in the wall. The hole in the wall is a maroon impulse made manifest—a fluid practice defined by its process rather than a predetermined expression. In so doing, we can disrupt our commitment to valuation through quantification. This is to say that elements like size, popularity, or duration cease to serve as the primary means of assessing the significance of these formations. What becomes important is how they function in the lives of those they serve. Waiters had such a positive experience there that he invites "somebody to go with me" in an attempt to share what he has found.

But what *did* he find that made him not want to leave? What did the dancing couples in Queen and Slim's juke joint discover in the dimly lit roadside bar? Was it entertainment alone that brought seekers to Liberation Lounge? What thirst was quenched? Can we name it? Must we? We know by now that there is more to Black life than the seen. Shadows become evidence of entire galaxies unknown. How may this maroon impulse drive us to places, times, and worlds not yet? The hole in the wall is one portal. Its significance extends beyond its materiality and into the psychic worlds of possibility and wonder that it opens up. To get there, we must also engage time differently.

The Under Land

In the summer of 2019, I was invited to perform at the Chale Wote Street Art Festival in Accra—the largest festival of its kind in West Africa. Each August, artists and thinkers from around the world gather for the two-week festival, where painting, photography, film, theater, and music pour into the streets of Jamestown. The festival ends with a two-night concert featuring performers from around the continent and Diaspora. I took the stage on the final night. A sea breeze washed over an ocean of Black faces. Where in the thousands did they number? Stage lights strobed and swept—left, right, front, back—as the crowd expanded with each swell. The impulse was there. We gathered around that year's festival theme of "Pidgin Imaginarium," or a "free-forming phenomenon of desire, intuition and ever-present multi-reality." Chale Wote identifies that the "so-called periphery has demonstrated over time, the existence of an Under-land Assemblage. . . . The under-land is a non-place of advanced care and accountability. This place silently rivals omens of modernity and re-centers philosophical contestation through a pidgin imaginarium" (Accra[dot] AltRadio 2019). These under-land lifeworlds, these counter-models for societies, are expressions of a maroon impulse that encourage us to understand the plain of possibility as extending into new spatial and imaginative territories. It is in line with Sun Ra's planet for Black people, which is "under different stars." The pidgin imaginarium's dwelling in non-space also implies a rupturing of time. It is Ra's alter-destiny, in which "we work on the other side of time" (Coney 1974).

   I am reminded of the time travel I would experience in a particular Brooklyn basement party that occurred once a month in the mid-aughts. Sounds of the Diaspora rolled out of above-head speakers making us dance from the inside as subwoofers shook the sweat-drenched floor beneath. We settled into the rhythm around midnight, laughing, flirting, and feeling. After what seemed like a few extended DJ mixes, there was always a collective shock when the music stopped and the lights came on. Four a.m. already? Caught in the rhythm, our Black mass sliced a portal into the fabric of master time. Dancing in the basement, we were an under-land assemblage that found entry through a hole in the wall. But my introduction to the potential of time travel through rhythm began much earlier. In junior high, my best friend watched me from the wall as I fumbled up and down a fretboard. Jimi Hendrix was patient, though. He stood square shouldered and dressed in a Royal Hussar British military jacket as I experimented with string, pickup, and vibration. Minor pentatonic. Barre chord. Open chord. Half-step bend. Whole-step bend. Blue note. The sun went down. I heard him ask, "Is that the stars in the sky, or is it rain falling down? Will it burn me if I touch the sun?"[5]

During that same time period, I would watch MTV in the morning before school. A slim, brown-skinned woman with big eyes and a big headwrap sang what sounded like the coolest . . . jazz? . . . I'd ever heard. Here name was Erykah Badu. The video for "On & On"[6]—the first single from her debut album, *Baduizm* (1997)—kept my attention each time it aired. In it, Badu is burdened with a family's worth of chores, which she has to complete before being able to go out. Along the way, her mother's emerald tablecloth catches her eye. In the next scene, Badu is the center of attention at a *Color Purple*–inspired juke joint, singing and shining in a stunning tablecloth turned dress. It was the video for Badu's second single, however, that helped me visualize time travel. "Next Lifetime" begins with a conundrum: "What am I supposed to do when I want you in my world? How can I want you for myself when I'm already someone's girl?"[7] The video the takes us on a transmillennial journey from Africa to the United States and back again in a series of missed romantic connections.

Both videos played with time in a way that engaged my imagination. In "On & On," Badu's voice was vintage yet new (the term *neo-soul* was only a whisper at that point). There were lyrics that my middle school mind couldn't comprehend ("Most intellects do not believe in God, but they fear us just the same"?), but I was willing to follow where she was leading us, made easier by the charming, rural, turn-of-the-twentieth-century aesthetic set to a hip-hop drum pattern. The colors, costumes, and creativity in "Next Lifetime" aligned with a small subgenre of videos out at the time (e.g., Missy Elliot's "Supa Dupa Fly" or Busta Rhymes's "Put Your Hands Where My Eyes Could See") but stood in stark contrast to most of the other videos in rotation. Further, cameos from Pete Rock, Method Man, and André 3000—influential hip-hop artists from Mount Vernon, Staten Island, and Atlanta, respectively—in the video suggested a collapsing of genre and geography.[8]

"I Think I See the Mothership Coming"

André 3000 was no stranger to space and time travel. A few months before *Baduizm* came out, his group, Outkast, released their second album,

ATLiens. Throughout, he and Big Boi, his partner, use otherworldliness as a metaphor for where they fit (or don't fit) in the rap game and beyond. These themes would continue throughout their work and find expression in the 2003 *Speakerboxxx/The Love Below*. The video for the fourth single, "Prototype," featured 3 Stacks and his family of "extra, extra-terrestrials" as they arrive on Earth. They exit their ship adorned in white jumpsuits and platinum hair. While familiarizing themselves with gravity, André senses a photographer taking their picture. He spots her and immediately experiences love, "the rarest of all human emotion."

I can't help but read the props of this family of extra, extra-terrestrials in the video as an homage to George Clinton and his P-Funk Mythology. The leader of it all was Dr. Funkenstein, King of the Funk or the Extra-Terrestrial Brotha. He had long, straight hair that reached down past his chest. On some occasions, that hair was the same platinum color as André 3000's. Parliament-Funkadelic created a world for its listeners with psychedelic-inspired embellishments, often hiding behind comedy to say things about Black life that may not have otherwise been so digestible. In an unprecedented feat, the cast of musicians landed a spaceship onstage as the culmination of their shows during the P-Funk Earth Tour. As the band sang "Swing down, Sweet chariot. Stop and let me ride," they offered a choral backdrop for an ad-libbing Glenn Goins, who, with all of the spirit and devotion of the Black church, would wail, "I think I see the Mothership coming!" The music would build before a spaceship would hover over the crowd and float toward the stage in a dazzling display of pyrotechnics and showmanship. It touched down, the doors opened, a Dr. Funkenstein–dressed George Clinton stepped out—hat and ankle-length coat made of fur—and the crowd lost it.

The Mothership landed for the first time on October 26, 1976, at the New Orleans Municipal Auditorium. The *concept* of the "mothership," however, has been present and prevalent in Black cultural traditions for centuries. Parliament-Funkadelic's own reference to the spiritual "Swing Low, Sweet Chariot" acknowledges and aligns with this tradition. The spiritual is at once a reference to the biblical story of the Prophet Elijah's ascent to heaven and a veiled set of instructions for enslaved Africans responding to a maroon impulse and seeking escape from the treacherous system of bondage. Parliament-Funkadelic was less concerned with the Christian theological aspects of the Mothership concept, however, than with the liberatory potential of the symbol. Two years earlier, Sun Ra's

Space Is the Place came out, featuring a music-powered spaceship that came to deliver an "alter-destiny" offering "Blackness without the void."[9] Erykah Badu makes reference to the concept, as well, in "On & On" when she sings, "the Mother Ship can't save you, so yo' ass is gon' get left." The song is laden with references to the philosophies and teachings of the Nation of Islam and its off shoot, the Nation of Gods and Earths, or the Five Percenters. Elijah Muhammad spoke of a "Mother of Planes," an aircraft capable of "staying in outer space six to twelve months" (Muhammad 2012, 6). This was Muhammad's interpretation of the biblical story of Ezekiel's wheel, whose arrival would signal the destruction of the white world and the creation of the Black man's heaven. Wayne Taylor (2005) points out that Malcolm X interpreted Muhammad's teaching as a "mother ship" that was part of Allah's final judgment. Both interpretations drew comparisons between the War of Armageddon and the mounting Cold War taking place between the United States and the Soviet Union. All of these cases—and I would add Marcus Garvey's Black Star Line—revolve around a real or symbolic vessel that would lead Black people to freedom. Sometimes that vessel came in the form of our own feet.

Janelle Monáe's *The ArchAndroid* (2010) was released in the early days of BlackStar. An album about love, escape, and pursuit, I kept it on repeat. There was one song, however, to which I found myself particularly drawn. It's called "Neon Valley Street" and functions as sort of an aria for this story of forbidden love and persecution. The song opens with a beautiful orchestral arrangement before Monáe's voice floats through the speakers with a prayer: "may this song reach your heart." Her melody is a soothing lullaby that is gently interrupted by a robotic voice recounting a love story that involved "running fast through time like Tubman and John Henry" as "an outlaw outrunning the law."

In "Neon Valley Street," Monáe offers a counterbalance to the somewhat ironic masculine conceptualizations of the Mothership discussed above. When an Oakland youth asks Sun Ra what he will do if they decide not to come with him, he (perhaps jokingly?) responds, "Then I'ma have to do you like they did you in Africa: chain you up and take you with me." In Monáe's formulation, there is no hint of coercion. Instead, she appeals to the impulse. Her voice is a beckoning call to her love from whom she is separated: "May the sound of my voice be your guide, bring you closer to me." It is at once an invitation and lighthouse illuminating the path to a life beyond what others have positioned as the war and destruction surrounding the Mothership's arrival. While "Neon Valley Street" is indeed a love song, it uses romantic love as a stand-in for wider forms of love: love of community, love of freedom. "For now," she sings, "I'll pretend I'm holding your hand." Listeners must make the journey alone, but they are cared for on their way.

Headed Home

Sun Ra, Erykah Badu, Outkast, George Clinton, and Janelle Monáe have almost become cliché figures in Afrofuturist literature.[10] They offer explicit examples of futurity and imagination as they draw on the past to help us reconceptualize the present. While their art is ripe for intellectualization, the ideas and sounds they've shared resonated with us and our audiences emotionally, both at Liberation Lounge and as we toured the juke joints and holes in the wall. "Prototype" was a mainstay on our set list. Tarriona "Tank" Ball, one of our singers, would do her best alien impression, stretching her voice beyond the human register and pulling the crowd into the palm of her hand. The song would swell to a guitar solo where I would channel Ernie Isley with phaser pedals, delays, and reverbs.[11] A cloud of heat and time would hang in the air as we collectively experienced what George Clinton calls "The One." Clinton got the musical idea from James Brown, who emphasized the first beat of a four-beat measure (ONE-two-three-four), as opposed to the second and fourth beats, or the back beat (one-TWO-three-FOUR), found in most popular music. Clinton, however, expanded The One into a cosmology in which, as Rickey Vincent observes, "everything and everyone in the universe is connected" (1996, 258). That is what we experienced in those moments onstage in the beautiful darkness of the non-space that is the hole in the wall. There was no band. There was no crowd. There was only The One. And the experience continued on with us.

In the hole in the wall, in the juke joint, in this place where Black people gather, we participate in a communal experience of our own creation and control. The hole in the wall, like our invisible man's hole in the ground, becomes a portal through which we may embody a sense of individual and collective fulfillment unavailable to us in the coffles and constraints of mainstream society—even if it only lasts until the sun rises; even if it only lasts for a song. It is, as Chale Wote promotes, evidence of a multi-reality of our creation. BlackStar Books and Caffé's Liberation Lounge, as its name suggests, contributed to an experience of freedom for a community of people gathered in the wake of yet another egregious display of the U.S. government's neglect of the residents of one of its Blackest cities and shared a collective desire to create something else for themselves. This is why Mel Waiters went back to the hole in the wall. This is why Queen and Slim sought temporary refuge in the juke joint. This is why people came from across the city to participate in Liberation Lounge. It was an underground assemblage of rhythm, an imaginarium of collectivity where common movement breached the space-time continuum and granted passage to a planet up under different stars.

Coda
BlackStar Forever

Then, as quickly as it came, it was gone. Kamali Academy closed its doors as an in-home school in 2015, when Samori repatriated to Ghana. BlackStar Books and Caffé ceased operations sometime in 2016. There was no official closing, just a series of extended closures. And while the school and shop may not exist in physical form anymore, the BlackStar community continues as a constellation of invisibility shining around the globe. Baakir has left New Orleans to start what he once referred to as "BlackStar City" with Baba El and a group of others on fifteen acres of land. In August 2012, community members gathered at Community Book Center for a meeting about homeschooling in the city. Several collectives emerged, with a few still active today. During the Covid-19 pandemic, as interest in homeschooling, culturally relevant curricula, and alternative educational models grew in popularity, there was a steep rise in the demand for Kamali's educational resources. Other members of the BlackStar community have started businesses in the city or left to grow families. The artists have continued their work. One band who cut their teeth at Liberation Lounge has received international notoriety and won a Grammy Award in 2025. High, Low, East, West. We all over the map.[1]

Throughout this book, I've shared a story of a group of people who, sensing an unarticulated dissatisfaction, sought to do something about it. I have identified the drive to escape this dissatisfaction in pursuit of a collective and individual fulfillment as a maroon impulse—a spark to create a positive and affirming form of community by extracting oneself from inhospitable social, political, and/or cultural arrangements. Sometimes that means moving. Other times, it means embracing the unseen presence right where you are. The BlackStar community acted on this impulse. And while I wish I could wrap this up with a happy ending, there isn't one. In fact, there is no ending at all. How do you offer any definitive determinant of something that is ongoing?

I realize, of course, it would be naive and irresponsible to believe or suggest that all we have to do is run away together, as if extraction alone would solve our issues. To suggest this would be to undermine one of the primary arguments of this book. Marronage opens up space for potential and possibility, but it is not a destination, nor a utopia. This has been my emphasis on *process*. Put differently, while marronage may lead us to an answer, it is not, in and of itself, *the* answer. It is simply a means to a new phase of collective exploration. Running away does not provide anything beyond the shortcomings of fugitivity I discussed in chapter 4. There are still tensions—many of them pragmatic—that remain unresolved. Samori and I were graduate students living off of fellowships and teaching gigs. Those resources freed up our time to be able to run a school out of our house. It also left us dependent on a system we were trying to escape. The school was not yet sustainable on its own. In fact, Kamali moved from its location across from Roberts High School because the house in which we were living/working went into foreclosure. We were notified not by the absentee landlord but by a large sticker on our front door one afternoon. A few months later, while eating lunch in the front yard with the students, the Sherriff's Department showed up to deliver our ninety-day notice. These are some of the limits of autonomy. For Kamali, we were autonomous to the extent that we weren't directly bound by state educational regulations. But how far can autonomy go when the material means of one's existence can be inhibited by outside forces at any time? We were kicked out of the facility that housed us.

While we were undeniably "in the system," however, we were also forging a space for ourselves and others outside of it. All of us—from teachers, to parents, to students—were operating within and engaging with mainstream society at several points throughout our day. Parents dropped their children off in the morning before heading off to work. Teachers had car loans, rent payments, or, as in the case of Mama Afivi, children to feed. Students were immersed in a media landscape saturated with violence, hypersexuality, and anti-Blackness. Between the hours of 8 a.m. and 3 p.m. at Kamali Academy, however, we strove to create a world of care and love, one in which they could imagine themselves outside of the limited possibilities presented to them in their neighborhoods, city, and country while offering them the tools to turn those possibilities into their reality. We were working toward a healthy and productive community based on mutually affirming relationships.

In speaking of Ella Baker, Barbara Ransby reminds us that revolution is "an ongoing process intimately bound up with one's vision of the future and with how one interacted with others on a daily basis" (2003, 251). It is founded on relationships and "the ways in which ordinary people could transform themselves and their communities" (113). This is not to imply some sort of abstract idealism in which everyone gets along. Rather, it is to reveal the protracted and collective nature of any effort worth working for, not as a continuous, linear movement, but as one of ups and downs, starts and stops. While I would not limit the expression of the maroon impulse to that of revolution, there is overlap here. Marronage is not necessarily about the creation of perpetual communities, but rather the *process* of building communities through which participants are brought together and, by such means, transformed. The successes or failures of such communities should not be measured solely by their duration but by the productivity of their existence.[2] This is certainly the case for the BlackStar community. The unseen presence requires a celestial vision beyond the pale of plain sight. In the quantitative nature of plain sight, institutional significance is measured by longevity, those companies that move from good to great and are built to last.[3] I consider this incorrect. Celestial vision understands time and experience as an inexhaustible well that continues to give. Quantifying BlackStar—examining it through plain sight—cannot capture its impact. It was a handful of people working together for a few years. Celestial vision, on the other hand, allows for a different mode of analysis sensitive to the perception of the unseen presence in the institutions' ongoing influence as part of a galaxy of movement through the spirocycle of time. By looking to the institutions and ideas of those who came before, Kamali identified its tradition, called upon it, and mobilized its lessons, values, and aspirations. Today, students and families have a K-12 curriculum worth of material to meet their educational and cultural needs. BlackStar Books and Caffé seized its time, recognizing that people in the city were primed for an alternative to the changing same (Baraka 2010). The relatively short physical lives of BlackStar Books and Caffé and Kamali Academy weigh little on these establishments' significance. The role they have played in the lives of their community persists.

A lot has changed in the time since Kamali and BlackStar closed. In 2019, New Orleans became the first school district in the United States to be completely made up of charter schools after the last traditional public school, McDonogh 35—namesake of the West Bank plantation owner—was converted. The school opened in 1917 as the first high school for Black students in the city. In the two decades since the state took over Orleans Parish schools and began issuing charters, many of the fears of parents and community members have come to pass. Charter schools in the city have been marked by a lack of accountability, changing standards, the absence of parental choice, and scandal. But it would be misleading to imply that charter schools are the problem any more than traditional public schools are. For the BlackStar community, these models did not meet our requirements for the type of education we envisioned or desired for our children.

A few months into the 2019 school year in New Orleans, all the schools were shut down as shelter-in-place mandates took over the world in response to the Covid-19 pandemic. Through necessity, the nation was forced to engage with home education. For the first time, parents had a direct view into the "classroom" of their students as remote education made its way into kitchens, living rooms, and bedrooms. Many were dissatisfied with what they saw and began considering other options. By week sixteen of the pandemic, as schools were reopening for the new school year, the number of Black families opting to homeschool rose by 16 percent—a larger increase than any other group (Eggleston and Fields 2021). In the time since, traditional homeschooling, learning pods, micro schools, and a host of alternative educational models have grown in a way that demonstrates a wider recognition of home education as a viable option. Samori has become a thought leader on Black home education. Today, in addition to curricular materials—from workbooks, to online classes, to K–12 self-paced curricula—Kamali is a virtual school with a student body spanning ten states and three countries.

In line with the processual nature of marronage, Baakir has expanded BlackStar Books and Caffé into the country. When the café opened, the city of New Orleans was experiencing a housing crisis that has only worsened in the fifteen years since. The higher cost of living, in conjunction with a dearth of affordable housing due to the rise of short-term rentals and an increased price in market rate long-term rentals, has forced many generational residents out. The tenability of life in the city wasn't promising, so Baakir and a group of others have built an intentional, off-the-grid town several hours outside of New Orleans. It is, in many ways, a continuation and maturation of the work started on General Meyer, able to meet even more of the needs of its members. Baakir is tapped into a national network of Black farmers—planting in plots ranging from window sills to acres—where he continues to work for autonomy and self-determination.

In *Under a Black Star,* I have shared a story about a group of people in New Orleans who sought to build a world for themselves: a world in which they could live as they desired; a world in which they could educate their children in accordance with those values they found to be most important; a world where they could be in communion with like-minded folks and be both serious and silly with no second thought. They built or maintained or attended or frequented a school and/or a bookstore. They sought friendships, companionships, and intimate partnerships in these spaces. They laughed, debated, dated, argued, agreed and disagreed. They fought and exited. They returned or stayed away. I was a member of this group of people. We were looking to meet life's demands on our own terms. This is the aspiration of the maroon impulse. The Congress of Afrikan People's call that "Kazi Is the Blackest of all" remains true. *Kazi,* or work, is the measurement of one's commitment to liberation, so we embraced work and sought to ensure that we were the beneficiaries of our labor. My intention in telling this story has not been to romanticize the experience. I could certainly do that. There was, after all, so much romance in it. The excitement of being a part of something that we perceived as larger than ourselves gave us all a greater sense of purpose and convinced us that the world we sought was not only possible but a matter of time. It kept us up at night and woke us early in the morning. It forced us to reckon with our ideals and ideas, especially when they stood at odds with our lived experience. It helped us imagine, envision, and rehearse what freedom felt like—and it felt so very good. We were powerful in our ability to bring ideas to life and were inspired by the lives we were living.

But I agree with David Scott (2004) here. Romance would not have been the best narrative frame for the telling of this story. In this instance, romance would have only served to euphemize. It would over-glorify those things that may ultimately be of greater use were they treated in a more sober manner. There was trial, error, and ego. There was bravado, obstinacy, and arrogance. There was naive idealism and glaring chauvinism. And, ultimately, this community did not sustain itself—at least not in the fashion we would most readily recognize. Romance, with its emphasis on longing and redemption, would not have allowed us to engage the breadth of questions needed to excavate all that was happening and could be learned from this relatively short-lived experiment. I take Scott's aim to heart: "to raise some questions about the continued efficacy of a mode of employment shaped by the mythos of romance, and to cast some doubt on the continued usefulness of a discursive strategy in which political change is thought in terms of a vindicationist narrative of liberation or a concept of revolution" (2004, 64–65). This certainly applies to the ways we were thinking about our work and ourselves, but this is also the space that marronage and maroons have come to occupy. This romantic mythos paints the maroons as fierce warriors or "rebel slaves"—as lexicologically primitive as the term may be—nobly pursuing a peaceful and isolated existence in the hills. While there are certainly identifiable incidents of this, it is by no means exhaustive. There are equal examples that do not lend themselves to such neat classification and may disrupt any claims made based on the former. Although it may be politically expedient to highlight the occurrences that reflect our values, I am curious as to how this romantic commitment tethers us to the very epistemological enclosures we are seeking to transgress.

While Scott proposes tragedy as a more appropriate frame for his purposes, I am not so quick to impose such a frame onto mine. It may be a bit pretentious to classify my telling as a "maroon" narrative format, but I certainly believe marronage's amorphousness allows for the nuance and erraticism necessary for the sharing of a story of Black autonomous community construction. It makes room for apparent contradiction, altered chronology, experimentation, and daring. Perhaps most importantly, it is not predicated on resolution. As a process, marronage itself is never final. There is no destination. Autonomy is a constant negotiation with self and environment, a perpetual pursuit of balance. And while it is beyond the parameters of this discussion, a notion of freedom on these terms—the very terms on which we were thinking at the time—must be reevaluated.

So, pretension aside, I have offered this story, which is part maroon narrative and part ethnographic memoir. I am still driven by the ideals that fueled BlackStar and Kamali. As a reflection of my commitment, I have sought to offer an honest story—as honest as one could be—designed to further understand and improve upon that in which I believe. Using marronage as a frame, I've traced a maroon impulse through the institutional lives of BlackStar Books and Caffé and Kamali Academy. The BlackStar community emerged within the context of a city attempting to wash itself of its Black residents—while maintaining their defining cultural contributions—in a most abject fashion. New Orleans's response to Hurricane Katrina is an exemplar for how cities around the country are dealing with their Black residents. BlackStar is an exemplar of how Black people—living beyond the gong—can deal with their cities.

Acknowledgments

What a city. I am honored to have been able to call New Orleans home for the short time I lived there. At one point, the thought of leaving never dawned on me, enraptured as I was in the humid passion of it all. Samori Camara was my friend since we first met in what was then the Center for African and African American Studies at the University of Texas at Austin. One of the first questions he asked me was, "What do you think we need to do to solve the problems facing Black people?" Talk about had-me-at-hello. We've been working toward answering—and reframing—that question ever since. He's the one who introduced me to Baakir Tyehimba. Baakir's capacity to love and support his people—both those he knows personally as well as complete strangers—is unparalleled. His laughter and the sheer hilarity of his storytelling are enough to encourage anyone on the darkest of days. He really believes in people. He's believed in me. I'm grateful. Both of these brothers are workers. They are action- and solution-oriented. Thank you for the apprenticeship.

I'm grateful for the scholarly and artistic communities I was a part of in the city. Mama Jennifer and Mama Vera from the Community Book Center on Bayou Road were always there as soundboard or springboard. Community was and continues to be a hub for Black intellectual activity, committed as they are to scholarship, research, and Black liberation . . . always with so much laughter. Then there are my musical partners from the BlackStar Bangas and Liberated Soul Collective: Jarred Savwoir, Norman Spence, Nate Cameron, Elliot Luv, Tarriona "Tank" Ball, Sybil Shanell. Tavia Osbey is behind the scenes, but there'd be no scene without her.

Jafar M. Pierre was kind enough to provide photographs for this book. There are also the poets: the great Sunni Patterson, Christopher "Wise Eye" Williams, Christine "CFreedom" Brown, and Asia Rainey. Aiji Daste was always there with vegan food and friendship. The Burrito Juke Joint was one of the illest holes in the wall in the city. Sister Akashi, Mama Nia, and several others are carrying on the tradition of independent, home education. We're in good hands.

Of course, I am grateful for the BlackStar community. While they are all in their late teens and twenties now, I still remember the students of Kamali as the high-energy—and at times, demanding—children running through my house. Mama Kendra, Mama Sauni, Baba El, Baba Q, brother Yimla, Krystle Cameron, and all the regulars at BlackStar Books and Caffé.

I've been fortunate to have a community of scholars who have supported and challenged me along the way. The Institute for Research in African American Studies at Columbia University is my foundation. As an undergrad, I had access to and built relationships with some of the top scholars in the field. Sam Roberts and Russell Rickford played the role of older brother well, keeping me in line when I started to waver and holding me to the potential they saw in me. David Scott gave me insight I am still chewing on today. He was patient and set in motion some of the very questions I engage in this book. Steven Gregory and Manning Marable were always there for my "quick questions." When I first heard that Robin D. G. Kelley was coming to Columbia, I nervously sent him a welcome email. He responded with an invitation to lunch. Sharon Byrd-Harris has been my day one, never failing to remind me of the seventeen-year-old boy I was when I walked in saying I wanted to be an African American studies major. Shawn Mendoza always had a job for me. Then there's Farah Jasmine Griffin. Queen Farah is a gift. She sent me off on my trip around the world with a hug and was there to greet me with the biggest smile when I returned. I read her work today and am so grateful to have had the opportunity to study under her. My peers kept my mind sharp: Simone Gaines, Talibah Newman, Gabe Feldman, and Kendra Tappin. Thank you. I'd also like to thank Pablo Herrera for finding me in the Havana heat, and Anónimo Consejo for the inspiration.

I'm grateful for the support of Ted Gordon, Leonard Moore, and Maria Franklin. João Costa Vargas and I have shared a passion for both liberation and music. Thank you for checking in and pushing me to think more profoundly. Molefi Asante has been in my corner, supporting me unwaveringly. Sonja Peterson-Lewis and Kimani Nehusi were always there to offer writing advice. Ajima Olaghere and the Junior Faculty Writing Collective provided a space for me to sit down and work, free from emails and unannounced office visits. I am particularly grateful to J. T. Roane for his close reading of and invaluable feedback on this manuscript. I'd also like to thank my anonymous reader who asked challenging questions that ultimately strengthened the manuscript.

Tafari Melisizwe and T'Shango Mbilishaka have served as intellectual companions on this journey. Nadine and Jacquie from Easton's Nook continue to encourage me. In Philly and beyond, I've found friendship in creativity and thought: Shaun, Jasmine, Kia, Mark, Ariel, Mama Afiya, Shanise, and Nadjah. I am particularly grateful for the Movement: Caleb Lucky, Malik Henry, Bets Charmelus, Ismail Abdus-Salaam, Marc Francois, Jaleel Jordan, Ali Richardson, and Kelly Thomas. Soular Rock is a beautiful place made all the more enjoyable by your presence.

Kwasi Konadu was first the author who had a significant impact on our thinking around independent schools and culturally centered education. Then, he was a member of my dissertation committee. Today, I consider him a friend. He has seen this book through each of its phases, offering ears to hear me think through ideas, eyes to read, and words to guide. Medaase.

Tata Mutá Imê, Mukkuiu. Desde sempre o senhor tá iluminando meu caminho. N'Zambi na kwa tesa.

I would like to thank my editor, Jason Weidemann. His first email response was so encouraging that I knew he was the right editor for this project. The time since has only confirmed my initial inclination. He also brought on Zenyse Miller, whose responsiveness and knowledge has made this such a pleasant process. Additionally, I'd like to thank the Faculty Board of the University of Minnesota Press. Their feedback and support pushed this project forward.

I began this book with my paternal grandfather, James Howard Johnson. I have so many more books that could come from the times I spent on the same couch from which we watched the aftermath of Hurricane Katrina play out. Yes, I wanted him to know all the beauty and power living and breathing in the city beyond the gong. But I also want him to know and experience all the blessings that continue to pave the way for his lineage. His son is doing an amazing job. His grandchildren have carried on his values of family and love. He never got to meet his great-grandchildren. Sometimes I imagine him sitting in the yard as they play: a slight smile as he follows their movements to and fro, peace and fulfillment blanketing his face. And while that is only in my imagination, they do know and speak his name: Papa Howard.

I was prepared to approach this study because of the world in which I was raised. It was a world of Diasporic Black people participating in life. Sometimes it was the life they chose. Sometimes it was the life that was chosen for them. At all times, though, they showed up. In the time since his transition, Papa Howard has been joined by his wife, Elnora, my grandmother, and their daughter, Aunty Ann. Nanny, my other grandmother, made her way, too. Aunt Sandy is there. We still can't make sense of Senyo's departure. To me, he was my little cousin, but to youth basketball in Brooklyn, he was a legend: Coach Two-Step. We live on in this world remembering them.

Precious has been one of my biggest supporters since I was a child. It has meant more than she may ever know. Aunt Florence is a woman who lives and models self-determination. She's made an art of it. To the cousins: Greg, Kenrick, Sena, Nakai, Darren, Kylie, Lashawnda, Latosha, Cynthia, Kemiya, Keenan, Landon, and Marcus. To Uncle Kenny and Aunt Barbara.

My Nangila family—Jason, Aiesha, Tracee, and Vasco—has been committed to community since high school. We continue this commitment as we raise our families together. Tracee is my sister. She was my copilot on that first drive through New Orleans. That was only one of the many we've shared. Thank you for riding with me. I met Mark Bolden when he was an RA at a summer program I was attending. After the opening ceremony, I approached him and said, "I have questions." His response: "You have curfew." Nearly thirty years later and he is still answering my queries while also keeping me focused. It's an honor to call you a friend.

Thank you to the Sanders, Jones, Mizzell, Bowers, and Thomas families for proving that family is more than blood. G and Dadoo have added me to their roster, and it feels like home. To Simunye, Joe, and Niko: thank you for counting me among your own. So much of what I know about life was first introduced to me by brother, Jeff. Thank you for continuing to clear the path. Crystal and Jeffrey Jr., it feels good to have folks cheering me on. You're both really good at it.

At Kamali, we used to repeat the proverb about bequeathing our children roots and wings. My parents, Mona and Turner, have given me both every day of my life. Mom and Dad, I pray that I may pass on at least a portion of what you have given—and continue to give—to me. Words could never be enough to express my gratitude.

And the reasons for it all: Noni and Omowale. You have made my dream come true. I am so joyful to be living this reality with you. To Grace: I knew who you were from the moment I saw you. How blessed am I to walk beside you? Thank you for being my compass and my sage.

With gratitude, I offer this book to all of those I passed along the way—both the known and the unknown, seen and unseen. Thank you.

Appendix
Kamali Academy Morning Meeting

The following are components of the Kamali Academy Morning Meeting. They were recited each morning to mark the official start of the school day. Students were expected to memorize and participate fully.

Afrikan Pledge

> We are an Afrikan people
> We will remember the humanity, glory and suffering of our ancestors.
> We will honor the struggles of our elders.
> We will strive to bring new values and new life to our people.
> We will have peace and harmony among us.
> We will be loving, sharing and creative.
> We will work, study and listen so we may learn, learn so we may teach
> We will cultivate self-reliance.
> We will struggle to resurrect and unify our homeland.
> We will have discipline, patience, devotion and courage.
> We will live as models to provide new directions for our people.
> We will be free and self-determining
> We are an Afrikan people,
> We will win, and we have won
> We will win, and we have won
> We will win, and we have won!
> Asé

Kamali Affirmations

Who are you?
I am the seed of my Ancestors. I am the hope of today. I am the builder for those unborn. I am the promoter of our Afrikan Way.

What is your purpose?
To use my personal skills and talents for the benefit of my community. To think of others first and build Umoja—Afrikan unity.

Where are you from?
Mama Afrika is my home. Liberation is my song. You can't steer me wrong. I'm Afrikan to the bone. Birth is not the beginning and death is not the end. I am because we are. Together we shall win.

RBG Pledge

We pledge allegiance to the Red, Black, and Green. Our flag, the symbol of our eternal struggle, and to the land we must obtain. One Nation of Black People, with one God of us all, totally united in the struggle for Black Love, Black Freedom, and Black Self-determination.

Kamali Academy Cultural Alphabet (Modified from Ahidiana)

A is for Afrika: land where our ancestors are from.
B is for Build: step by step, one by one.
C is for Create: to make things better.
D is for Determination. We won't give up ever.
E is for Example: to be what we believe.
F is for Focus: to pay attention to our needs.
G is for Growth: to change from good to best.
H is for History: we've been put to the test.
I is for Identity. Afrikan people are we.
J is for Journey: our Maafa on land and sea.
K is for Knowledge: to fill our minds.
L is for Love of self and kind.
M is for Many, both young and old.
N is for Nation: our own land to control.
O is for Organize: to get it together.
P is for Power: the more the better.

Q is for Question: to know the how, what, where, why, and when.
R is for Reliance: to be strong from beginning to end.
S is for Struggle: to fight our enemies toe to toe.
T is for Teach: to pass on to our people whatever we know.
U is for Unity, together both day and night.
V is for Values: to know the wrong from right.
W is for Work, which is our best hope.
X is for the unknown, which is the negro.
Y is for Youth. The future are we.
Z is for Zero, which is all we get free.

Notes

Introduction

1. In all of my studies of Black history in the United States, I had never heard anything like this. The absurdity was nearly unbelievable. When I moved to New Orleans and formed a friendship with Mama Jennifer, a respected elder from the Community Book Center on Bayou Road, her immediate response was, "Which was one was it? There were so many. That's why my Daddy never let us go to the white theaters."

2. President Bush's mother, former first lady Barbara Bush, visited New Orleans residents evacuated to Houston after the storm. After her visit, she commented, "And so many of the people in the arena here, you know, were underprivileged anyway, so this is working very well for them." See *New York Times* 2005.

3. Paul Vallas was the superintendent of the Recovery School District in 2007 and 2008. After his tenure, he was hired as an education consultant following the 2010 earthquake in Haiti. See Flaherty 2010.

4. Cedric Robinson argues that the Black radical tradition consists of disengagement, flight, and marronage. I am deeply indebted to his profound scholarship. As I will explore throughout this book, I argue that disengagement and flight are themselves parts of marronage, with the third part being reengagement into a community working toward a shared goal of the construction and maintenance of autonomy. See Robinson 2000.

5. See Bilby 2008; Bledsoe 2017; Counter and Evans 1981; Diouf 2014; Dunham 1946; Fouchard 1981; Herskovits and Herskovits 1934; Hueman 1986; Hurston 1990; C. James 2002; Lalla 1996; Leaming 1995; Manigat 1977; Moura 1993, 2001; Nascimento 1980; Nevius 2020a, 2020b; Price and Price 1999; Price 1975, 1996, 2002; Carey Robinson 1971; Sayers 2015; A. O. Thompson 2006; Winston 2021.

6. This concept—*vem e vai*, coming and going—prevalent in the practice and philosophy of the African-Brazilian tradition of *capoeira*, suggests the flux

and reflux of life, time, and the very nature of the universe. It refers to a balance that appears off balance, an engagement that conceals, and necessary practices of deceit and cunning used to protect. More broadly, it speaks to the spirocyclic nature of time. For more, see Fu-Kiau 2001.

7. This literature is generally described as Afropessimism. See Wilderson 2010, 2020; Sharpe 2016; Sexton 2008.

8. We also find this idea of Black as extending beyond sociological race in the Congress of African People, who in 1972 adopted the slogan "Kazi Is the Blackest of All." One's "Blackness"—one's seriousness and dedication to liberation—was measured by one's commitment to *kazi*, Kiswahili for "work." Ahidiana, whom I discuss in chapter 3, placed *kazi* at the center of their curriculum and philosophy. They also defined *Black* as consisting of "color, culture, and consciousness." For more, see Christopher Johnson 2012; Rickford 2016a; and Simanga 2015.

9. Jayna Brown's *Black Utopias* (2021) explores alternate states of being and the speculative through the works of Sun Ra, Alice Coltrane, Octavia Butler, and others.

10. I am grateful for feedback from João Costa Vargas, who suggested that Kamali might be a more appropriate research site for the questions I was asking.

1. No Place in Babylon

1. I first came across the following statement from Fanon when studying with an organization I was a part of in high school called Nangila: "Each generation must, out of relative obscurity, discover its mission, fulfill it, or betray it" (1963, 206). This gave us a sense of purpose, and this idea traveled with me throughout the Diaspora, where I encountered other youth on a shared quest.

2. My use of the term "plantation complex" extends beyond the built environment to include its cultural and psychic dimensions. See Curtin 1998 and Wynter 1971.

3. See Sayers 2015; C. J. Robinson 1997; A. O. Thompson 2006; Reis 1995; Fouchard 1981.

4. A *quilombola* is one who lives in a *quilombo*, which is the Brazilian equivalent of a maroon community. The term *quilombo* is believed to come from the Kimbundo word *kilombo,* which roughly translates to "war camp."

5. Nehanda Abiodun, interview with author, Havana, June 17, 2004.

6. Translated by Nafeesah Allen and Amari Johnson.

7. These are female and male Santería initiates, respectively.

8. Translated by Nafeesah Allen and Amari Johnson.

9. For more on this, see Brathwaite 1994.

2. West Bank Is the Best Bank

1. Philippe II, Duke of Orléans (after the whom the city is named), became regent for the five-year-old King Henry XV, who inherited the monarchy after the death of his great-grandfather King Henry XIV. In 1717, Philippe granted a

monopoly charter to the Company of the West for the development of its North American colony. The three-thousand-mile territory stretched from current-day Louisiana into Canada.

2. For an in-depth discussion on the changes made in the 1724 document specific to Louisiana, see J. M. Johnson 2020.

3. This influx would reach a peak in 1809 after the Spanish banished the French from Cuba following Napoleon's invasion of Spain during the Peninsular War. By this point New Orleans was part of the United States, which was struggling with the multilingual, multicultural city. By 1810 the refugees—divided almost perfectly into thirds as free people of color, enslaved Africans, and whites—numbered nearly ten thousand, doubling the population of New Orleans. See Rebecca Scott 2012 and Ferrer 2014.

4. There is, however, a reference to Le Page that calls his character into question. Wilson writes: "In one case, dated May 18, 1729, Phillipe François Vellard, a carpenter, complained that Le Page had falsely accused him of theft" (1990, 175). It appears that Le Page is inserting himself into a thwarted rebellion that occurred in June 1731, when a Bambara working with the Natchez and Chickasaws arrived in New Orleans recruiting other Bambara to massacre the French and join the British, where they would gain their freedom. According to Gwendolyn Hall, nearly four hundred Bambara joined the plot. Governor Étienne Périer who questioned an enslaved domestic worker in the city and discovered the plans. Several conspirators were killed on the wheel, and one woman was hung. Périer later confessed that he had his doubts as to whether the conspiracy was real or not. See Hall 1992.

5. Samba, also known as Samba Bambara, has a fascinating personal history. It is believed that he is from Senegal and worked as a translator for the French on the West Coast of Africa. When the judge recited Samba's life history, Samba demanded to know who told him. The judge begrudgingly informed him that it was Le Page, to which he responded, "Oh yes, Mr. Page. The devil who knows everything" (Hall 1992, 110). For more detail on the life of Samba and the rebellious presence of Bambaras in Louisiana, see chapter 4 in Hall 1992.

6. "St. Malo" could refer to the port in France of the same name. It could also be the Spanish *malo*, which translates to "bad," but as Hall points out, the Spanish documents place an accent over the "o," which is not present in *malo*. Hall does offer the Bambara word *malo*, meaning "charismatic leader who defies the social order" (Hall 1992, 213). The Bambara had a strong presence in early Louisiana, so it is possible that the name could have come from the language (Bambara, Bamana, Bamanankan), but it is unclear where Hall got this translation. Bambara is part of the Mande language family, in which term *malo* translates as "shame" (Bird and Kendall 1980). Hall wonders if *St. Malo* could actually be the creolized *sans malo*, or "without shame" (Hall 1992, 81).

7. In his memoir, McDonogh outlines his practice of repatriating the formerly enslaved to Liberia. See McDonogh 1862.

8. I am reminded of the Dead Prez lyric "Dying over streets you don't even own anyway. / You could get bucked off any day. / We behind enemy lines." See Dead Prez 2000.

9. See Ballard 2015 and Capitol News Bureau 2015.

10. Like most southern states, Louisiana was resistant to school desegregation. In the spring of 1960, six years after *Brown v. Board of Education* outlawed school segregation, a federal district court judge ordered that Orleans Parish schools develop a plan for the desegregation of its public schools. After a tussle with Governor James Davis, a staunch segregationist, the deadline was set for November 1960. Six Black students were initially chosen to enter white schools, but two of them decided not to go through with it. On the morning of November 14, 1960, four Black girls desegregated the New Orleans Public Schools: Leona Tate, Tessie Prevost, Gail Etienne, and Ruby Bridges. Bridges was eternalized in Norman Rockwell's painting *The Problem We All Live With*. Each of the girls was in the first grade, with the first three attending McDonogh 19. Bridges attended William Frantz. The white response was overwhelmingly contrary. Many of the parents with children at the two now desegregated schools refused to send their children, leaving the girls many times in class alone (Bridges 1999).

11. See Bradley 2020 and Purpura 2008.

12. Henry Glover's bones were discovered in a burned car left near the levee. A video shot by the man who discovered the vehicle clearly shows severe damage to his skull. By the time the remains arrived at the coroner, the skull was missing. It would turn out that a New Orleans police officer shot Glover. When his brother and a stranger who stopped to help brought him to a police auxiliary station, they were handcuffed and beaten while Glover lay dying in the car. Police officers then drove the stranger's car, with Glover in the back, to the levee, where they took photographs and then set the car on fire. A. C. Thompson's research provided federal investigators with what they needed to bring charges against some of the officers involved. Only one was convicted.

13. Rescue crews made use of FEMA's search code (also known as X-code) protocol whereby X's would be spray-painted onto houses to indicate that these locations had been searched. The left quadrant designated what party completed the search. The upper quadrant told the time and date. The right quadrant described any hazards discovered. The bottom quadrant indicated if there were any survivors or corpses. It is important to note that, due to the pandemonium following the storm, there were wide variations in search efforts and their documentation.

3. Black Star, Keep Shining

1. TIA was an acronym for "This is Africa," a concept drawn from the song "T.I.A." by the Somali-born, Toronto-based artist K'naan. See K'naan 2009.

2. Outkast had an explicit influence on BlackStar's physical aesthetic, sonic possibility, and ideological exploration. "Spottieottiedopalicious" (1998) was a popular song on the sound system. Its catchy horn line and driving rhythm evoked a meditative spirit that settled over the atmosphere.

3. bell hooks's concept of "homeplace" is helpful here. hooks describes homeplace as a "site where one could freely confront the issue of humanization, where one could resist." It's a place where "Black women resisted by making homes where all black people could strive to be subjects, not objects, where we could be affirmed in our minds and hearts despite poverty, hardship, and deprivation, where we could restore to ourselves the dignity denied us on the outside in the public world" (1990, 42). Homeplace represents Black autonomy within the private sphere. At BlackStar we were seeking to expand the private into a semipublic sphere, while maintaining that autonomy and subjecthood.

4. This is how departing guests were sent on their way. It was an invitation to return both to BlackStar and to a cultural state of being.

5. This was a continuation of a national trend set in motion by the No Child Left Behind Act of 2001.

6. Local Algiers legend holds that "Who Dat?," the phrase that has come to characterize the New Orleans Saints, was originally started by Quack as a rally cry for L. B. Landry High School.

7. Baakir Tyehimba, text correspondence, New Orleans, June 9, 2022.

8. The Krewe of NOMTOC (New Orleans' Most Talked Of Club) is a Mardi Gras parade held in Algiers each year by the Jugs Social Club.

9. BlackStar benefited from the influence and support of other cultural institutions, namely, Community Book Center and Ashé Cultural Arts Center, both located on the east bank.

10. When Liberation Lounge started out it was held on the second and fourth Sundays of each month. Demand grew rather quickly, so we decided to hold it every week.

11. Keep in mind that this was in the early period of cell phone navigation.

12. Baakir expounds on these influences: "Garvey's influence symbolizes our virtual capacity to travel to and from the mother continent while imposing the flag of actuality where we are, since the whole world we inhabit as Africans is Africa. Thus TIA, much in the way the Black Star Line was intended—the Pan-Africanist intention. The line was set to work as a cruise (the pleasure) and cargo (the work). So, even as a brick and mortar, BlackStar Caffé as well as the *shule* (school) would allow for a pleasant work experience." Garvey was mentioned regularly in the shop. Tony Martin's *Race First: The Ideological and Organizational Struggles of Marcus Garvey and the Universal Negro Improvement Association* (1986) was a mainstay on our bookshelf. The work is a masterful study on the complexities and expansiveness of the Universal Negro Improvement Association. Kwame Nkrumah was the second influence: "Nana Nkrumah and his leadership as a national chief to unify the whole diaspora of Africans under the BlackStar set the anchor for the ultimate and optimal African World Order." Kwame Nkrumah became the president of Ghana in 1957, when it became the first African nation to gain independence from colonial rule. His administration chose a national flag designed by stateswoman Theodosia Salome Okoh. The

black star placed at the center of the red, yellow, and green flag is the "Lodestar of African Freedom," drawing from Garvey's Black Star Line and meant to symbolize Ghana as a beacon of hope for the liberation of Africa. Elijah Muhammad was the third influence: "The Black family is equated/associated to the universe (sun, moon, and stars). He assigned the stars, being the most plentiful, to the child/children. Since it started as a school/shule, I determined we'd impart African knowledge, wisdom, and understanding to Black children/stars. Thus, we also used two African youth—one male and one female—dressed as alchemists who merge to produce the six pointed BlackStar (two juxtaposed triangles representing the male and female principles that is and produces light/life) as our logo." Baakir was, at one time, a member of the Nation of Islam. Wallace D. Fard Muhammad founded the Nation, as it is known, in 1930. When he mysteriously disappeared in 1934, Elijah Muhammad assumed leadership and opened mosques across the country, spreading messages of clean living and knowledge of self to "downtrodden" Black people and communities across the country. Baakir Tyehimba, text correspondence with author, November 14, 2019.

13. The use of the letter "k" in the spelling of "Afrika" recognizes that "Africa" is not the true name of the continent. In so doing, these groups are engaging in a cultural redefinition of self and kind.

14. These concepts of nationalism and Americanism came directly from the teachings of Malcolm X, whose speeches were read and played regularly in the café.

15. For more on this internal colony theory, see R. Allen 2005; Woodard 1999; Blauner 1972; and Ture and Hamilton 1967.

16. See chapter 6.

17. Du Bois's (1907) study traced the history of social and economic cooperation among Black communities dating back to the 1700s. From schools, to grocery stores, to social aid and benevolent societies, to churches, Du Bois documents the widespread nature of these operations that sustained communities despite external pressure. For a more recent study on cooperatives and cooperation, see Gordon Nembhard 2014.

18. Samori eventually took over the opening shift to ensure that the shop opened at the stated time.

19. I have benefited from the field of Black geographies, which has provided new insights and directions for inquiry. See McKittrick 2011; McKittrick and Woods 2007; Gilmore 2007.

20. That which is not seen is part of Browne's dark matter. See Browne 2015.

21. Krista Thompson's *Shine: The Visual Economy of Light in African Diasporic Aesthetic Practice* (2015) is a fascinating study of the role that light and illumination play in the "visual economy" of diasporic aesthetics. Browne's "black luminosity" is also relevant here, which she defines as a "form of boundary maintenance occurring the site of the Black body, whether by candlelight, flaming torch, or the camera flashbulb that documents the ritualized terror of a lynch mob" (2015, 67).

22. Ghani and Ganesh (2004) define warm data as "deeply personal but non-identifying information that spoke to the lived experience of being subjected to political invisibility of various kinds." My father's memories occupy a space unaccounted for in the historical record.

23. Baakir used this spelling of Afraka, which was composed of the components *af/afu* (flesh/body), *ra* (light of the creator), and *ka* (spirit/soul).

24. In 2022 the New Orleans City Council voted to rename Slidell Street "Red Allen Way" after Black, Algiers-born jazz musician Henry James "Red" Allen Jr.

25. This is reminiscent of a standoff between the MOVE organization and the city of Philadelphia. The police department was commanded to forcibly remove the organization from their residence in the city's Powelton Village neighborhood. As things escalated, the city sent in a mediator who informed John Africa, MOVE's leader, that Quakers had offered the group land outside of the city. John Africa offered a simple response: "Why don't the city move?" Several years later, in May 1985, the city of Philadelphia would drop a bomb on another MOVE residence, killing eleven men, women, and children. See Garry and McKenna 2004.

26. At the time of this writing, the images are still available on Google Maps.

27. This is consistent with what Darius Scott describes as Black spatial humanities, which recognizes "radically different understandings of space" predicated on place more than cartographic positioning (2021, 477).

28. Robert O'Meally makes this point about Ellison's novel when he writes that "the 'obscure' references to black life and lore make all the sense in the world: Here too the point is to communicate intimately with those sharing the author's particular cultural background" (1988, 10).

29. See Miller and Rivera 2008.

4. "They Ain't Talkin' 'bout Nothin', Y'heardme?"

1. Enclosures include "social mechanisms that construct notions of race, gender, class, and sexuality; and . . . embodies the removal/withdrawal/denial of services and programs that are key to the stability and long-term well-being of communities" (Sojoyner 2016, xii–xiii).

2. A similar sentiment would appear in Buju Banton's "Murderer" from his 1995 *'Til Shiloh* album: "Murderer, blood is on your shoulders. Kill I today, you cannot kill I tomorrow." See Banton 1995.

3. This was Henson's second year. The school opened with grades six and nine and added two grades per year until they were operating grades six through ten.

4. In 2005 there had been two districts operating in the city: the Orleans Parish School Board (OPSB) and the RSD. The RSD was completely charter since 2015. The OPSB was completely charter by 2019. See Newmark and DeRugy 2006; Lehrer 2005.

5. See C. Johnson 2015; Kee 2015; Sanders 2015.

6. Out of 7,500 school employees, 400 teachers were fired when the state took over New Orleans's school system. Since then, nonprofit teacher-training

organizations provide the city with young, inexperienced teachers. See Goodman 2006 and Lipsitz 2015.

7. See C. Johnson 2015 and Rosario-Moore 2015.
8. Mama Tamieka, interview with author, New Orleans, November 11, 2011.
9. Kamal, interview with author, New Orleans, October 7, 2011.
10. Kamal interview.
11. This teacher was a Black Teach for America Fellow who had graduated from Dartmouth the spring before arriving at Henson.
12. Kamal, interview with author, December 15, 2011.
13. Kamal interview.
14. Kamal interview.
15. See Sullivan and Morgan 2010.
16. By 2004, New Orleans ranked among the worst school districts in the country. Forty percent of the city's adults—the same percentage living below the poverty line—could not read beyond an elementary school level. The city's dropout rate was slightly over 70 percent, the same percentage of Louisiana state inmates who did not have a high school diploma (D. Cooper 2008; Morelli 2008). The city's educational system suffered from the same corruption and back-door dealing that affected the city at large (ABA Center on Children and the Law 2009; Liu et al. 2011). By the time of the storm, twenty-four school district leaders had been indicted for fraud and corruption since 2002. In 2004, Superintendent Anthony Amato set up an FBI corruption investigation unit in the New Orleans Public School (NOPS) headquarters (D. Cooper 2008). There was so much foul play in the NOPS that the state of Louisiana plotted a takeover. Hurricane Katrina aided their plans. As Kee points out, however, at the very least, "Neighborhood schools were valued historic sites of community pedagogy" (2015, 257).
17. See C. Johnson 2015.
18. Mama Afivi, interview with author, New Orleans, January 26, 2012.
19. Several parents feared that the schools imposed limitations on their children's expressions/learning styles in a way that could stunt their growth. Baba Ali told me: "That system, like I said—they want to take all of the . . . square pegs and make them fit into a round hole, when really you gotta let a square peg be a square peg, you know? And you got to let an octagon be an octagon. You can't make an octagon into a circle, because it's no longer what it was, you know? And you can't shape a person into what you want that person to be." Baba Ali, interview with author, New Orleans, January 12, 2012.
20. Baba Mukasa, interview with author, New Orleans, December 19, 2012.
21. See Flaherty 2011. The harsh disciplinary tactics were made evident by the spike in security spending. During the 2004–5 school year (before the storm) the Orleans Parish School Board spent nearly $46 per student on security. During the 2006–7 school year the RSD spent an average of $2,100 per student. Even though the RSD reduced security spending the following year, they still spent

approximately $690 per student (Sullivan and Morgan 2010). The increase in spending also led to a greater presence of armed security guards in schools. On May 4, 2010, a security officer at Sarah T. Reed Elementary shackled a six-year-old boy to a chair after he failed to follow his teacher's directions. Two days later, a different security officer handcuffed the same boy for arguing in the cafeteria (Chang 2010). Although the RSD ruled it an isolated incident, there were at least two other reported incidents at other schools.

Families and Friends of Louisiana's Incarcerated Children is one organization that has taken up the fight against the militarization of New Orleans schools and the criminalization of students. In the spring of 2010 they published a report titled *Pushed Out: Harsh Discipline in Louisiana Schools Denies the Right to Education: A Focus on the Recovery School District in New Orleans,* which highlights the disproportionate punishment of students of color, particularly through suspension and expulsion, as well as the creation of prison-like environments. They write: "This significant allocation of resources towards security in schools is favoring the criminalization of student behavior over an investment in supportive interventions and professional school staff that could better meet the needs of students and create healthy school environments" (Sullivan and Morgan 2010, 19). These "healthy school environments," unfortunately, do not appear to be a priority for school officials.

22. Gil Scott-Heron's song "Who'll Pay Reparations on My Soul?" questions the possibility of healing and redress for the irreparable, sentient damage done through enslavement and continuing white terror and domination. See Scott-Heron 1971.

23. There was a show on Court TV called *Bait Car*. The premise was that camera crews would film a staged car left in a high-traffic area. To entice people, the police would perform a mock arrest to catch the attention of passersby. Witnesses would then see an abandoned vehicle with keys in the ignition. Once someone tried to drive it away, the engine would lock up and police would swarm the car. One morning, a teacher at Henson said he had a student he wanted me to connect with. The student had just returned to school after being locked up. I met the young man that afternoon. He had been arrested in a *Bait Car* incident. His charges were dismissed after the judge cited entrapment.

5. The Seed of Our Ancestors

1. This call-and-response is what we called the "Kamali Affirmations" and was a central part of our morning meeting. For more, see the appendix.

2. Morning meeting was one of the ways Kamali engaged what Imani Perry calls "black formalism," or "ritual practices with embedded norms, codes of conduct, and routine, dignified ways of doing and being" (2018, 7).

3. By replacing the "his" of "history" with "our," the term comes to reflect an approach to the study of the past that centers those studying it, that is, African people.

4. It was an exciting time for all involved and suggested a growing interest in independent education. As I will discuss shortly, these independent schools emerged during the Black Power period. There was a resurgence in independent, African-centered schools in the United States during the late 1980s and early 1990s, reflective of the larger cultural trend of Afrocentricity (Akoto 1992; Asante 1989). As the decade drew to a close, however, the interest in independent schools declined and many schools either closed or converted to charter schools. See Rickford 2016a and Hotep 2001.

5. Kwasi Konadu (2009) offers a nuanced conversation about how this played out in the organizational context of New York City. Rickford (2016a) offers a wider context in his examination of independent schools across the United States during the Black Power era.

6. Many of these formations were members of the Council of Independent Black Institutions (CIBI), which is a network of "Pan African nationalist educational institutions rooted in not only academic excellence, but also self-reliance and self-definition, not for mainstream integration, but for independent nation building" (Hotep 2001, 35). At its height, CIBI offered teacher-training programs, annual conferences, publications, and support to its members. For an in-depth discussion of the CIBI, see Hotep 2001 and Afrik 1974. For more on independent schools, see Konadu 2009; Shujaa 1998; Kifano 1996; Lomotey 1992; Ratteray and Shujaa 1987.

7. We spent the summer leading up to the new school year in constant dialogue while diving deeper into our study of independent schools. Samori was in regular contact with members of Ahidiana, who offered insight and advice. I reached out to some friends in New York who had attended African-centered schools as children, including Shule Ya Mapinduzi, Little Sun People, and the most robust of all, Uhuru Sasa Shule. Ahidiana's Work/Study Center and The East's Uhuru Sasa Shule exemplified the type of community-based, independent institution we were seeking to build. Teachers, parents, and students worked together as a functioning whole pursuing collective goals. In addition to our conversations, we also reached out to people across the country for any archival materials that could better inform our efforts. We held study groups on books such as Kwame Agyei Akoto's *Nationbuilding: Theory and Practice in Afrikan Centered Education* (1992). We knew Baba Agyei as a founding member of Washington, D.C.'s, NationHouse, one of the oldest independent African-centered schools in the country. Kwasi Konadu's *A View from the East: Black Cultural Nationalism and Education in New York City* (2009) served as somewhat of a handbook for us. While centered around Uhuru Sasa, the text outlines the various initiatives, successes, and challenges of The East—many of which matched the aspirations of our own BlackStar community.

8. Similar means were employed in Cincinnati, where a group of people "desiring to give their children the benefit of a school" mounted an experiment in 1820. They would take small subscriptions, rent a room, and hire a teacher. It

only lasted a few weeks, but eventually "the schools in Cincinnati continued to flourish, and the Negro population in the state increased till many other schools were established" (Du Bois 1907, 75).

9. In the late nineteenth century, national debates and conferences were dedicated to the issue of the newly "emancipated Negro's" education. Often working against Black self-identified priorities, the white benefactors hosting these conferences ultimately decided on an industrial education that essentially locked Black pupils into a state of peonage. This was accomplished through the control of teacher-training intuitions, which recognized that trained teachers would have a direct influence on the students. The Hampton Institute was one of the flagship institutions of this philosophy, "deliberately teaching" economic values to Black educators that were "detrimental to the objective economic interests of black workers" (J. D. Anderson 1998, 52), which was, above all else, self-reliance. This was why Kamali was so adamant about offering an alternative to the charter schools rampant in the city.

10. This was on display earlier in 1864 and 1865 when the Freedmen's Bureau took over schools in New Orleans. After proving themselves unprepared for the task, they withdrew support. Black communities, concerned with the education of their children, however, pooled resources and maintained the schools themselves. For these communities to refuse to abdicate control to the government suggests they believed that they had a better grasp on their needs than the "Yankees" who showed up to an already functioning system. Beyond this, for them to regularly contribute to local educational formations via subscription, even if they did not directly benefit, speaks to a larger investment in their understanding of and dedication to their community. They were committed to self-reliance.

11. This self-reliance was not limited to schools. For example, Special Field Order No. 15—popularly known "Forty Acres and a Mule"—was issued by William T. Sherman on January 16, 1865. The order was to transfer 400,000 acres of land on the coasts of South Carolina, Georgia, and Florida to Black families in forty-acre plots. The idea, however, was not Sherman's. He received it from a group of Black clergymen, representatives of larger communities in the region, with whom he met four days prior. The spokesman was the sixty-seven-year-old, self-emancipated Garrison Frazier. When asked how the group believed the newly emancipated Africans could take care of themselves, Frazier replied, "The way we can best take care of ourselves is to have land, and turn it and till it by our own labor–that is, by the labor of the women and children and old men; and we can soon maintain ourselves and have something to spare." The follow-up question asked how they would rather live, "whether scattered among the whites or in colonies by yourselves." Frazier responded, "I would prefer to live by ourselves, for there is a prejudice against us in the South that will take years to get over; but I do not know that I can answer for my brethren." All but one of the accompanying nineteen men agreed. See Berlin et al. 2012.

12. Baba El, interview with author, New Orleans, October 6, 2011.

13. One of the cofounders of Take 'em Down NOLA, a coalition dedicated to the removal of Confederate monuments in the city, often through direct action, frequented BlackStar Books and Caffé.
14. Mama Tamieka, interview with author, New Orleans, November 8, 2011.
15. Mama Kia, interview with author, New Orleans, December 15, 2011.
16. Kamali's dietary guidelines limited the amount of meat and junk food that students were allowed to consume during school hours. In "Be Healthy," from their album *Let's Get Free!* (2000), Dead Prez rap, "I don't eat no meat. / No dairy, no sweets. / Only ripe vegetables, fresh fruit, and whole wheat." They continue, "Be careful how you season and prepare your foods / 'cause you don't wanna lose vitamins and minerals / and that's the jewel. / Life brings life, it's valuable / so I eat what comes from the ground. / It's natural." Understanding the wide-ranging impact of diet on health, particularly for Black people living in impoverished neighborhoods where access to affordable healthy options is severely limited, Kamali worked to challenge students and parents to prioritize healthy eating.
17. Mama Kia interview.
18. Mama Afivi, interview with author, New Orleans, October 6, 2011.
19. Yao, interview with author, New Orleans, February 3, 2012.
20. One day, one of the students, who had a rich, dark complexion, called another student of equal hue a "Black monkey." I immediately stopped class to address the issue. Rather than reproach the student, I chose to give him an opportunity to explain his position. I asked him if he felt that he, too, was a "Black monkey." He quickly refused the title. As the conversation progressed and other students joined in, he became aware of his contradiction. From there, we were able to explore colorism. We used Baba Malcolm's "dictionary experiment" whereby we looked up the definitions of "black" and "white." We also watched a video on Dr. Kenneth and Mamie Clark's doll experiments alongside an episode Samori and I had done through our YouTube channel on the color complex. It was not the last time we would hear comments such as these, but it was the start of the establishment of an environment where such attitudes and values were questioned and replaced by affirmative ideas.
21. In this instance, "public school system" refers to the public charter system in place in the city.
22. Kwame, interview with author, New Orleans, February 3, 2012.
23. Ayana, interview with author, New Orleans, February 3, 2012.
24. Mama Jamila, interview with the author, New Orleans, January 9, 2012.
25. Mama Kia interview.
26. Mama Naima, interview with author, New Orleans, October 6, 2011.
27. Mama Esi, interview with author, New Orleans, January 13, 2012.
28. Baba Ali, interview with author, January 12, 2012.
29. Mama Kia interview.
30. Kamali's first math teacher was sister Akosua, who left the position because the travel was unmanageable. Samori then began teaching the class. In the fall of

2011 a young sister took some of the younger students and began teaching them in order to provide more individualized attention. She stopped a few months later, however, when she moved out of the city. One of Samori's male students from his class at the community college then came to the school. He taught math to the older students, while Samori taught the younger ones. Availability was a large factor that determined who taught what. When sister Akosua, for instance, showed up, we asked her what she could teach and placed her accordingly. My conversation here, however, is informed by general trends.

31. See Ray 2009, 2015, 2024; and Fields-Smith and Kisura 2013.

32. Kofi, interview with the author, New Orleans, October 13, 2011.

6. Black in the Whirlwind

1. William DeVaughn's "Be Thankful for What You Got" (1974) was a crowd favorite at Liberation Lounge. It was an icebreaker of sorts for first-time visitors, who, enveloped in the communal atmosphere of joy and familiarity, would settle into the evening.

2. One of the regulars at Liberation Lounge was Elliot Luv. He shot a music video for his song "Run n Hide" at BlackStar, which is an accurate representation of the Liberation Lounge experience. At the time of this writing, the video is still available on YouTube.

3. See Baraka 2000 and Hazzard-Gordon 1990.

4. Davis 2011 and Baraka 2000 also speak to class conflict and the moral economy of Black folk culture at the turn of the century. This is also exhibited in *The Color Purple* (1982).

5. See Hendrix 1967.

6. See Badu 1997b.

7. See Badu 1997a.

8. Pete Rock, from Mount Vernon, New York, is a hip-hop producer responsible for shaping the sound of East Coast hip-hop throughout the 1990s. Method Man, from Staten Island, is a member of Wu Tang Clan, one of the most innovative and influential groups in hip-hop. André 3000 is a member of Outkast, a duo from Atlanta responsible for putting southern hip-hop on the map. While the sounds of the South became central to hip-hop by the time I was moving around New Orleans, that was not the case in the 1990s, when the genre was dominated by both coasts. Hip-hop out of California was heavily infused with samples and interpolations of Parliament-Funkadelic sounds, while New York rappers and producers preferred harder-hitting drums and grittier samples. Tensions mounted on both sides of the country—partially stoked by media sensationalism—and was put on full display at the 1995 Source Awards, held at Madison Square Garden's Paramount Theater. When Outkast won Best New Artist they were booed all the way to the stage. A frustrated André 3000 took the mic and ended his speech with the now iconic words "The South got something to say."

9. Sun Ra, too, would make use of Christian lore in his promotion of liberation. Graham Lock offers an in-depth discussion of Sun Ra's tensions with Christianity in *Blutopia* (1999).

10. See Aghoro 2018; R. Anderson and Jones 2017; Campbell and Hall 2016; David 2007; Gipson 2016; English and Kim 2013; Eshun 2003; Lock 1999; Murchison 2018; Ramsby 2013; Valnes 2017; Van Veen 2013; Womack 2013; Zamalin 2019.

11. Jimi Hendrix was once a hired gun for the Isley Brothers. He even lived with them for a spell, during which time the young Ernie Isley soaked up as much as he could. He credits Hendrix as heavily influential.

Coda

1. See Mos Def 1999.

2. I am indebted here to Robin D. G. Kelley's thinking in *Freedom Dreams* (2002), which focuses on the architecture of the dream as a site of validation separate from material success or failure.

3. See Collins 2001 and Collins and Porras 1994.

Bibliography

ABA Center on Children and the Law. 2009. *Children, Law, and Disasters: What We Have Learned from Katrina and the Hurricanes of 2005.* Chicago: ABA Publishing.

Accra[dot]AltRadio. 2019. "Chale Wote Street Art Festival—Pidgin Imaginarium." Accra[Dot]Alt Radio. https://allaboutaccra.wordpress.com/2019/05/07/the-call-for-artists-chale-wote-arts-festival-2019/.

Advancement Project. 2005. *Education Lockdown: The Schoolhouse to Jailhouse Track.* Advancement Project.

Afrik, Hannibal. 1974. "Point of View for Black Education." *Council of Independent Black Institutions Newsletter* 1 (2): 3.

Afrik, Hannibal. 1981. *Education for Self-Reliance, Idealism to Reality: An Analysis of the Independent Black School Movement.* Stanford, Calif.: Council of Independent Black Institutions.

Aghoro, Nathalie. 2018. "Agency in the Afrofuturist Ontologies of Erykah Badu and Janelle Monáe." *Open Cultural Studies* 2 (1): 330–40. https://doi.org/10.1515/culture-2018-0030.

Agorsah, Emmanuel K. 1994. *Maroon Heritage.* Barbados: Canoe Press.

Aharone, Ezrah. 2008. *Sovereign Evolution: Manifest Destiny from "Civil Rights" to "Sovereign Rights."* Bloomington, Ind.: Authorhouse.

Ahidiana. n.d. "Ahidiana Work/Study Center: A Black Independent and Affirmative Institution of Vital Education." https://www.ahidiana.com/_files/ugd/10ecaa_88c79758b4b6452b91839a621c9c00dc.pdf.

Ahidiana. 1985. "Document Prepared for the 1985 Annual Conference of the National Association for the Education of Young Children." New Orleans, November 16, 1985.

Ahmad, Muhammad. 2007. *We Will Return in the Whirlwind: Black Radical Organizations, 1960–1975.* Chicago: Charles H. Kerr.

Akoto, Kwame Agyei. 1992. *Nationbuilding: Theory and Practice in Afrikan Centered Education.* Washington, D.C.: Pan Afrikan World Institute.

Akoto, Kwame Agyei, and Akun Nson Akoto. 2000. *The Sankofa Movement.* Washington, D.C.: Yoko Infocom.

Allen, Diane Jones. 2022. "Living Freedom through the Maroon Landscape." *Places Journal,* Septemer 2022. https://doi.org/10.22269/220922.

Allen, Robert L. 2005. "Reassessing the Internal (Neo) Colonialism Theory." *The Black Scholar* 35 (1): 2–11. https://doi.org/10.1080/00064246.2005.11413289.

Anderson, Benedict. 1991. *Imagined Communities: Reflections on the Origin and Spread of Nationalism.* London: Verso.

Anderson, James D. 1988. *The Education of Blacks in the South, 1860–1935.* Chapel Hill: University of North Carolina Press.

Anderson, Reynaldo, and Charles E Jones, eds. 2017. *Afrofuturism 2.0: The Rise of Astro-Blackness.* New York: Lexington Books.

Anderson, Robert Nelson. 1996. "The Quilombo of Palmares: A New Overview of a Maroon State in Seventeenth-Century Brazil." *Journal of Latin American Studies* 28 (3): 545–66. https://doi.org/10.1017/s0022216x00023889.

Ani, Marimba. 1992. *Let the Circle Be Unbroken.* Lawrenceville, NJ: Red Sea Press.

Anónimo Consejo. "Afrolucha Continua." Track 5 on *Hablando de Algo.* 2007.

Anónimo Consejo. "Loma y Machete." Track 3 on *Hablando de Algo.* 2007.

Armah, Ayi Kwei. 1995. *Osiris Rising.* Popenguine, Senegal: Per Ankh.

Armah, Ayi Kwei. 2000. *Two Thousand Seasons.* Popenguine, Senegal: Per Ankh.

Armah, Ayi Kwei. 2006. *The Healers: A Novel.* Popenguine, Senegal: Per Ankh.

Armstrong, Louis. "Black and Blue." Track 25 on *Jazz & Blues: 36 Outstanding Tracks.* Weston-Wesgram, 2001, streamed.

Asante, Molefi Kete. 1989. *Afrocentricity.* Trenton, N.J.: Africa World Press.

Avildsen, John G, dir. 1989. *Lean on Me.* Warner Brothers.

Badu, Erykah. 1997a. "Next Lifetime." Track 6 on *Baduizm.* Universal Records.

Badu, Erykah. 1997b. "On & On." Track 2 on *Baduizm.* Universal Records.

Ballard, Mark. 2015. "Bills Would Allow Algiers to Secede from City of New Orleans; Here's What's Next." *The Advocate,* May 15, 2015. https://www.theadvocate.com/baton_rouge/news/politics/legislature/article_aa9ddc81-1442-56f9-a9ae-4dcc171811ae.html.

Bambara, Toni Cade, and Eleanor W Traylor. 2005. *The Black Woman an Anthology.* New York: Washington Square Press.

Banton, Buju. 1995. *'Til Shiloh.* Island Records.

Banton, Buju. 1997. *Inna Heights.* Island Records.

Baraka, Amiri. 1999. *The LeRoi Jones/Amiri Baraka Reader.* New York: Basic Books.

Baraka, Amiri. 2000. *Blues People: Negro Music in White America.* New York: Perennial.

Baraka, Amiri. 2010. *Black Music.* New York: Akashic Books.

Bibliography

Baralt, Guillermo A. 2014. *Slave Revolts in Puerto Rico.* Princeton: Markus Wiener.
Barnes, Sandra T. 1997. *Africa's Ogun.* Bloomington: Indiana University Press.
Beckles, Hilary. 1989. *Natural Rebels.* New Brunswick: Rutgers University Press.
Berlin, Ira, Steven F. Miller, Joseph P. Reidy, and Leslie S. Rowland, eds. 2012. "Meeting between Black Religious Leaders and Union Military Authorities, January 12, 1865." In *Freedom: A Documentary History of Emancipation, 1861–1867,* series 1, vol. 3, *The Wartime Genesis of Free Labor: The Lower South,* 331–38. Cambridge: Cambridge University Press.
Best, Stephen, and Saidiya Hartman. 2005. "Fugitive Justice." *Representations* 92 (1): 1–15. https://doi.org/10.1525/rep.2005.92.1.1.
Biko, Steve. 2017. *I Write What I Like: A Selection of His Writings.* Northlands, Johannesburg: Picador Africa.
Bilby, Kenneth M. 2008. *True-Born Maroons.* Gainesville: University Press of Florida.
Birch, Eugenie L., and Susan M. Wachter. 2006. *Rebuilding Urban Places after Disaster: Lessons from Hurricane Katrina.* Philadelphia: University of Pennsylvania Press.
Bird, Charles S., and Martha B. Kendall. 1980. "Modes of Thought: The Mande Hero." In *Explorations in African Systems of Thought,* edited by Ivan Karp and Charles S. Bird, 13–26. Bloomington: Indiana University Press.
Black Star. 1998. "Astronomy (8th Light)." Track 2 on *Mos Def and Talib Kweli Are Black Star.* Rawkus Entertainment.
Blassingame, John W. 1979. *The Slave Community.* New York: Oxford University Press.
Blassingame, John W. 2008. *Black New Orleans, 1860–1880.* Chicago: University of Chicago Press.
Blauner, Robert. 1972. *Racial Oppression in America.* New York: Harper & Row.
Bledsoe, Adam. 2017. "Marronage as a Past and Present Geography in the Americas." *Southeastern Geographer* 57 (1): 30–50. https://doi.org/10.1353/sgo.2017.0004.
Bledsoe, Adam, and Willie Jamaal Wright. 2018. "The Pluralities of Black Geographies." *Antipode* 51 (2): 419–37. https://doi.org/10.1111/anti.12467.
Bonilla, Yarimar. 2015. *Non-sovereign Futures.* Chicago: University of Chicago Press.
Bradley, Ed. 2020. "2005—A City Blocks Pedestrians Fleeing Hurricane Katrina." 60 Minutes.
Brand, Dionne. 2000. *At the Full and Change of the Moon: A Novel.* New York: Grove Press.
Brathwaite, Kamau. 1994. "Nanny, Palmares, and the Caribbean Maroon Connection." In *Maroon Heritage: Archaeological, Ethnographic, and Historical Perspectives,* edited by E. Kofi Agorsah, 119–38. Barbados: Canoe Press.
Bridges, Ruby. 1999. *Through My Eyes.* New York: Scholastic Press.
Brinkley, Douglas. 2006. *The Great Deluge.* New York: Harper Perennial.

Brooks, Rosa. 2005. "Our Homegrown Third World." *Los Angeles Times,* September 7, 2005.

Brown, Jayna. 2021. *Black Utopias: Speculative Life and the Music of Other Worlds.* Durham: Duke University Press.

Brown, Scot. 2003. *Fighting for US: Maulana Karenga, the US Organization, and Black Cultural Nationalism.* New York: New York University Press.

Browne, Simone. 2015. *Dark Matters: On the Surveillance of Blackness.* Durham: Duke University Press.

Camp, Stephanie M. H. 2002. "'I Could Not Stay There': Enslaved Women, Truancy, and the Geography of Everyday Forms of Resistance in the Antebellum Plantation South." *Slavery & Abolition* 23 (3): 1–20. https://doi.org/10.1080/714005245.

Camp, Stephanie M. H. 2004. *Closer to Freedom: Enslaved Women and Everyday Resistance in the Plantation South.* Chapel Hill: University of North Carolina Press.

Campanella, Richard. 2019. "Algiers at 300: The Early Years." *New Orleans Advocate,* March 10, 2019.

Campanella, Richard. 2020. *The West Bank of Greater New Orleans: A Historical Geography.* Baton Rouge: Louisiana State University Press.

Campbell, Bill, and Edward A. Hall. 2016. *Mothership.* Greenbelt, Md.: Rosarium Publishing.

Campt, Tina Marie. 2012. *Image Matters: Archive, Photography, and the African Diaspora in Europe.* Durham: Duke Univeristy Press.

Campt, Tina Marie. 2017. *Listening to Images.* Durham: Duke University Press.

Campt, Tina Marie. 2019. "Black Visuality and the Practice of Refusal." *Women & Performance: A Journal of Feminist Theory* 29 (1): 79–87. https://doi.org/10.1080/0740770x.2019.1573625.

Capitol News Bureau. 2015. "Algiers Breakaway Bill Clears House." *The Advocate,* June 2, 2015. https://www.theadvocate.com/baton_rouge/news/politics/legislature/algiers-breakaway-bill-clears-house/article_39c2f8cb-8969-5861-8031-574bd80d4811.html.

Carneiro, Edison. 1958. *O Quilombo dos Palmares.* São Paulo: Companhia Editora Nacional.

Carneiro, Edison. 2001. "Singularidades dos Quilombos." In *Os Quilombos na dinânima social do Brasil,* edited by Clóvis Moura, 11–20. Maceió: Edufal.

Chang, Cindy. 2010. "Father of First-Grader Handcuffed at Sarah T. Reed Files Lawsuit against RSD." *Nola.com,* July 8, 2010.

Chenier, Cierra. 2020. "Algiers Is Very Much New Orleans; Was Often the Soil Where Enslaved Ancestors First Stepped Foot." *Noir 'N Nola,* February 4, 2020. https://www.noirnnola.com/post/algiers-is-very-much-new-orleans-was-often-the-soil-where-enslaved-ancestors.

Cleaver, Kathleen, and George N. Katsiaficas. 2001. *Liberation, Imagination, and the Black Panther Party: A New Look at the Panthers and Their Legacy.* New York: Routledge.

Collins, Jim. 2001. *Good to Great: Why Some Companies Make the Leap . . . and Others Don't*. New York: Harper Business.

Collins, Jim, and Jerry I. Porras. 1994. *Built to Last: Successful Habits of Visionary Companies*. New York: Harper Business.

Coney, John, dir. 1974. *Space Is the Place*. Rhapsody Films.

Cooper, Carolyn. 1995. *Noises in the Blood: Orality, Gender and the "Vulgar" Body of Jamaican Popular Culture*. Durham: Duke University Press.

Cooper, Christopher, and Robert Block. 2007. *Disaster*. New York: Henry Holt.

Cooper, Drea, dir. 2008. *Reborn: New Orleans Schools*. CreateSpace.

Copeland-Carson, Jacqueline. 2004. *Creating Africa in America Translocal Identity in an Emerging World City*. Philadelphia: University of Pennsylvania Press.

Corzo, Rosa. 2003. *Runaway Slave Settlements in Cuba: Resistance and Repression*. Chapel Hill: University of North Carolina Press.

Counter, S. Allen, and David L. Evans. 1981. *I Sought My Brother: An Afro-American Reunion*. Cambridge, Mass.: MIT Press.

Curtin, Philip D. 1998. *The Rise and Fall of the Plantation Complex: Essays in Atlantic History*. New York: Cambridge University Press.

Dallas, Robert C. 2010. *The History of the Maroons: From Their Origin to the Establishment of Their Chief Tribe at Sierra Leone*. New York: Cambridge University Press.

Datta, Ansu K., and R. Porter. 1971. "The Asafo System in Historical Perspective." *Journal of African History* 12 (2): 279–97. https://doi.org/10.1017/s0021853700 010689.

David, Marlo. 2007. "Afrofuturism and Post-Soul Possibility in Black Popular Music." *African American Review* 41 (4): 695. https://doi.org/10.2307/25426985.

Davis, Angela Y. 1983. *Women, Race, and Class*. New York: Vintage.

Davis, Angela Y. 2011. *Blues Legacies and Black Feminism*. New York: Vintage.

Dawdy, Shannon L. 2008. *Building the Devil's Empire: French Colonial New Orleans*. Chicago: University of Chicago Press.

Dead Prez. 2000. "Be Healthy." Track 10 on *Let's Get Free*. Loud Records.

Deal, Carl, and Tia Lessin, dirs. 2008. *Trouble the Water*. Zeitgeist.

DeBerry, Jarvis DeBerry. 2019. "Delayed Justice Makes It Something Other than Justice." *Nola.com*, February 27, 2019. https://www.nola.com/opinions/delayed-justice-makes-it-something-other-than-justice/article_84134bc6-68f1-5dbd-8f78-79784433fb8c.html.

Department of Justice. 2019. "New Orleans Man Sentenced for Hate Crime in Shooting of Three African-American Men Attempting to Evacuate after Hurricane Katrina." Justice.gov, February 14, 2019. https://www.justice.gov/opa/pr/new-orleans-man-sentenced-hate-crime-shooting-three-african-american-men-attempting-evacuate.

Dessens, Nathalie. 2010. *From Saint-Domingue to New Orleans: Migration and Influences*. Gainesville: University Press of Florida.

DeVaughn, William. 1974. "Be Thankful for What You Got." Single. Roxbury Records.

DeVore, Donald E., and Joseph Logsdon. 1991. *Crescent City Schools: Public Education in New Orleans, 1841–1991*. Lafayette: University of Southwestern Louisiana.

Din, Gilbert C. 1980. "'Cimarrones' and the San Malo Band in Spanish Louisiana." *Louisiana History: The Journal of the Louisiana Historical Association* 21(3): 237–62.

Diop, Cheikh Anta. 1989. *The Cultural Unity of Black Africa*. Trenton, N.J.: Red Sea Press.

Diouf, Sylviane A. 2003. *Fighting the Slave Trade: West African Strategies*. Athens: Ohio University Press.

Diouf, Sylviane A. 2014. *Slavery's Exiles: The Story of the American Maroons*. New York: New York University Press.

Dubois, Laurent, and John D. Garrigus. 2017. *Slave Revolution in the Caribbean, 1789–1804: A Brief History with Documents*. Boston: Bedford/St. Martin's, Macmillan Learning.

Du Bois, W. E. B. 1907. *Economic Co-operation among Negro Americans*. Atlanta: Atlanta University Press.

Dunham, Katherine. 1946. *Katherine Dunham's Journey to Accompong*. Illustrated by Ted Cook. New York: Henry Holt & Company.

Edwards, Bryan. 2014. *The History Civil and Commercial, of the British Colonies in the West Indies*. Nabu Press.

Edwards, Bryan. 2017. *The Proceedings of the Governor and Assembly of Jamaica, in Regard to the Maroon Negroes*. Forgotten Books.

Eggleston, Casey, and Jason Fields. 2021. "Homeschooling on the Rise during COVID-19 Pandemic." United States Census Bureau, March 22, 2021. https://www.census.gov/library/stories/2021/03/homeschooling-on-the-rise-during-covid-19-pandemic.html.

Ellison, Ralph. (1952) 1995. *Invisible Man*. New York: Knopf Doubleday.

English, Daylanne K., and Alvin Kim. 2013. "Now We Want Our Funk Cut: Janelle Monáe's Neo-Afrofuturism." *American Studies* 52 (4): 217–30. https://doi.org/10.1353/ams.2013.0116.

Eshun, Kodwo. 2003. "Further Considerations of Afrofuturism." *CR: The New Centennial Review* 3 (2): 287–302. https://doi.org/10.1353/ncr.2003.0021.

Evans-Winters, Venus E. 2011. *Teaching Black Girls: Resiliency in Urban Classrooms*. New York: P. Lang.

Fanon, Frantz. 1963. *Wretched of the Earth*. Translated by Constance Farrington. New York: Grove Press.

Fanon, Frantz. 1994. *Black Skin, White Masks*. Translated by Constance Farrington. New York: Grove Press.

Fernandes, Adrienne L., and Thomas Gabe. 2024. *Disconnected Youth: A Look at 16- to 24-Year Olds Who Are Not Working or in School*. April 1, 2024. Washington, D.C.: Congressional Research Service.

Ferrer, Ada. 2014. *Freedom's Mirror: Cuba and Haiti in the Age of Revolution*. Cambridge: Harvard University Press.

Fields-Smith, Cheryl, and Monica Wells Kisura. 2013. "Resisting the Status Quo: The Narratives of Black Homeschoolers in Metro-Atlanta and Metro-DC." *Peabody Journal of Education* 88 (3): 265–83. https://doi.org/10.1080/0161956x.2013.796823.

Flaherty, Jordan. 2010. *Floodlines: Community and Resistance from Katrina to the Jena Six.* Chicago: Haymarket Books.

Flaherty, Jordan. 2011. "Sojourner Truth Academy Suspends 20% of Its Senior Class for Singing." *Louisiana Justice Institute,* December 7, 2011. https://louisianajusticeinstitute.blogspot.com/2011/12/sojourner-truth-academy-suspends-20-of.html.

Floyd, Samuel. 1996. *The Power of Black Music: Interpreting its History from Africa to the United States.* New York: Oxford University Press.Fouchard, Jean. 1981. *The Haitian Maroons.* New York: Edward W Blyden Press.

Frontline. 2010. "Law & Disorder." PBS.

Fu-Kiau, Kia B. 2001. *African Cosmology of the Bântu-Kôngo.* New York: Athelia Henrietta Press.

Fu-Kiau, Kia B. 2007. *The Mbongi: An African Traditional Political Institution: A Eureka to the African Crisis.* Atlanta: African Djeli Publishers.

Funari, Pedro Paulo Abreu, and Aline Viera de Carvalho. 2005. "O patrimônio em uma perspectiva crítica: O caso do Quilombo dos Palmares." *Diálogos* 9 (1): 33–47.

Garry, Ben, and Ryan McKenna, dirs. 2004. *Move.* Cohort Media.

Garvey, Marcus. 1986. *The Philosophy and Opinions of Marcus Garvey; or, Africa for the Africans.* Compiled by Amy Jacques Garvey. Dover, Mass.: Majority Press.

Gaspar, David B., and David P. Geggus. 1997. *A Turbulent Time: The French Revolution and the Greater Caribbean.* Bloomington: Indiana University Press.

Gay, Geneva. 2010. *Culturally Responsive Teaching: Theory, Research, and Practice.* 3rd ed. New York: Teachers College Press.

Genovese, Eugene D. 2006. *From Rebellion to Revolution: Afro-American Slave Revolts in the Making of the Modern World.* Baton Rouge: Louisiana State University Press.

Genovese, Eugene D. 2011. *Roll, Jordan, Roll: The World the Slaves Made.* New York: Vintage.

Gerima, Haile, dir. 1993. *Sankofa.* Mypheduh Films.

Germany, Kent B. 2011. *New Orleans after the Promises.* Athens: University of Georgia Press.

Ghani, Mariam, and Chitra Ganesh. 2004. "How Do You See the Disappeared? A Warm Database." Net Art Anthology. https://anthology.rhizome.org/how-do-you-see-the-disappeared-a-warm-database.

Gilmore, Ruth W. 2007. *Golden Gulag: Prisons, Surplus, Crisis, and Opposition in Globalizing California.* Berkeley: University of California Press.

Gipson, Grace D. 2016. "Afrofuturism's Musical Princess: Psychedelic Soul Message Music Infused with a Sci-Fi Twist." In *Afrofuturism 2.0,* edited by Reynaldo Anderson and Charles E. Jones, 91–108. New York: Lexington Books.

Glissant, Édouard. 1997. *Poetics of Relation.* Translated by Betsy Wing. Ann Arbor: University of Michigan Press.

Golden, Kathryn Benjamin. 2021. "'Armed in the Great Swamp': Fear, Maroon Insurrection, and the Insurgent Ecology of the Great Dismal Swamp." *Journal of African American History* 106 (1): 1–26. https://doi.org/10.1086/712038.

Gomes, Flávio dos Santos. 2010. "Africans and Slave Marriages in Eighteenth-Century Rio de Janeiro." *The Americas* 67 (2): 153–84. https://doi.org/10.1353/tam.2010.0022.

Goodman, Amy. 2006. "All New Orleans Public School Teachers Fired, Millions in Federal Aid Channeled to Private Charter Schools." *Democracy Now,* June 20, 2006. http://www.democracynow.org/2006/6/20/all_new_orleans_public_school_teachers.

Gordon Nembhard, Jessica. 2014. *Collective Courage: A History of African American Cooperative Economic Thought and Practice.* University Park: Pennsylvania State University Press.

Gottlieb, Karla. 2000. *The Mother of Us All.* Trenton, N.J.: Africa World Press.

Graythen, Chris. 2005. Agence Frace-Presse/Getty Images photo. August 29, 2005.

Greenfield-Sanders, Timothy, dir. 2019. *Toni Morrison: The Pieces I Am.* Perfect Day Films.

Griffin, Farah Jasmine. 1996. *Who Set You Flowin? The African-American Migration Narrative.* New York: Oxford University Press.

Griffin, Farah Jasmine. 2021. *Read until You Understand: The Profound Wisdom of Black Life and Literature.* New York: Norton.

Gyekye, Kwame. 1995. *An Essay on African Philosophical Thought: The Akan Conceptual Scheme.* Philadelphia: Temple University Press.

Hahn, Steven. 2009. *The Political Worlds of Slavery and Freedom.* Cambridge, Mass.: Harvard University Press.

Hall, Gwendolyn M. 1992. *Africans in Colonial Louisiana: The Development of Afro-Creole Culture in the Eighteenth Century.* Baton Rouge: Louisiana State University Press.

Harris, Gardiner. 2005. "Police in Suburbs Blocked Evacuees, Witnesses Report." *New York Times,* September 10, 2005. https://www.nytimes.com/2005/09/10/us/nationalspecial/police-in-suburbs-blocked-evacuees-witnesses-report.html.

Hart, Philip S. 2007. *African Americans and the Future of New Orleans: Rebirth, Renewal, and Rebuilding.* Phoenix: Amber Communications Group.

Hartman, Chester W., and Gregory D. Squires. 2006. *There Is No Such Thing as a Natural Disaster: Race, Class, and Hurricane Katrina.* New York: Routledge.

Hartman, Saidiya V. 1997. *Scenes of Subjection: Terror, Slavery, and Self-Making in Nineteenth-Century America.* New York: Oxford University Press.

Hartman, Saidiya V. 2007. *Lose Your Mother: A Journey along the Atlantic Slave Route.* New York: Farrar, Straus, and Giroux.

Hartman, Saidiya V. 2019. *Wayward Lives, Beautiful Experiments: Intimate Histories of Social Upheaval.* New York: Norton.

Hazzard-Gordon, Katrina. 1990. *Jookin': The Rise of Social Dance Formations in African-American Culture*. Philadelphia: Temple University Press.

Heitz, Dianna. 2010. "Duncan: Katrina Was Good for New Orleans Schools." Politico, January 31, 2010. https://www.politico.com/blogs/politico-now/2010/01/duncan-katrina-was-good-for-new-orleans-schools-024700.

Hendrix, Jimi. 1967. "Love or Confusion." Track 4 on *Are You Experienced*. Experience Hendrix, LLC.

Hernon, Peter. 2005. *A Terrible Thunder: The Story of the New Orleans Sniper*. New Orleans: Garrett County Press.

Herskovits, Melville J., and Frances S. Herskovits. 1934. *Rebel Destiny: Among the Bush Negroes of Dutch Guiana*. New York: McGraw-Hill.

Heuman, Gad. 1986. *Out of the House of Bondage*. London: Cadd.

Hilliard, David, and Huey Newton. 2008. *The Black Panther Party: Service to the People Programs*. Albuquerque: University of New Mexico Press.

Hirsch, Arnold R., and Joseph Logsdon. 1992. *Creole New Orleans: Race and Americanization*. Baton Rouge: Louisiana State University Press.

Holm, Ramsus, dir. 2006. *Welcome to New Orleans*. Fridthjof Films.

Honychurch, Lennox. 2017. *In the Forests of Freedom*. London: Papillote Press.

hooks, bell. 1990. *Yearning: Race, Gender, and Cultural Politics*. New York: Routledge, Taylor & Francis Group.

Hoover, Mary Eleanor Rhodes. 1992. "The Nairobi Day School: An African American Independent School, 1966–1984." *Journal of Negro Education* 61 (2): 201. https://doi.org/10.2307/2295416.

Hosbey, Justin, and J. T. Roane. 2021. "A Totally Different Form of Living: On the Legacies of Displacement and Marronage as Black Ecologies." *Southern Cultures* 27 (1): 68–73. https://doi.org/10.1353/scu.2021.0009.

Hotep, Uhuru. 2001. "Dedicated to Excellence: An Afrocentric Oral History of the Council of Independent Black Institutions, 1970–2000." Doctoral diss., Duquesne University.

Hueman, Gad. 1986. *Out of the House of Bondage: Runaways, Resistance and Marronage in African and the New World*. London: Cadd.

Hunt, Alfred N. 2006. *Haiti's Influence on Antebellum America: Slumbering Volcano in the Caribbean*. Baton Rouge: Louisiana State University Press.

Hurston, Zora Neale. 1990. *Tell My Horse: Voodoo and Life in Haiti and Jamaica*. New York: Harper.

Hutton, Clinton A. 2005. *The Logic and Historical Significance of the Haitian Revolution and the Cosmological Roots of Haitian Freedom*. Kingston: Arawak.

Ingersoll, Thomas N. 1999. *Mammon and Manon in Early New Orleans: The First Slave Society in the Deep South, 1718–1819*. Knoxville: University of Tennessee Press.

Institute on Metropolitan Opportunity. 2010. "The State of Public Schools in Post-Katrina New Orleans: The Challenge of Creating Equal Opportunity." https://scholarship.law.umn.edu/imo_studies/84/.

Isaacs, Gregory. 2006. "Border." Track 10 on *One Man Against the World*. VP Records.

James, C. L. R. 2012. *History of Pan-African Revolt*. Oakland: PM Press.

James, Cynthia. 2002. *The Maroon Narrative: Caribbean Literature in English, across Boundaries, Ethnicities, and Centuries*. Portsmouth, N.H.: Heinemann.

Johnson, Cedric. 2011. *The Neoliberal Deluge: Hurricane Katrina, Late Capitalism, and the Remaking of New Orleans*. Minneapolis: University of Minnesota Press.

Johnson, Cedric. 2015. "Gentrifying New Orleans: Thoughts on Race and the Movement of Capital." *Souls* 17 (3–4): 175–200. https://doi.org/10.1080/109999 49.2015.1125219.

Johnson, Christopher. 2012. "The Spirit That Protects the Youth from Death: Maroonage, African-Centered Education, and the Case of Kamali Academy in New Orleans, Louisiana." Doctoral diss., University of Texas at Austin.

Johnson, Jessica Marie. 2020. *Wicked Flesh: Black Women, Intimacy, and Freedom in the Atlantic World*. Philadelphia: University of Pennsylvania Press.

Jones Allen, Diane. 2022. "Living Freedom through the Maroon Landscape." *Places Journal*, no. 2022 (September). https://doi.org/10.22269/220922.

Joseph, Peniel E. 2007. *The Black Power Movement: Rethinking the Civil Rights–Black Power Era*. New York: Routledge.

Joseph, Peniel E. 2010. *Neighborhood Rebels: Black Power at the Local Level*. New York: Palgrave Macmillan.

Kamali Academy. 2011. *Kamali Academy* (blog). https://kamaliacademy.word press.com.

Katrina Reader Team. 2008. "A Katrina Reader: Readings by & for Anti-Racist Educators and Organizers." https://katrinareader.cwsworkshop.org/.

Kee, Jessica Baker. 2015. "No Excuses or No Equity? Narrative and Counternarrative Themes within Educational Discourse in New Orleans." *Souls* 17 (3–4): 248–62. https://doi.org/10.1080/10999949.2015.1127110.

Kelley, Robin D. G. 2002. *Freedom Dreams: The Black Radical Imagination*. Boston: Beacon Press.

Kent, R. K. 1996. "Palmares: An African State in Brazil." In *Maroon Societies: Rebel Slave Communities in the Americas*, edited by Richard Price, 170–90. Baltimore: John Hopkins University Press.

Kifano, Subira. 1996. "Afrocentric Education in Supplementary Schools: Paradigm and Practice at the Mary McLeod Bethune Institute." *Journal of Negro Education* 65 (2): 209. https://doi.org/10.2307/2967314.

Kly, Y. N. 2006. *The Invisible War: The African American Anti-Slavery Resistance from the Stono Rebellion through the Seminole Wars*. Atlanta: Clarity Press.

K'naan. 2009. "T.I.A." Track 1 on *Troubadour*. Interscope Records.

Knabb, Richard D., Jamie R. Rhome, and Daniel P. Brown. 2023. "Tropical Cyclone Report: Hurricane Katrina." *National Hurricane Center*, January 4, 2023.

Konadu, Kwasi. 2004. "The Cultural Identity of Africa and the Global Tasks of Africana Studies." *African Studies Quarterly* 7 (4): 33–40.

Konadu, Kwasi. 2009. *A View from the East: Black Cultural Nationalism and Education in New York City.* Syracuse: Syracuse University Press.

Konadu, Kwasi. 2019. *Our Own Way in This Part of the World: Biography of an African Culture, Community, and Nation.* Durham: Duke University Press.

Kopytoff, Barbara K. 1978. "The Early Political Development of Jamaican Maroon Societies." *The William and Mary Quarterly* 35 (2): 287. https://doi.org/10.2307/1921836.

Kunzelman, Michael. 2010. "Witness: Officer Laughed after Burning Man's Body." Ravalli Republic. Associated Press. November 18, 2010. https://ravallirepublic.com/article_5f7a7176-f350-11df-879d-001cc4c03286.html.

Lalla, Barbara. 1996. *Defining Jamaican Fiction: Marronage and the Discourse of Survival.* Tuscaloosa: University of Alabama Press.

Landers, Jane. 1999. *Black Society in Spanish Florida.* Urbana: University of Illinois Press.

Leaming, Hugo P. 1995. *Hidden Americans: Maroons of Virginia and the Carolinas. 1.* New York: Garland.

Lee, Trymaine. 2010. "Rumor to Fact in Tales of Post-Katrina Violence." *New York Times,* August 26, 2010. http://www.nytimes.com/2010/08/27/us/27racial.html?_r=1&pagewanted=all.

Lehrer, Jim. 2005. "New Orleans Schools before and after Katrina." *PBS News,* November 1, 2005. https://www.pbs.org/newshour/show/new-orleans-schools-before-and-after-katrina.

Le Page du Pratz, Antoine-Simon. 2015. *The History of Louisiana, or of the Western Parts of Virginia and North Carolina.* Project Gutenberg. https://www.gutenberg.org/cache/epub/9153/pg9153-images.html.

Lipman, Pauline. 2011. "Neoliberal Education Restructuring: Dangers and Opportunities of the Present Crisis." *Monthly Review* 63 (3): 114. https://doi.org/10.14452/mr-063-03-2011-07_13.

Lipsitz, George. 2015. "Challenging Neoliberal Education at the Grass Roots: Students Who Lead, Not Students Who Leave." *Souls* 17 (3–4): 303–21. https://doi.org/10.1080/10999949.2015.1125185.

Liu, Amy, Roland V. Anglin, Richard M. Mizelle, and Allison Plyer. 2011. *Resilience and Opportunity: Lessons from the U.S. Gulf Coast after Katrina and Rita.* Washington, D.C.: Brookings Institution Press.

Lock, Graham. 1999. *Blutopia: Visions of the Future and Revisions of the Past in the Work of Sun Ra, Duke Ellington, and Anthony Braxton.* Durham: Duke University Press.

Lockley, Timothy J. 2009. *Maroon Communities in South Carolina: A Documentary Record.* Columbia: University of South Carolina Press.

Lomotey, Kofi. 1992. "Independent Black Institutions: African-Centered Education Models." *Journal of Negro Education* 61 (4): 455. https://doi.org/10.2307/2295363.

Malm, Andreas. 2018. "In Wildness Is the Liberation of the World: On Maroon Ecology and Partisan Nature." *Historical Materialism* 26 (3): 3–37. https://doi.org/10.1163/1569206x-26031610.

Manigat, Leslie F. 1977. "The Relationship between Marronage and Slave Revolts and Revolution in St. Domingue-Haiti." *Annals of the New York Academy of Sciences* 292:420–38. https://doi.org/10.1111/j.1749-6632.1977.tb47761.x.

Mann, Eric. 2006. *Katrina's Legacy: White Racism and Black Reconstruction in New Orleans and the Gulf Coast*. Los Angeles: Frontlines Press.

Martin, Chris. 2005. Associated Press photo. August 29, 2005.

Martin, Tony. 1986. *Race First: The Ideological and Organizational Struggles of Marcus Garvey and the Universal Negro Improvement Association*. Dover, Mass.: Majority Press.

Matskoukas, Melina, dir. 2019. *Queen & Slim*. Universal Pictures.

McCarthy, Brendan. 2010. "Former Algiers Resident Pleads Not Guilty in Racial Shooting in Chaos after Katrina." *Nola.com*, August 12, 2010. http://www.nola.com/crime/index.ssf/2010/08/former_algiers_resident_pleads.html.

McCarthy, Brendan. 2011. "Former Algiers Man Is Mentally Unfit to Stand Trial in Shooting of Three Black Men after Hurricane Katrina, Judge Rules." *Nola.com*, September 21, 2011. http://www.nola.com/crime/index.ssf/2011/09/former_algiers_resident_is_men.html.

McDonogh, John. 1862. *Self-Emancipation: A Successful Experiment on a Large Estate in Louisiana. Internet Archive.* The Library of Congress. https://www.loc.gov/item/ca30001167/.

McKittrick, Katherine. 2006. *Demonic Grounds: Black Women and the Cartographies of Struggle*. Minneapolis: University of Minnesota Press.

McKittrick, Katherine. 2011. "On Plantations, Prisons, and a Black Sense of Place." *Social & Cultural Geography* 12 (8): 947–63. https://doi.org/10.1080/14649365.2011.624280.

McKittrick, Katherine, and Clyde A. Woods. 2007. *Black Geographies and the Politics of Place*. Cambridge, Mass.: South End Press.

Meléndez Guadarrama, Fabiola. 2009. "Negro en rebeldía: De esclavo fugado a apalencado: Casos comparados entre el Palenque de San Basilio y el Palenque de San Lorenzo de Los Negros, siglo XVII." Master's thesis, Universidad Nacional Autónoma de México. Facultad de Filosofía y Letras.

Merrow, John. 2005. "New Orleans Schools before and after Katrina." PBS NewsHour, November 1, 2005. https://www.pbs.org/newshour/show/new-orleans-schools-before-and-after-katrina.

Miller, Demond Shondell, and Jason David Rivera. 2008. *Hurricane Katrina and the Redefinition of Landscape*. Lanham, Md.: Lexington Books.

Mintz, Sidney W., and Richard Price. 2011. *The Birth of African-American Culture an Anthropological Perspective*. Boston: Beacon Press.

Monáe, Janelle. 2010. "Neon Valley Street." Track 13 on *The ArchAndroid*. Bad Boy Records.

Moore, Leonard N. 2010. *Black Rage in New Orleans: Police Brutality and African American Activism from World War II to Hurricane Katrina*. Baton Rouge: Louisiana State University Press.

Morelli, Vincent, dir. 2008. *Left Behind: The Story of the New Orleans Public Schools*. MedArt Productions.

Mos Def. 1999. "Hip Hop." Track 2 on *Black on Both Sides*. Rawkus Records.

Moura, Clóvis. 1993. *Quilombos: Resistência ao escravismo*. São Paulo, Brazil: Ática.

Moura, Clóvis. 2001. *Os Quilombos na dinâmica social do Brasil*. Maceió, Brazil: Edufal.

Muhammad, Elijah. 2012. *Message to the Blackman in America*. Chicago: The Final Call.

Mullin, Gerald. 1974. *Flight and Rebellion: Slave Resistance in 18th Century Virginia*. New York: Oxford University Press.

Murchison, Gayle. 2018. "Let's Flip It! Quare Emancipations: Black Queer Traditions, Afrofuturisms, Janelle Monáe to Labelle." *Women and Music: A Journal of Gender and Culture* 22: 79–90.

Mutabaruka. 1996. *The Ultimate Collection*. Shanachie.

Nascimento, Abdias do. 1980. *Quilombismo: An Afro-Brazilian Political Alternative*. New York: State University of New York at Buffalo.

Neighbors, Jim. 2002. "Plunging (Outside of) History: Naming and Self-Possession in 'Invisible Man.'" *African American Review* 36 (2): 227. https://doi.org/10.2307/1512257.

Nelson, Alondra. 2002. "Introduction: Future Texts." *Social Text* 20 (2): 1–15.

Nevius, Marcus P. 2020a. *City of Refuge: Slavery and Petit Marronage in the Great Dismal Swamp, 1763–1856*. Athens: University of Georgia Press.

Nevius, Marcus P. 2020b. "New Histories of Marronage in the Anglo-Atlantic World and Early North America." *History Compass,* no. 31 (March): 1–14. https://doi.org/10.1111/hic3.12613.

Newmark, Kathryn, and Veronique DeRugy. 2006. "Hope after Katrina: Will New Orleans Become the New City of Choice?" *Education Next* 6 (4): 12–21.

New York Times. 2005. "Barbara Bush Calls Evacuees Better Off." September 7, 2005. https://www.nytimes.com/2005/09/07/us/nationalspecial/barbara-bush-calls-evacuees-better-off.html.

Nyerere, Julius. 1967. *Education for Self-Reliance*. Dar es Salaam: United Republic of Tanzania.

O'Meally, Robert G. 1988. *New Essays on "Invisible Man."* New York: Cambridge University Press.

Outkast. 1996. *ATLiens*. Arista.

Outkast. 1998. "SpottieOttieDopaliscious." Track 12 on *Aquemini*. LaFace.

Outkast. 2003. *Speakerboxxx/the Love Below*. Streamed. Arista.

Owens, Imani D. 2023. *Turn the World Upside Down*. New York: Columbia University Press.

Parliament. 1975. *Mothership Connection (Star Child)*. Casablanca/Island Def Jam.
Patterson, Orlando. 2018. *Slavery and Social Death: A Comparative Study*. Cambridge, Mass.: Harvard University Press.
Paul, Dierdre G. 2003. *Talkin' Back: Raising and Educating Resilient Black Girls*. Westport, Conn.: Praeger.
Perry, Imani. 2018. *May We Forever Stand: A History of the Black National Anthem*. Chapel Hill: University of North Carolina Press.
Podair, Jerald E. 2002. *The Strike That Changed New York: Blacks, Whites, and the Ocean Hill–Brownsville Crisis*. New Haven: Yale University Press.
Price, Richard. 1975. *Saramaka Social Structure: Analysis of a Maroon Society in Surinam*. Río Piedras, Puerto Rico: Institute of Caribbean Studies.
Price, Richard. 1979. *Maroon Societies: Rebel Slave Communities in the Americas*. Baltimore: Johns Hopkins University Press.
Price, Richard. 1996. *Maroon Societies: Rebel Slave Communities in the Americas*. 3rd ed. Baltimore: Johns Hopkins University Press.
Price, Richard. 2002. *First-Time: The Historical Vision of an African American People*. Chicago: University of Chicago Press.
Price, Richard, and Sally Price. 1999. *Maroon Arts: Cultural Vitality in the African Diaspora*. Boston: Beacon Press.
Purifoy, Danielle. 2021. "The Parable of Black Places." *Transactions of the Institute of British Geographers* 46 (4): 829–33. https://doi.org/10.1111/tran.12502.
Purifoy, Danielle M., and Louise Seamster. 2021. "Creative Extraction: Black Towns in White Space." *Environment and Planning D: Society and Space* 39 (1): 47–66. https://doi.org/10.1177/0263775820968563.
Purpura, Paul. 2008. "Two Testify about Gretna Police Bridge Blockade after Hurricane Katrina." *Nola.com*, September 25, 2008. https://www.nola.com/news/two-testify-about-gretna-police-bridge-blockade-after-hurricane-katrina/article_9061459f-e9aa-59bb-b559-be959b763308.html.
Quashie, Kevin. 2021. *Black Aliveness, or A Poetics of Being*. Durham: Duke University Press.
Rambsy, Howard, II. 2013. "Beyond Keeping It Real: OutKast, the Funk Connection, and Afrofuturism." *American Studies* 52 (4): 205–16. https://doi.org/10.1353/ams.2013.0113.
Rameau, Max. 2013. *Take Back the Land: Land, Gentrification, and the Umoja Village Shantytown*. Edinburgh: AK Press.
Ransby, Barbara. 2003. *Ella Baker and the Black Freedom Movement: A Radical Democratic Vision*. Chapel Hill: University of North Carolina Press.
Ratteray, Joan D., and Mwalimu Shujaa. 1987. *Dare to Choose: Parental Choice at Independent Neighborhood Schools*. Washington, D.C.: Institute for Independent Education.
Ray, Brian D. 2009. "Homeschooling across America: Academic Achievement and Demographic Characteristics." National Home Education Research Institute. August 10, 2009. http://www.nheri.org/research/nheri-news/homeschool

ing-across-america-academic-achievement-and-demographic-characteristics.html.
Ray, Brian D. 2015. "African American Homeschool Parents' Motivations for Homeschooling and Their Black Children's Academic Achievement." *Journal of School Choice* 9 (1): 71–96. https://doi.org/10.1080/15582159.2015.998966.
Ray, Brian D. 2024. "Homeschooling: The Research." National Home Education Research Institute. May 29, 2024. http://www.nheri.org/research/research-facts-on-homeschooling.html.
Reed, Betsy. 2006. *Unnatural Disaster: The Nation on Hurricane Katrina*. New York: Nation Books.
Regis, Helen A. 2006. *Caribbean and Southern: Transnational Perspectives on the U.S. South*. Athens: University of Georgia Press.
Reid, Vic. 1983. *Nanny-Town*. Kingston: Jamaica Publishing House.
Reis, João J. 1993. *Slave Rebellion in Brazil: The Muslim Uprising of 1835 in Bahia*. Baltimore: Johns Hopkins University Press.
Reiter, Bernd. 2015. "Palenque de San Basílio: Citizenship and Republican Traditions of a Maroon Village in Colombia." *Journal of Civil Society* 11 (4): 333–47.
Rickford, Russell J. 2016a. *We Are an African People: Independent Education, Black Power, and the Radical Imagination*. New York: Oxford University Press.
Rickford, Russell J. 2016b. "'Kazi Is the Blackest of All': Pan-African Nationalism and the Making of the 'New Man,' 1969–1975." *Journal of African American History* 101 (1–2): 97–125. https://doi.org/10.5323/jafriamerhist.101.1-2.0097.
Roane, J. T. 2018. "Plotting the Black Commons." *Souls* 20 (3): 239–66. https://doi.org/10.1080/10999949.2018.1532757.
Roberts, Neil. 2015. *Freedom as Marronage*. Chicago: University of Chicago Press.
Robinson, Carey. 1971. *The Fighting Maroons of Jamaica*. Jamaica: William Collins and Sangster.
Robinson, Carey. 1993. *The Iron Thorn: The Defeat of the British by the Jamaican Maroons*. Kingston: Kingston Publishers.
Robinson, Cedric J. 1997. *Black Movements in America*. New York: Routledge.
Robinson, Cedric J. 2000. *Black Marxism: The Making of the Black Radical Tradition*. Chapel Hill: University of North Carolina Press.
Rooks, Noliwe M. 2006. *White Money/Black Power: The Surprising History of African American Studies and the Crisis of Race in Higher Education*. Boston: Beacon Press.
Rosario-Moore, Alexios. 2015. "OneApp, Many Considerations: Black Social Capital and School Choice in New Orleans." *Souls* 17 (3–4): 231–47. https://doi.org/10.1080/10999949.2015.1127105.
Sanders, Raynard. 2015. "New Orleans Publicly Funded Private School System: Unbelievable Claims, Undemocratic, Unmasked Inequity, Unaccountable Cash Cow Schools, and Chronic Failure All under the Guise of School Reform." *Souls* 17 (3–4): 201–10. https://doi.org/10.1080/10999949.2015.1125173.

Sayers, Daniel O. 2015. *A Desolate Place for a Defiant People: The Archaeology of Maroons, Indigenous Americans, and Enslaved Laborers in the Great Dismal Swamp.* Gainesville: University Press of Florida.

Schafer, Judith K. 2003. *Becoming Free, Remaining Free: Manumission and Enslavement in New Orleans, 1846–1862.* Baton Rouge: Louisiana State University Press.

Scott, Darius. 2021. "Normalized Alterity: Visualizing Black Spatial Humanities." *GeoHumanities* 7 (2): 475–93. https://doi.org/10.1080/2373566x.2021.1904788.

Scott, David. 1991. "That Event, This Memory: Notes on the Anthropology of African Diasporas in the New World." *Diaspora: A Journal of Transnational Studies* 1 (3): 261–84. https://doi.org/10.1353/dsp.1991.0023.

Scott, David. 1999. *Refashioning Futures Criticism after Postcoloniality.* Princeton: Princeton University Press.

Scott, David. 2004. *Conscripts of Modernity: The Tragedy of Colonial Enlightenment.* Durham: Duke University Press.

Scott, Rebecca. 2012. *Freedom Papers: An Atlantic Odyssey in the Age of Emancipation.* Cambridge: Harvard University Press.

Scott-Heron, Gil. 1971. "Who'll Pay Reparations on My Soul?" Track 13 on *Small Talk at 125th and Lenox.* Ace Records.

Sexton, Jared. 2008. *Amalgamation Schemes: Antiblackness and the Critique of Multiracialism.* Minneapolis: University of Minnesota Press.

Sexton, Jared. 2012. "Ante-Anti-Blackness." *Lateral* 1 (1). https://doi.org/10.25158/l1.1.16.

Shange, Savannah. 2019. *Progressive Dystopia: Abolition, Antiblackness, and Schooling in San Francisco.* Durham: Duke University Press.

Sharpe, Christina. 2016. *In the Wake: On Blackness and Being.* Durham: Duke University Press.

Shujaa, Mwalimu J. 1992. "Afrocentric Transformation and Parental Choice in African American Independent Schools." *Journal of Negro Education* 61 (2): 148. https://doi.org/10.2307/2295412.

Shujaa, Mwalimu J. 1995. "Cultural Self Meets Cultural Other in the African American Experience: Teachers' Responses to a Curriculum Content Reform." *Theory into Practice* 34 (3): 194–201. https://doi.org/10.1080/00405849509543679.

Shujaa, Mwalimu J. 1998. *Too Much Schooling, Too Little Education: A Paradox of Black Life in White Societies.* Trenton, N.J.: Africa World Press.

Silk, Garnett. 1993. "Zion in a Vision." Track 33 on *Reggae Anthology: Music Is the Rod.* VP Records.

Simanga, Michael. 2015. *Amiri Baraka and the Congress of African People: History and Memory.* New York: Palgrave Macmillan.

Sojoyner, Damien M. 2016. *First Strike: Educational Enclosures in Black Los Angeles.* Minneapolis: University of Minnesota Press.

Sojoyner, Damien M. 2017. "Another Life Is Possible: Black Fugitivity and Enclosed Places." *Cultural Anthropology* 32 (4): 514–36. https://doi.org/10.14506/ca32.4.04.

South End Press. 2007. *What Lies beneath: Katrina, Race, and the State of the Nation.* Cambridge, Mass.: South End Press.

Spielberg, Steven, dir. 1985. *The Color Purple.* Warner Brothers Pictures.

Stanonis, Anthony J. 2009. *Creating the Big Easy: New Orleans and the Emergence of Modern Tourism, 1918–1945.* Athens: University of Georgia Press.

Stedman, John G. 2015. *Narrative of a Five Years Expedition against the Revolted Negroes of Surinam: Transcribed for the First Time from the Original 1790 Manuscript.* New York, NY: Open Road Integrated Media.

Stevens, Matt. 2019. "White Man Who Shot Black Men after Hurricane Katrina Dies Days after Sentencing." *New York Times,* February 27, 2019.

Stuckey, Sterling. 2014. *Slave Culture: Nationalist Theory and the Foundations of Black America.* New York: Oxford University Press.

Students at the Center. 2011. *The Long Ride.* CreateSpace.

Sublette, Ned. 2008. *The World That Made New Orleans: From Spanish Silver to Congo Square. Google Books.* Chicago: Chicago Review Press. https://books.google.com/books?id=zCOhLy9ojyYC&printsec=frontcover&source=gbs_ge_summary_r&cad=0#v=onepage&q&f=false.

Sullivan, Elizabeth, and Damekia Morgan. 2010. "Pushed Out: Harsh Discipline in Louisiana Schools Denies the Right to Education." https://dignityinschools.org/wp-content/uploads/2017/10/Pushed-Out-Harsh-Discipline-in-Louisiana-Schools-Denies-the-Right-to-Education-2010.pdf.

Swanson, Betsy. 2004. *Historic Jefferson Parish: From Shore to Shore.* Gretna, La.: Pelican.

Taylor, Eric R. 2009. *If We Must Die: Shipboard Insurrections in the Era of the Atlantic Slave Trade.* Baton Rouge: Louisiana State University Press.

Taylor, Wayne. 2005. "Premillennium Tension: Malcolm X and the Eschatology of the Nation of Islam." *Souls* 7 (1): 52–65. https://doi.org/10.1080/10999940590910041.

Tedla, Elleni. 1995. *Sankofa: African Thought and Education.* New York: Peter Lang.

Thevenot, Brian. 2009. "Local School Principals' Pay Reaches New Heights." *Nola.com,* May 17, 2009. http://www.nola.com/news/index.ssf/2009/05/local_school_principals_pay_re.html.

Thompson, A. C. 2008a. "Katrina's Hidden Race War." *The Nation,* December 17, 2008. https://www.thenation.com/article/archive/katrinas-hidden-race-war/.

Thompson, A. C. 2008b. "NOPD Responds to Nation Investigation." *The Nation,* December 26, 2008. https://www.thenation.com/article/archive/nopd-responds-nation-investigation/.

Thompson, A. C. 2009. "New Evidence Surfaces in Post-Katrina Crimes." *The Nation,* July 11, 2009. https://www.thenation.com/article/archive/new-evidence-surfaces-post-katrina-crimes/.

Thompson, A. C. 2010a. "Feds Charge Man as New Orleans Inquiry Turns to Vigilante Violence." ProPublica. July 15, 2010. http://www.propublica.org/article/feds-charge-man-as-new-orleans-inquiry-turns-to-vigilante-violence.

Thompson, A. C. 2010b. "Jury Convicts Three, Acquits Two in Post-Katrina Police Shooting." *The Nation,* December 10, 2010. https://www.thenation.com/article/archive/jury-convicts-three-acquits-two-post-katrina-police-shooting/.

Thompson, Alvin O. 2006. *Flight to Freedom: African Runaways and Maroons in the Americas.* Kingston: University of the West Indies Press.

Thompson, Krista A. 2015. *Shine: The Visual Economy of Light in African Diasporic Aesthetic Practice.* Durham: Duke University Press.

Thornton, John K. 1991. "African Dimensions of the Stono Rebellion." *The American Historical Review* 96 (4): 1101. https://doi.org/10.2307/2164997.

Tompkins, Christien. 2015. "There's No Such Thing as a Bad Teacher: Reconfiguring Race and Talent in Post-Katrina Charter Schools." *Souls* 17, nos. 3–4 (2015): 211–30. https://doi.org/10.1080/10999949.2015.1147905.

Trouillot, Michel-Rolph. 1995. *Silencing the Past: Power and the Production of History.* Boston: Beacon Press.

Ture, Kwame, and Charles V. Hamilton. 1967. *Black Power: The Politics of Liberation in America.* New York: Vintage Books.

United States Attorney's Office, Eastern District of Louisiana. 2010. "New Orleans Man Charged with Shooting African-Americans in the Aftermath of Hurricane Katrina." Justice.gov, July 15, 2010. https://www.justice.gov/opa/pr/new-orleans-man-charged-shooting-african-americans-aftermath-hurricane-katrina.

Valnes, Matthew. 2017. "Janelle Monáe and Afro-Sonic Feminist Funk." *Journal of Popular Music Studies* 29 (3). https://doi.org/10.1111/jpms.12224.

Vansina, Jan. 1996. "Quilombos on São Tomé, or in Search of Original Sources." *History in Africa* 23 (January): 453–59. https://doi.org/10.2307/3171955.

Van Veen, Tobias C. 2013. "Vessels of Transfer: Allegories of Afrofuturism in Jeff Mills and Janelle Monáe." *Dancecult* 5 (2): 7–41. https://doi.org/10.12801/1947-5403.2013.05.02.02.

Vargas, João Helion Costa. 2008. *Never Meant to Survive: Genocide and Utopias in Black Diaspora Communities.* Lanham, Md.: Rowman & Littlefield.

Vargas, Ramon A. 2018. "White Man Charged with Shooting at Black Men Post-Katrina Again Faces Trial, Despite Prior Health Worries." *Nola.com*, June 22, 2018. https://www.nola.com/news/crime_police/white-man-charged-with-shooting-at-black-men-post-katrina-again-faces-trial-despite-prior/article_1cb3c069-9339-5dd6-9da7-cdc40bbcecf7.html.

Vargas, Ramon A. 2019. "Man Who Admitted to Racist, Post-Katrina Triple Shooting Receives 10-Year Prison Sentence." *Nola.com*, February 14, 2019. https://www.nola.com/news/crime_police/man-who-admitted-to-racist-post-katrina-triple-shooting-receives-10-year-prison-sentence/article_19fdd319-5df1-5e8a-a7e8-0fd2b27089c5.html.

Vincent, Rickey. 1996. *Funk: The Music, the People, and the Rhythm of the One.* New York: St. Martin's Griffin.

Waiters, Mel. 1999. "Hole in the Wall." Track 3 on *Material Things.* Waldoxy Records.

Walker, Alice. (1983) 2017. *The Color Purple.* London: Weidenfeld & Nicolson.

Walters, Wendy W. 1997. "'One of Dese Mornings, Bright and Fair, / Take My Wings and Cleave de Air': The Legend of the Flying Africans and Diasporic Consciousness." *MELUS* 22 (3): 3–29. https://doi.org/10.2307/467652.

Wilderson, Frank B. 2010. *Red, White, and Black: Cinema and the Structure of U.S. Antagonisms.* Durham: Duke University Press.

Wilderson, Frank B. 2020. *Afropessimism.* New York: Norton.

Williams, Heather A. 2009. *Self-Taught: African American Education in Slavery and Freedom.* Chapel Hill: University of North Carolina Press.

Wilson, Samuel, Jr. 1990. "The Plantation of the Company of the Indies." *Louisiana History: The Journal of the Louisiana Historical Association* 31(2): 161–91. https://www.jstor.org/stable/4232789.

Winston, Celeste. 2021. "Maroon Geographies." *Annals of the American Association of Geographers* 111 (7): 2185–99. https://doi.org/10.1080/24694452.2021.1894087.

Witt, Howard. 2008. "Katrina Aftermath Still Roils Gretna." *Chicago Tribune*, September 4, 2008. https://www.chicagotribune.com/nation-world/chi-gretna_wittsep04-story.html.

Womack, Ytasha L. 2013. *Afrofuturism: The World of Black Sci-Fi and Fantasy Culture.* Chicago: Lawrence Hill Books.

Woodard, Komozi. 1999. *A Nation within a Nation.* Chapel Hill: University of North Carolina Press.

Woods, Clyde A. 1998. *Development Arrested: The Cotton and Blues Empire of the Mississippi Delta.* New York: Verso.

Woods, Clyde A. 2017. *Development Drowned and Reborn: The Blues and Bourbon Restorations in Post-Katrina New Orleans.* Athens: University of Georgia Press.

Woodson, Carter G. 2018. *The Mis-Education of the Negro.* Seattle: Vert Volta Press.

Wright, Willie Jamaal. 2019. "The Morphology of Marronage." *Annals of the American Association of Geographers* 110 (4): 1134–49. https://doi.org/10.1080/24694452.2019.1664890.

Wynter, Sylvia. n.d. "Black Metamorphosis: New Natives in a New World." Unpublished manuscript.

Wynter, Sylvia. 1971. "Novel and History, Plot and Plantation." *Savacou*, no. 5: 95–102.

X, Malcolm. 1990. *Malcolm X Speaks: Selected Speeches and Statements.* New York: Pathfinder.

X, Malcolm. 1992a. *By Any Means Necessary: Speeches, Interviews, and a Letter.* New York: Pathfinder Press.

X, Malcolm. 1992b. *February 1965.* New York: Pathfinder Press.

Ya Salaam, Kalamu. 1974. "The Right and Responsibility to Educate Black Children Is Finally Ours Alone!" *Council of Independent Black Institutions Newsletter* 1 (2): 4–5.

Young, Jason R. 2007. *Rituals of Resistance: African Atlantic Religion in Kongo and the Lowcountry South in the Era of Slavery.* Baton Rouge: Louisiana State University Press.

Zamalin, Alex. 2019. *Black Utopia: The History of an Idea from Black Nationalism to Afrofuturism.* New York: Columbia University Press.

Zips, Werner. 1999. *Black Rebels: African-Caribbean Freedom Fighters in Jamaica.* Princeton: Markus Wiener Publishers.

Index

Abiodun, Nehanda, 30
Africa: variations in spelling, 156n13, 157n23
African Americans. *See* Blacks
African Diaspora, 37, 127, 152n1, 156n21; black star as symbol of, 60, 64, 155–56n12; marronage as tradition of, 7–8, 9, 18, 22, 24, 29; quest for liberation, 3, 10
African people: marronage in lives of, 18, 23, 37; quests for freedom, 24–25, 27–28. *See also* Blackness; Blacks; enslaved Africans/enslaved people; maroons; marronage; spirituality, African
"Afrocubano Soy Yo" (song, Anónimo Consejo), 30–33
agency, Black, 47, 64; juke joints and holes in the wall as sites of, 118, 122–23, 126. *See also* autonomy, Black; self-determination, Black
Ahidiana (work), 152n8
Ahidiana's Work/Study Center (independent Black school, New York City), 101, 160n7
Alexander, Marcel: survivor of racial violence following Hurricane Katrina, 54

Algiers (New Orleans neighborhood), 39–58; history of, 18, 40–51; Hurricane Katrina's effects on, 51–56; maps of, 50 (fig.), 57 (fig.); maroons in, 41–46; unseen presence and, 40, 51, 56–58. *See also* BlackStar Books and Caffé; Kamali Academy; West Bank, Mississippi River
Americanism, 65, 156n14
Anderson, James D.: on Black self-determination through education, 101, 102
Andre 3000 (hip-hop artist), 128–29, 163n8
Angola Prison. *See* Louisiana State Penitentiary (aka Angola Prison)
Anónimo Consejo (rap duo), 30–33, 34
anti-Blackness, 11–12. *See also* Blackness
Armah, Ayi Kwei: on white road of death, 110
Ashé Cultural Arts Center: support for BlackStar Books, 155n9
autonomy, Black, 50, 94, 122, 134, 137, 155n3; leveraging invisibility for, 60, 73–74; marronage as pursuit of, 2, 6–7, 8, 23, 29, 123, 126, 138–39. *See*

also agency, Black; communities, Black: building autonomous; freedom, Black; independence, Black; liberation, Black; self-determination, Black

Babatunde Omowale (band), 119, 121, 125, 131
Badu, Erykah (singer/songwriter), 131
Baker, Ella (civil rights activist), 135
Bambara, Samba, 42, 153n5
Bambaras, 153n3, 153n4, 153n5, 153n6
Baraka, Amiri, 100–101
Bas du Fleuve, Louisiana, 43–44
bayous: maroons in, 41–46, 123
"Be Healthy" (rap, Dead Prez), 162n16
Best, Stephen: on escape, 90
"Be Thankful for What You Got" (song, DeVaughn), 163n1
Bey, Yasiin (rapper and actor). See *Mos Def and Talib Kweli Are Black Star* (album, Def and Kweli)
black holes concept, 67
Blackness, 69–70, 130, 152n8, 156n21; universal, 13, 66. *See also* anti-Blackness
Black Power movement, 4, 30; independent schools operating during, 100–101, 160n4, 160n5. *See also* civil rights movement; nationalism, Black
Blacks, 9, 25, 47–48. *See also* African people; Black world
black star: symbolism of, 9–10, 18–19, 60, 64, 66–68, 70, 76, 155–56n12
BlackStar Bangas (band), 118–19
BlackStar Books and Caffé, 3–6, 59–76; activities at, 62–63, 73–74; closing of, 133; creating community, 64–66, 73, 75; description of, 59–60; as engagement with marronage, 6–9, 139; founding of, 16, 60–63;

greeting and farewell, 59, 64, 76, 155n4; as a hole in the wall, 125; hours of operation, 67, 156n18; Kamali Academy to be funded by, 98, 99; legacy of, 135–36; maintaining Black autonomy, 155n3, 155–56n12; mission of, 119, 139; move into the country, 136–37; relocation of, 74–75; strategic use of invisibility, 10, 63–64, 67, 68, 69, 73–74, 123; street sign near, 74 (fig.). *See also* Liberation Lounge (BlackStar Books and Caffé open-mic night); Tyehimba, Baaki
BlackStar community, 3–6, 12; emergence of, 62, 78, 87, 139; as expression of maroon impulse, 40, 134; goals of, 10, 13–14, 16, 17, 18, 104, 136, 160n7; street sign erected by, 74 (fig.). *See also* BlackStar Books and Caffé; Kamali Academy
BlackStar Educational Cooperative (homeschool collective), 14, 15, 61, 64, 96–99, 103. *See also* Kamali Academy
Black Star Line (Universal Negro Improvement Association), 9, 130, 155–56n12. *See also* Garvey, Marcus (political activist)
"BlackStar Rising" (song, Tyehimba), 119–21
Black Utopias (book, Brown), 152n9
Black world, 9, 10, 11–14, 18, 70, 119. *See also* African people; Blacks
Bledsoe, Adam: on maroon communities, 9
Bonilla, Yarimar: strategic entanglement concept, 6
Brazil: maroons in, 23, 34
Bridges, Ruby: and desegregation of New Orleans Public Schools, 154n10

Brown, James (singer), 131
Brown, Jayna: on perceiving the universe, 70
Browne, Simone: dark sousveillance concept, 69, 156n21
Bush, Barbara: visit to Hurricane survivors in Houston, 151n2
Butler, Octavia (author), 152n9

Camara, Samori, 3, 57–58, 97 (fig.), 109; and BlackStar Educational Cooperative, 14, 15, 96–99; and Kamali Academy, 4, 15–16, 95, 96–100; leader in Black homeschool movement, 136; pursues PhD, 110–11; repatriates to Ghana, 133; work at BlackStar Books and Caffé, 156n18
Camp, Stephanie: rival geographies concept, 47; truancy formulation, 27
Campanella, Richard, 47
Campt, Tina: fugitivity insights, 78, 90
Carneiro, Edison: on marronage, 28
Chale Wote Street Art Festival (Accra, Ghana), 127, 131–32
charter schools, 79–82, 157n3, 160n4; concern with test scores, 15, 61, 86; negative impact of, 5, 15, 19, 89–90, 158n19, 161n9; New Orleans becomes all-charter-school city, 5, 14, 80, 136, 157n4; public, 73, 77, 97; spending on security, 158–59n21. *See also* Henson Academy (pseudonym, charter school); Roberts High School (pseudonym, charter school)
chattel enslavement. *See* enslaved Africans/enslaved people; plantations
civil rights movement, 51, 73, 154n10. *See also* Black Power movement

Clinton, George (singer/songwriter), 129, 131
Code Noir, 41, 45
Collins, Chris: survivor of racial violence following Hurricane Katrina, 54
Coltrane, Alice (musician), 152n9
Common Ground Relief (relief organization), 55
communities, Black: building autonomous, 2, 4–5, 8–9, 10, 14, 16–17, 58, 64–68, 75, 138–39, 151n4; cooperation among, 156n17; Kamali Academy building, 105–6, 115–16; maroon, 7, 9, 32; marronage as pursuit of, 6, 23, 94, 133–34, 135; strategic use of invisibility by, 70–71, 76; use of term, 60–61. *See also* BlackStar community
Community Book Center: support for BlackStar Books and Caffé, 155n9
Company of the Indies, 41–43
Company of the West, 40, 152–53n1. *See also* Company of the Indies
Company Plantation, 40, 41, 42–43, 47, 48. *See also* plantations
Congo, Louis, 48–49
Cooper, Carolyn: on marronage, 6
Council of Independent Black Institutions (CIBI), 160n6
culture: African Diasporic, 7, 37; Black, 109, 114, 152n8, 163n4; French, 41; hole-in-the-wall, 124; homeschool, 103–6; jook, 123; New Orleans, 14, 46; Rastafari, 25

Def, Mos. *See Mos Def and Talib Kweli Are Black Star* (album, Def and Kweli)
desegregation, 73, 154n10
Diaspora. *See* African Diaspora

Diouf, Sylviane: on relationships between maroons and Africans on plantations, 27, 28
disengagement, Black: and Black fugitivity, 15, 90–91; marronage as, 6, 9, 19, 20, 23, 91, 118, 151n4; of students and faculty, 78, 84, 112, 114
Dominica: maroons in, 34
DuBois, W. E. B., 101–2, 156n17

East's Uhuru Sasa Shule, The (Freedom Now School, independent Black school, New York), 101, 160n7
education: independent Black, 19, 89–90, 94, 100–104, 160n4, 160n5, 160n7, 160–61n8, 161n9. *See also* charter schools; New Orleans: state of education in; *and individual schools*
enclosures, 78, 89, 157n1
engagement, Black, 83, 90; with marronage, 6–9, 10; with self-determination, 100–101, 151–52n6. *See also* disengagement, Black; reengagement, Black
enslaved Africans/enslaved people: brought to New Orleans from Africa, 40–48, 57, 153n3; marronage linked to, 7–8, 24–25, 28–29, 32, 122; plantation slaves' relationship with maroons, 26–28, 44, 48; repatriation to Liberia, 153n7. *See also* plantations

Families and Friends of Louisiana's Incarcerated Children, 158–59n21
Fanon, Frantz, 152n1
Fard Muhammad, Wallace D.: founding of Nation of Islam by, 155–56n12
Faubourg Tremé (New Orleans neighborhood), 46, 47, 49

Federal Emergency Management Agency (FEMA), 2, 154n13
Fields-Smith, Cheryl: on resistance to racism, 103
Flaherty, Jordan: on charter schools, 89
flight, Black: marronage as, 6, 20, 23, 28, 90–91, 118, 151n4; from violence, 45. *See also* fugitivity, Black
Floyd, Samuel: on juke joints, 123, 124
Frazier, Garrison, 161n11
freedom, Black, 66, 72, 91; African people's quest for, 24–25, 27–28; marronage as pursuit of, 6, 27, 28, 29, 32, 36; power and, 73–75; vision of, 137, 139. *See also* autonomy, Black; independence, Black; liberation, Black; self-determination, Black
Freetown (New Orleans neighborhood), 46
fugitivity, Black, 77–92; disengagement and, 90–91, 115; as liberation praxis, 19, 78, 95; marronage's relationship to, 9, 91; shortcomings of, 134. *See also* flight, Black

Ganesh, Chitra: warm data defined, 157n22
Garvey, Marcus (political activist), 9, 14, 64, 74, 120–21, 155n12; painting of, 59–60. *See also* Black Star Line (Universal Negro Improvement Association)
geographies, Black, 8–9, 68, 73, 75–76
Gerima, Haile: *Sankofa,* 26–28
Ghana, 133, 155–56n12
Ghani, Mariam: warm data defined, 157n22
Glissant, Édouard: on transparency, 17
Glover, Henry: killed by racial violence, 154n12

Index

Goins, Glenn (singer), 129
Graduation Exit Exam (GEE), 80–81
grand marronage, 24, 28
Grandy Nanny (maroon leader), 34–36

Hall, Gwendolyn M.: on Bambaras, 153n4, 153n6; on maroons of southeastern Louisiana, 44, 45
Hampton Institute (Virginia), 161n9
Hartman, Saidiya: on afterlife of slavery, 8; on escape, 90; on holes in the wall, 118
Hazzard-Gordon, Katrina: "jook continuum" concept, 121–22, 123, 124, 126
Hendrix, Jimi (musician), 164n11
Henson Academy (pseudonym, charter school), 14–15, 16–17, 19, 79–87, 89, 90, 91, 157n3
Herrera, Pablo (hip-hop producer), 29–30
Herrington, Donnell: survivor of racial violence following Hurricane Katrina, 54, 56
hip-hop music, 29–33, 163n8
"Hole in the Wall" (song, Waiters), 124–25, 126
holes in the wall, 19–20, 118, 122, 124–26, 127, 131–32. *See also* juke joints
homeschool cooperatives/homeschools, 10, 103, 104, 133, 136. *See also* BlackStar Educational Cooperative (homeschool collective); Kamali Academy
hooks, bell: homeplace concept, 155n3
Hurricane Katrina: New Orleans' response to, 1–2, 5, 11–12, 63, 83, 94, 139, 151n2, 154n3; violence following, 18, 51–56

identity, Black: African cultural, 3, 5, 108–10; of BlackStar, 64–65; diasporic, 29; of French Quarter, 52; group, 30, 33; self-defined, 13, 69, 75
"I'll Take You There" (song, Staple Singers), 124
independence, Black, 34–35, 63; building communities of, 2, 67, 94. *See also* autonomy, Black; freedom, Black
invisibility, 133, 157n22; BlackStar Books and Caffé's strategies use of, 10, 63–64, 67, 68, 69, 73–74, 123; cloak of, 17, 60, 70–71, 75, 76, 126; leveraging for Black autonomy, 60, 73–74; in literature and cinema, 68–73; role in Blackworld-making, 18–19, 73. *See also* unseen presence
Invisible Man (novel, Ellison), 68–70, 71, 157n28
Isaacs, Gregory (musician), 26

Jamaica: maroons of, 33–34, 35
Jenkins, Patryce: survivor of violence following Hurricane Katrina, 53
Johnson, Jessica Marie: on Louis Congo, 48–49
juke joints, 19, 118, 121–24, 128, 131, 132. *See also* holes in the wall

Kamali Academy, 3–6, 93–116; building relationships, 106–12, 115, 135; challenges for, 49, 113–14; closing of, 133–34; culture of, 103–6; curriculum, 108, 159n3; daily rituals, 93–94, 159n1, 159n2; development of, 10, 15, 16, 96–100; dietary guidelines, 109, 162n16; different approach to education, 94–95, 161n9; as engagement with marronage, 6–9, 19, 139; fostering an African-centered identity, 108–10; as nation-building initiative, 104, 115; relocation of, 134; as response to maroon impulse, 19,

96, 111–12, 139; teachers, 104, 105, 111–12, 162–63n30, 188; transformation to virtual school, 136. *See also* BlackStar Educational Cooperative (homeschool collective)
"Katrina's Hidden Race War" (article, Thompson), 53–56, 154n12
kazi (work), 137, 152n8
Kee, Jessica Baker: on neighborhood schools, 158n16
King's Plantation, 41–42. *See also* plantations
Kisura, Monica Wells: on resistance to racism, 103
Kokino (Adeyeme, rapper), 30. *See also* Anónimo Consejo (rap duo)
Konadu, Kwasi, 64, 160n5
Krewe of NOMTOC (New Orleans' Most Talked Of Club), 155n8
Kuumba Academy, 100
Kweli, Talib. *See Mos Def and Talib Kweli Are Black Star* (album, Def and Kweli)

Lean on Me (film), 83–84
Le Page du Pratz, Antoine-Simon, 42, 45, 51, 153n4, 153n5
liberation, Black: African Diaspora as quest for, 3, 10; black star as symbol of, 9–10, 60; dedication to, 152n8; fugitivity as praxis of, 19, 78, 95; Kamali Academy advancing, 3–4, 115; marronage as pursuit of, 6, 23, 29, 137. *See also* autonomy, Black; freedom, Black
Liberation Lounge (BlackStar Books and Caffé open-mic night), 4, 15, 19–20, 63, 117–23, 131, 132, 155n10; performers at, 133, 163n1, 163n2. *See also* BlackStar Books and Caffé
Little Afraka Street Festival, 17 (fig.), 74, 97 (fig.)

Little Sun People, 160n7
"Loma y Machete" (song, Anónimo Consejo), 30–33. *See also* machetes
Louisiana. *See* bayous; New Orleans
Louisiana Educational Assessment Program (LEAP) test, 80
Louisiana Purchase, 49
Louisiana State Penitentiary (aka Angola Prison), 61

machetes, 33, 35, 37. *See also* "Loma y Machete" (song, Anónimo Consejo)
Malcolm X, 117, 130, 156n14; painting of, 59–60
Malvin, John (free colored preacher), 102
marginalization: of invisibility, 60, 75; of juke joints, 123; of race and class, 122; of students, 78, 81, 112
maroon impulse, 21–37; applied to Black homeschooling, 104; Black fugitivity as factor in, 78; BlackStar community an expression of, 14, 40; and community formation, 18, 23, 94, 133–34; definition of, 22–24; enslaved Africans responding to, 129; flourishing under unseen presence, 10, 60, 75; juke joints and holes in the wall as expression of, 118, 125, 126, 127; Kamali Academy as response to, 19, 96, 111–12; liberation through, 137; revolution overlapping with, 135; unseen presence as expression of, 10, 16, 60, 75; as urge to pursue, 45–46
maroons: in the bayous, 41–46, 123; beliefs about the land, 33–34, 49; cultural traditions of, 34, 36; formation of, 7, 28–29; of Jamaica, 33–34, 35; literature of, 24–28; relationship with Africans on plantations, 26–28, 44, 48; romantic mythos of, 138

Index

Maroon Societies (book, Price), 24–25, 27, 32
marronage, 2–3, 27, 33, 115, 151n4; as African Diasporic tradition, 7–8, 9, 18, 22, 24, 29; amorphous nature of, 23, 95; beliefs about the land, 34–37, 49; and Black autonomy, 6–7, 29; and Black freedom, 28, 32, 45–46; chattel enslavement linked to, 7–8, 24–25, 28–29, 32; in colonial era, 43–46; definition of, 18, 23–24; engagement with, 6–9, 10; flight as, 6, 20, 23, 28, 90–91, 118, 151n4; fugitivity as, 9, 91; legacies of, 2–3, 14, 135; as liberation pursuit, 6, 23, 29, 137; in lives of African people, 18, 23, 37; manifestations of, 122, 134; mobility of, 35–37; power of, 6, 8, 17; processual nature of, 19, 36–37, 115, 126, 136–37, 138–39; self-determination through, 7, 18; sketches of, 6–9. *See also* autonomy, Black: marronage as pursuit of; disengagement, Black: marronage as; reengagement, Black: marronage as
McDonogh, John: legacy of, 46, 153n17
McDonoghville (New Orleans neighborhood), 46, 47
McKittrick, Katherine: on Black geographies, 68, 69, 73; on non-cartographic mapping, 47
Method Man (hip-hop artist), 163n8
mobility, Black, 35–37, 60, 122
Monáe, Janelle (singer/songwriter), 131
Mos Def and Talib Kweli Are Black Star (album, Def and Kweli), 9
mothership, concept of, 129–31
Moura, Clóvis: on marronage, 28–29, 33, 34
MOVE organization: standoff with Philadelphia police, 157n25

Muhammad, Elijah, 64, 97, 130, 155–56n12; painting of, 59–60
"Murderer" (song, Banton), 157n2
Mutabaruka (poet and musician), 26
Mynameisphlegm, 39

Nanny-Town (novel, Reid), 34–37
nationalism, Black, 64, 95, 156n14. *See also* Black Power movement
Nationbuilding (book, Akoto), 160n7
NationHouse (independent Black school, Washington, D.C.), 160n7
Nation of Islam, 97, 130, 155–56n12
Nèg Mawon (*Le Marron Unconnu*, statue), 32–33
"Neon Valley Street" (song, Monáe), 130–31
New Orleans, 20, 153n3; author's move to, 14–17; becomes all-charter-school city, 5, 14, 80, 136, 157n4; employment limitations for Blacks in, 112; housing crisis in, 137; incarceration rate in, 91; map of, 50 (fig.); progress made by, 37; school desegregation in, 154n10; seasonal activities in, 15–16; segregation in, 1, 20, 72–73, 151n1; state of education in, 19, 87, 90, 94, 96–97, 157–58n6; treatment of Black people in, 4–5, 18, 19, 51–56, 112. *See also* Algiers (New Orleans neighborhood); Faubourg Tremé (New Orleans neighborhood); Hurricane Katrina; McDonoghville (New Orleans neighborhood); West Bank, Mississippi River
"Next Lifetime" (song and video, Badu), 128
Nkrumah, Kwame, 64
No Child Left Behind Act of 2001, 80, 155n5

O'Meally, Robert: on *Invisible Man*, 157n28
"On & On" (song and video, Badu), 128, 130
ourstory (Kamali Academy subject), 108, 114, 159n3
Outkast (hip-hop duo), 128–29, 131, 163n8
Owens, Imani, 24

palenque. See communities, Black: maroon
Palmares (Brazilian maroon settlement), 23, 34
Parliament-Funkadelic (hip-hop group), 129, 163n8
Patterson, Orlando: socially dead formulation, 28
Patterson, Sunni, 77
Peninsular War, 153n3
Périer, Étienne: and Bambara plot, 153n4
petit marronage, 26–28, 48
Philippe II, Duke of Orléans, 152–53n1
plantation complex, 6–7, 24, 28–29, 33, 152n2
plantations: autonomous communities outside of, 24–25, 48, 122; concept of earth associated with, 34; impact of marronage on, 2, 29; master time on, 67, 68; relationship between maroons and Africans on, 26–28, 44, 48. *See also* chattel enslavement; Company Plantation; King's Plantation; slavery/slaves
Prevost, Tessie: and desegregation of New Orleans schools, 154n10
Problem We All Live With, The (painting, Rockwell), 154n10
"Prototype" (song and video, Outkast), 129

Quashie, Kevin: Black world imagined by, 11, 12–13
Queen & Slim (film), 70–73
quilombo: definition of, 152n4

Race First (book, Martin), 155n12
Rahim, Malik (Common Ground Relief director): on Algiers, 51, 55
Ransby, Barbara: on Ella Baker, 135
Rastafari (social and religious movement), 25
Ratteray, Joan: on social protest, 104
reengagement, Black: Kamali Academy facilitating, 112, 115; marronage as, 6, 19, 20, 23, 91, 95, 118, 151n4. *See also* disengagement, Black; engagement, Black
Reid, Vic, 21, 33. *See also Nanny-Town* (novel, Reid)
religion, African. *See* spirituality, African
Rickford, Russell J.: examination of independent schools, 160n5
Roane, J. T.: black holes concept, 67
Roberts, Neil: on marronage, 28
Roberts High School (pseudonym, charter school), 16–17, 19, 77–78, 79 (fig.), 80, 87, 90, 91, 94
Robinson, Cedric: on Black radical tradition, 29, 31, 151n4
Rock, Pete (hip-hop producer), 163n8
"Run n Hide" (song and video, Luv), 163n2

schools. *See* charter schools; education; homeschool cooperatives/homeschools; *and individual schools*
Scott, Darius: on noncartographic mapping, 47, 157n27
Scott, David, 138

segregation. *See* civil rights movement; desegregation; New Orleans: segregation in
self-determination, Black: Baakir Tyehimba's work for, 137; BlackStar community building, 17, 64–66; through education, 94, 100–4; engagement with, 100–101, 151–52n6; Marcus Garvey's work for, 120–21; through marronage tradition, 7, 18. *See also* agency, Black; autonomy, Black; independence, Black
self-reliance, Black, 100–103, 160n6, 161n9, 161n10, 161n11
Shine (study, Thompson), 156n21
Shujaa, Mwalimu: schooling vs. education, 89; on social protest, 104
Shule Ya Mapinduzi, 160n7
slavery/slaves. *See* enslaved Africans/enslaved people; plantations
sling-shot towns, 35–37
Sojoyner, Damian: enclosure concept of, 78, 89; fugitivity insights, 90
space, 24, 67–68, 118, 157n27
Space Is the Place (film), 13
space travel, 10, 24, 128–30
spirituality, African, 25, 26, 31; beliefs about the land, 33–34, 35, 49
"Spottieottiedopalicious" (song, Outkast), 154n2
St. Malo: origin of term, 153n6
St. Malo, Jean (aka Juan San Maló), 43–46
Sun Ra (musician and poet), 1, 14, 127, 129–30, 131, 152n9, 164n9
Suriname: maroons in, 34
survival, Black, 66, 123
"Swing Low, Sweet Chariot" (song), 129

Take 'em Down NOLA coalition, 162n13

Tate, Leona: and desegregation of New Orleans Public Schools, 154n10
Taylor, Wayne: on Malcolm X, 130
"TIA" ("This is Africa," song, Knaan), 154n1
Timberlane (private country club, New Orleans), 51
time: at BlackStar Books and Caffé, 67, 68; spirocycle of, 34, 135, 151–52n6
time travel, 10, 19, 24, 118, 127, 128–29
Treaty of Fontainebleau (1762), 41
truancy: use of term, 27
Tyehimba, Baakir, 17 (fig.); and BlackStar Books and Caffé, 4, 16, 60–63, 65, 67, 98, 136–37, 155n12; and BlackStar Educational Cooperative, 14, 96–98; "BlackStar Rising" composed by, 119–21; membership in Nation of Islam, 155–56n12; starts new community, 133, 137

Uhuru Sasa Shule (independent Black school, New York City), 160n7
Umoja, Sekou (singer). *See* Anónimo Consejo (rap duo)
Universal Negro Improvement Association, 9, 155–56n12
unseen presence, 13, 46, 123; Algiers and, 40, 51, 56–58; maroon impulse flourishing under, 10, 16, 60, 75; providing refuge and community, 71–72, 76; role in Black worldmaking, 18–19, 73, 134; working in BlackStar community, 10, 135. *See also* invisibility

Vallas, Paul (school district superintendent), 151n3
Vellard, Phillipe François (carpenter), 153n4
vem e vai (coming and going), 151–52n6

View from the East, A (book, Konadu), 160n7

Vincent, Rickey: on George Clinton's cosmology, 131

violence, 45, 47, 73; following Hurricane Katrina, 18, 51–56

visibility, 66–67, 71. *See also* invisibility

Waiters, Mel, 132. *See also* "Hole in the Wall" (song, Waiters)

warm data: definition of, 157n22. *See also* invisibility

Welcome to New Orleans (film), 55

West, Kanye: on George W. Bush, 2

West Bank, Mississippi River, 39–58; history of, 40–51; map of, 50 (fig.); post-Hurricane Katrina violence on, 18, 51–56. *See also* Algiers (New Orleans neighborhood)

"Who'll Pay Reparations on My Soul?" (song, Scott-Heron), 159n22

Williams, Heather Andrea: on Black determination to get education, 102

Wilson, Samuel, Jr., 42, 153n5

Winston, Celeste: on marronage, 9

Woods, Clyde: on New Orleans, 87

Wright, Willie Jamaal: on marronage, 7

Wu Tang Clan (hip-hop group), 163n8

Wynter, Sylvia: on African spirituality, 33–34, 35, 36

AMARI JOHNSON is an independent scholar, filmmaker, and musician based in Philadelphia.